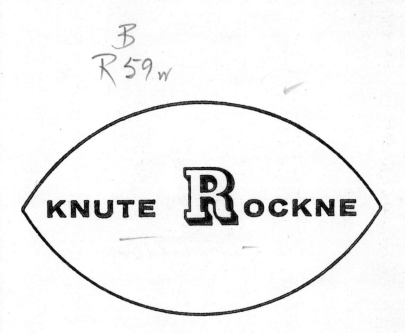

KNUTE ROCKNE

by Francis Wallace

Doubleday & Company, Inc.

Garden City, New York

1960

To JIM ARMSTRONG
who in his own field and in a quiet way
has become another *rock*
in the edifice of Notre Dame

I

Knute Kenneth Rockne was perhaps the greatest of America's Horatio Alger heroes.

He was a speck of the European fallout that drifted to our shores. Free to follow instinct, he took from the soil and the winds the nourishment needed to develop in size and strength.

He had a mind that touched genius, a blowtorch spirit, physical courage, infectious humor, rare charm. He was a hungry, talented immigrant, eager to prove that he belonged. He was a battleground of emotion and intellect, of moods and feuds. He could be petty, secretive, suspicious; but there was in him neither malice nor hate; and mostly he was naïve, generous, kind. He used his voice as a weapon or a sedative. His eyes could express the simple charm of a child; or a terrifying inner force.

He had no great design but lived from day to day, doing the things he thought should be done. When opportunity came he was always ready; and he closed with the opportunity that came, using the weapons available. He thought quicker and moved faster than his competitors. Had he been consistently wrong he could have been in much trouble. But he was amazingly right—and a success in a remarkable variety of categories.

He became a football coach by necessity, when he could not become a doctor. He remained a coach by choice, dignified all sport by proving sport could demand and absorb, and to the fullest, just about every mental, emotional, spiritual, and physical resource a

human possesses. As a coach he was a teaching perfectionist; a practicing psychologist, a brilliant actor, an intellectual competitor who
functioned best in the white heat of urgency.

He might have been outstanding in any of the fields in which he
was gifted—as a chemist, writer, salesman, orator, diplomat, fighter,
executive. Created for leadership, he knew the secret paths to the
hearts of men. His football, reflecting the man, was a skillful blend
of science and the liveliest of the arts that realized the Grecian ideal
of the sound mind in the sound body.

Very few other coaches have records comparable to his thirteen-
year span of 105 victories, twelve defeats, five ties and five undefeated seasons; but none has even approached the unique place
Rockne held in the national imagination in the twenties when life
was juicy fat and we were supposedly forever done with war. It
wasn't just what he did but how. Every game was a production, every
season flared with special drama. Operating from the off-Broadway
theater of Notre Dame, he became, and still remains, the unequaled
impresario of our Outdoor Stage.

In 1920 the snows of Christmas powdered the grave of his Thanksgiving hero—and George Gipp became an authentic gridiron immortal. In 1924, having lost only three games and tied one in six
years, Rockne produced the all-time glamour eleven, the Four Horsemen and Seven Mules. In 1928 even his lone "bad" year (five victories and four defeats) brought his most electrifying single triumph,
as sophomore Johnny "One-Play" O'Brien came off the bench for a
single play that was the winning touchdown; and the New York
Daily News carried a back-page headline, *GIPP'S GHOST BEATS
ARMY*, for my exclusive story of Rockne's emotional dressing-room
talk which took off from there to become part of football lore.

In 1929, laid low by phlebitis, he coached dramatic triumphs from
a wheel chair, by long-distance phone and by two personal appearances which violated doctor's orders and put his life in actual jeopardy. In 1930, when his final squad staggered under burdens and
injuries, he won a second consecutive national championship with a
masterpiece of psychological coaching to which I will later give
attention.

Behind the glitter of Rockne, the coach, an astounding job was
done by Rockne, the director of athletics. He took over in 1918 with

a home seating capacity of 2500. In 1930 he built a stadium holding almost 58,000. During his thirteen-year period, Notre Dame had become the undisputed box-office champion and held crowd records in all sections.

Rockne became one of the standard newspaper names of his era as his activities overflowed sport. He developed from a shy tyro to a forceful and popular speaker. He published two books, wrote magazine and syndicated articles, did movie shorts, appeared on radio.

About 1928 he had begun giving inspirational sales talks to salesmen of the Studebaker Corporation whose main automobile plants and home offices were located in South Bend, Indiana. Twelve days before his death he had signed as sales promotion manager and would have become vice-president of the Rockne Motor Corporation which was already developing a Rockne car.

He could reach either hand, in 1931, and pluck one of the contracts business was dangling for some share of the talents of this multiple man. The Hearst newspapers were offering $75,000 annually; RKO was "talking $50,000" for him to play the part of the coach in its movie version of the stage musical *Good News*. He had already declined an offer from David O. Selznick to appear in a picture to be made from my novel *Huddle*. He was working on a third book.

His welded, over-all talent was an intuitive knowledge of human behavior. In his Studebaker activities (Paul Hoffman said they were notably successful) he simply talked to salesmen as he talked to football players; and transposed the language of football into business.

His greatest usefulness to the country would have been in politics. He laughed at the idea when I suggested it; but he loved new fields, new adventures, new challenges. In all sincerity, I think Rockne had the talents necessary to handle Khrushchev. He could outtalk him, outthink him, outfight him, outstare him, outshout him, outact him, and if necessary, outfinagle him. He could beat him, pick him up, brush him off, and send him home reasonably happy about things.

On March 31, 1931, Rockne took a plane at Kansas City, heading for Los Angeles and investigation of some of the big money that people were waving at him. Two hours later the plane fell down on a Kansas farm.

His friend Will Rogers wrote: "It takes a mighty big calamity to shock this country all at once, but Knute, you did it."

The little things behind the big things came out, as usually they do, after his death. Rockne had been to men a symbol of victory; to women a symbol of virile manhood; to youth almost an archangel. Behind the glamour, the magic, and the uproar was a simple, modest man who loved people; and people, knowing it, loved him in return.

Rock went out at the top, where he always fought to be.

There is no Great Lover here—unless you count absolute devotion to family, loyalty to friends, and a willingness to give of himself to strangers.

Nor is there any extortionate ego here. He liked praise, as all true artists do, for his *work:* but he seldom spoke or wrote about Rockne; nor did he want people probing around for the real Rockne, not even with friendly probes.

Westbrook Pegler once described a Rockne speech as ". . . a battered old oil can giving off champagne." This phrase was generally supposed to have started one of Rock's most bitter feuds; but I think what really kicked it off was this further quotation from the same column: "I see Mr. Rockne as a modest man who does not think much of himself, who is constantly amazed to find himself a great national celebrity and who wants to make all the money he can while he can lest the public suddenly get next to him." As a friend of both, and toastmaster at the dinner from whence the column came, I've always thought Rock was really mad because Peg had looked into his secret room.

This was a shy lion who seemed to run away from his fame and ahead of his applause. And he did have that deep respect for and mistrust of money which come to the man who has always had to scratch for it. Before he left South Bend on that final trip to see about all that big money that was being waved at him, he had left a pair of tan shoes with Augie Backun, a bellhop at the Oliver Hotel, to be half-soled. He would believe that money when he had it in his hands. Right about most things, about the big money he was dead right.

Nobody has ever called for those shoes. Nobody has come close to filling them, at Notre Dame or in all of football.

I have a fine drawing of him by Ray Shanahan which appeared

about 1925 in the New York *Post*. It portrays Rockne as a sphynx. At the time I thought the artist had missed the mark because nobody seemed more simple or easier to read than Rockne.

But now, almost thirty years after his death, I think the artist was more perceptive than those of us who had been close to the man. There was a Rockne riddle: something within him that seemed to have a fuller, more complete, almost instantaneous picture of the problem at hand; that had an almost terrifying knowledge of human hearts, that spoke at crucial moments and was always so right.

I believe Rockne felt it, knew it was there, was uncomfortable with the knowledge; which was why he ran from it. But it was his; he respected it, so he tried to protect it.

We won't get much help from him in probing into Rockne. He didn't approve of my first novel *Huddle*, a fictional account of Notre Dame with a character modeled after Rockne, even though—or perhaps because—in the words of the publisher, the book apotheosized him.

I'm hoping that he would feel about this effort as he seemed, finally, to feel about my newspaper story of his dressing-room speech about Gipp. The first time he saw me after that he gave me a quizzical look and said calmly: "Frank, you did something you never did before—you broke a confidence."

"It didn't come to me as a confidence," I said. "Though ordinarily I would have considered it as such. But I thought this was something that belonged to the tradition."

He looked at me, thought a little, half-nodded as if saying, Perhaps, I hadn't thought of it that way.

II

The bodily temple in which Rockne resided was unimpressive. His five-feet eight inches was undersized for an athlete. His legs were spindly. He was prematurely bald; his face was round and flat, his nose had been spread by the enthusiastic application of a baseball bat in happy high-school days around the Chicago Logan Square neighborhood then vigorously inhabited by Irish and Nordics.

He was an intense perfectionist. There was only one way with him, the right way; any deviation brought questioning, disapproval, or fierce criticism in proportion to the enormity. He was so hungry for competition that to be his friend was almost automatically to be a vocal sparring partner. He seldom had the whisper of a disciplinary problem; his players were satisfied to just keep even, to avoid the whips of scorn and barbs of humor he could lay on with his scythe-like voice.

His smile was all the more effective because it brought relief from this aura of tension. But it was a good smile, forceful and total as all his emanations. His generous mouth upturned, all his wrinkles crinkled, the eyes released warm, good feeling. Everybody who knew him called him Rock because, as Johnny "Butch" Niemiec, one of his great stars, said, "You almost had to because he was so—*intimate*." Rock could be that way with his players because they knew that one transgression might immediately transform intimacy into stern remoteness. He had that sort of force.

I first met him in the early rainy dark of an October evening in 1919 when, with other freshmen, I waited under a tree for the storied old Hill Street trolley. A car stopped to pick us up. Rock was driving. Things had evidently not gone too well at practice. In the back seat we sat rigidly, feeling the explosive power of the man up front, ready to roar at the first spark. But the fact that he had stopped to pick us up was typical. Rock was sometimes "taken" by the hitchhikers he picked up along his various roads; but about this he never seemed to learn.

Our next contact was almost a year later, in early September 1920, in the anteroom of the office of Rev. James A. Burns, the president of Notre Dame. Gipp was with him and they were on serious business. The captain-elect of the football squad, something of a gambler, (as we shall later see) had bet he could absent himself from more than the permissible number of classes in the law school. He had lost, been declared ineligible for athletics. Now he and Rockne had come to petition the court of last resort. Father Burns, tall, straight and stern, was no reed to bend in a wind. But he had been a varsity baseball catcher and he knew the ways of students and athletes.

Rock, knowing his man, as he always did, had come not to plead for mercy but with a sporting proposition: Give Gipp a chance to prove he had absorbed the classwork, even if he had been lax in attendance. Let him take an oral examination *now* without a chance for cramming—and let his performance decide.

Permission was granted. Gipp, always at his best under fire, came through. His captaincy was not restored. What happened that day became important to football history; but much more important to me was the other thing Father Burns did. I needed a job to stay in school. I had brashly come to the president, who practically created a job that was to put me in the newspaper business. Within three months I would be writing the story of George Gipp's funeral; and within six months would be working for Rockne.

The incident reveals the paterfamilias character of the Notre Dame of that time—a perfect background for the operations of a brilliant ad-libber like Rockne.

J. P. McEvoy, the writer, often quipped that at Notre Dame he had been of "the lowest form of collegiate life—a student waiter who waited on other student waiters." The job Father Burns had given to me was equally humble. I went about the campus scraping crumbs of news off the bulletin boards for the South Bend *News-Times;* and on Sunday afternoons I covered Interhall football. Notre Dame is a male boarding school without fraternities. Life is organized about the residence halls, including teams in every sport. The program absorbs the young men, not good enough for the varsity, who still like the "rough go." Rock himself had come from Interhall football to the varsity; and he always watched the Sunday games hopefully. But there was no chitchat between us because I wore the uniform of the *News-Times* with which he was then feuding.

Notre Dame news had always been furnished to big outside newspapers by correspondents from the *News-Times* and the other South Bend newspaper, the *Tribune*. Since this was done at space rates, the rivalry was economic, as well as journalistic. As Notre Dame news had become more marketable, the writing had become more fanciful; there were times when inaccurate stories antagonized other schools and endangered the Rockne job of schedule-building. With typical astuteness, he solved the problem by appointing an official correspondent through whom Notre Dame news would be cleared and who would be responsible to him. The job went to Arch (then Archie) Ward, an experienced sports writer from the Rockford, Illinois, *Star* who had been recommended by Charles "Gus" Dorais, Rockne's assistant.

The metropolitan dailies were pleased with the arrangement; as was the *Tribune,* which published only in the afternoon. But the *News-Times* was not happy because, since it had both morning and afternoon editions, it figured, in a free market, to get the first shot at fresh news. After a short period the *News-Times* told Ward to choose between it and the *Tribune.* Irritated at this interference with his plans, Rock advised Ward to go with the *Tribune* and promised him the exclusives. Freeman "Mike" Scully, sports editor of the *News-Times,* covered varsity football; but when the 1920 season was over I was made responsible for all Notre Dame news, including varsity sport.

I went to Rockne who received me courteously enough, said I could cover whatever was open to public inspection, including varsity games and practices; but that the *News-Times* would get nothing else from him. I understood there was nothing personal in his attitude; but I still dreamed of the day when the cub reporter would scoop everybody concerned, including this proud and haughty man. So one afternoon, just after lunch, I walked into a Spanish class and *there it was.*

The Athletic Board had met at noon in this handy room, just around the corner from Rock's office. He had written the 1921 football schedule, big news of the year, on the blackboard—and forgotten to rub it off. I copied it; and did some thinking which had little to do with irregular Spanish verbs.

After class I bearded the gruff lion in the little office which was then the athletic department. He was on his feet, as he usually was, and alone, which he seldom was; he gave me the glare which reminded me I was out of bounds, that whatever it was I wanted, I wouldn't get.

"Rock—I've got your next year's schedule."

Now I was getting from the glaring eyes the full candlepower usually reserved for Yost, Pegler, or some other Enemy of the Moment. I do not recall his exact words; but the general reaction was amazement at such brazen effrontery by a cub reporter. So I read the schedule to him.

The inference now was that I had picked his pocket, rifled his desk or perpetrated some other outrage to be expected of the *News-Times*.

"Where did you get that?"

"You forgot to rub it off the blackboard."

This was "the most unkindest cut." Rockne, the perfectionist, had fumbled, left his flank unguarded and himself naked to the enemy. His face was always mobile, and his eyes always expressive. While he was in this weak defense I made my proposition: I could use the schedule that afternoon; but I would hold it to share with Ward and the *Tribune* if Rockne would give me an even break on the important news thereafter.

He agreed, after hardly a pause; and kept his word. He may have already known that Arch Ward would soon be leaving; and that, if he appointed me, the *News-Times* would have to dig up another man or go along. That was what happened. The *News-Times*, after trying it out, gave me the same choice it had given Ward. I went with Rockne, the *Tribune* and its then sports editor Gene Kessler. The *News-Times* lined up against us with an aggressive city editor, a sports editor, and another student correspondent.

We had a right merry war for three years. It blew up with a mighty explosion on the day I was leaving South Bend. Rock, as usual, was in the middle of it.

Arch Ward became sports editor of the Chicago *Tribune* where he pioneered the annual baseball All-Star game, the College All-Star game against the pros and other important promotions. He was the first in a group of Rockne-trained student sports writers including, following me, George Strickler, now assistant sports editor of the Chicago *Tribune;* Paul Butler, who absconded to politics; Joe Petritz, a Chicago publicist; and Walter (Globe Trotter) Kennedy. Rockne either recognized budding talent, or infected us, as he did his players, with that feverish desire to be best.

I did not then realize that I was to be a camera in the tail of the Rockne comet that would blaze gloriously through the national sky for the next decade.

Rockne's keen interest in casuals is further revealed in a recent

letter from Walter Trohan, Washington correspondent of the
Chicago *Tribune:* "I met him in my first week at school when he
picked me up as I was trudging out to the campus from town. He
asked me my name, which I told him—he knew I was a freshman—
and then said, 'How are things going?' I said, 'They've got a tough
line in there, Coach—Father Carroll in English, Professor Hines in
history, Professor Kaczmarek in biology, and Professor Cooney in
journalism.' Rock laughed heartily. All through my four years, whenever he spotted me in a group, he would say, 'Hello, Walter.' In my
freshman year particularly this used to astound my brethren. They
used to say: 'Do you know Rockne?' I would tell them I did and
that he was saving me for the Army game. Years later, when I got
on the *Tribune,* he would visit the Tower and would always drop
by, pull up a chair and ask: 'Walter, how's that line you have to
crack?' "

III

One of Rock's favorite stories concerned a professional game between
Canton and Massillon in 1919. It portrayed him as a mosquito end
who had been annoying herculean Jim Thorpe with irritating tackles.
Finally the colorful Indian ran the little end down as a truck might
demolish a bicycle. On his way back from the touchdown, he paused
to help Rock to his feet with this consoling remark: "That's a good
boy, Rock. You let Big Jim run. The people pay to see Big Jim run."

That's the way Rock told it at banquets, coaching schools and
pep talks to salesmen; and it always got a big laugh. But this is the
way Stan Cofall, who was the Massillon coach–captain, said it really
happened: "My regular end was hurt so I sent a distress call to Rock
because he could always handle Thorpe. He had just finished his
second season as head coach at Notre Dame, and was not in playing
shape; but he said he would give it a try, partially, I suspect, to get
another crack at Thorpe who had been one of his favorite sparring
partners. He did all right until he ran out of gas, but Thorpe finally
did get around him; and did make that crack about letting Big Jim

run. It was the way they kidded each other. But Rock, as usual, had the last word. He called to me, so Thorpe could hear: 'Take me out, Stan. When Thorpe can get around me it's time to quit.' And he did quit. That was the last game of football he ever played."

The true version has its points. Rock would go a long and often improvident way for a friend, or a friend of a friend. He was hungry for competition in any form, loved to handle the big guys, to beat brawn with nimble brilliance. He liked to laugh and have that last word. He never tried to ignore a fact; or argue away truth. He was a realist with a mind trained in science.

But he was also an artist; an actor who would never allow a small fact to spoil a good punch line; a writer who would cheerfully adjust chronology to bolster up a premise; a speaker who used an anecdote to illustrate a point; a man so secure in reputation that he could laugh at himself. Rockne was usually the goat, rather than the hero of his stories. One of his favorite and most effective phrases, used often and altered to fit circumstances, was: "The only guy dumber than a dumb Irishman is a smart Norwegian." This one had the double effect of chiding the Irish, with whom he was usually dealing, while making them think the gag was really at the expense of his own nationality. He used humor for definite purposes. His players copied him in all this; and their players; which explains why some of them, even to this day, are apt to answer a request for the time of day with a puzzling whimsicality. Rockne football was a philosophy, a way of life, a personality.

For our immediate purposes, all of this means that any yarn he told about himself must be suspect, especially those with humorous aspect. In his autobiography, a collection of eight articles printed in *Collier's* in 1930, he dismisses the first five years of his life thus:

"The traditional venturesomeness of the Norsemen, aided by infiltrations of Irish blood acquired when the earlier and hardier Vikings invaded Ireland looking for trouble and returned to Norway with colleens for wives, breaks out at intervals. With my father it broke out when I was about five. The World's Fair was to be held in Chicago. Dad, by profession a stationary engineer and by avocation a carriage builder, wanted to show his wares at the World's Fair. He went to America. Later he sent for his family. My mother took her daughters and her only son to New York and we were duly admitted to Castle Garden. My only equipment for life in the new country was a Norwegian vocabulary, a fervent memory of home-cooking combined with pleasant recollections of skiing and skating among the Voss mountains. How my mother ever managed that tedious voyage which I still recall with qualms; how she guided us through the intricacies of entry, knowing nothing of English, and took us into the heart of a new, strange and bewildering country without mishap—how, in brief, she achieved the first step in our Americanization unaided by anybody, is one of the millions of minor miracles that are of the stuff and fabric of America."

Having made this personal concession to literary form, he proceeded to a more typical account of how, on his first day at the Fair, this "white-haired Nordic, fresh from the original source of supply," toured "the Elysium of the World's Fair" and finally wound up among the jet-haired Indian papooses until that night, "a weary copper, passing the Indian reservation, beheld a blond head surmounted by feathers, bobbing through a scampering mob of Indian kids, wielding a wooden tomahawk and yelling for scalps. They promptly collected me, stripped me of Indian finery and restored me to my puzzled parents."

A likely story which no doubt titillated audiences; but a mild caper compared with others from the family lore and archives. As a boy of four, young Knute (pronounced Kan-ute), while fishing through ice, drifted on a floe into a lake twenty miles long and required the effort of the entire town to rescue him. In true Western style, he hung around livery stables and rode a rebellious horse named Satan. On the trip to the United States he was lost in the embarking town of Bergen, fell in the water and was fished out by sailors. In New York, when ready to leave the ship, Knute Kenneth turned up missing again and was finally located in the crow's nest where "the future King of Sport was enthroned literally on what seemed like the top of the world—almost flung like a pennant from the top of the ship."

Mother Rockne herself remembered that, while waiting to debark, Knute and his two sisters were bound by strong ribbons to her waist. So the roughest part of the "tedious journey" might well have been keeping Knute the towhead, in reasonable corral; which could be prime symbolism because just about everybody else he was to contact in the new country—from tackles to faculties—was to have that same trouble.

Rockne wrote of his ancestry: "It's on an elaborately inscribed piece of parchment that looks like a map outline of all the football plays ever invented. This, on close perusal, informs me that I'm descended—among others—from one Enidride Erlandson of Losna, Norway. When her celebrated Majesty Queen Margaret of Norway merged the three kingdoms of Norway, Sweden, and Denmark, she did not retain the best features of each. At least my *pride of ancestry* won't permit me to believe that she did. For the Erlandsons of Losna refused to have anything to do with the merger, retiring, in a collective huff, to the town of Voss and there establishing themselves in the hills. Generations elapsed, the hills remained the same, but it became harder and harder to make a good living."

Voss, near the west coast of Norway between Bergen and Oslo, nestles among rivers, lakes, and mountains and is on the tourist route today. The high, steep hills are dotted with farms and lodges and the district has long had some reputation as a health resort. Presumably the Erlandsons continued their one-sided feud with the descendants of her celebrated Majesty Queen Margaret. Four hundred years later the coach's great-grandfather Knute Lars (Louis) Rokne (there is no c-k conjunction in Norwegian and the name is pronounced Rok-nuh) was still a farmer in the hills; and the first twinkle of the Rockne star may have come when his great-grandfather, awaking from the long family sleep in the hills, constructed a farm vehicle with wheels to replace the runners which had been in use until that time.

His son Knute Knutson Rokne moved down into the town in 1852, set himself up as blacksmith, machinist, and hardware merchant—and began to build wagons and buggies with seats. In 1882 Rock's father, Lars Knutson Rokne, who added woodworking to the family skills, began to manufacture two-wheeled vehicles called *stolkjerre* and *kariol* (carryall). These became so popular that Emperor Wilhelm of Germany, a frequent visitor to the healthy hills, became one of his customers. English noblemen among his clients induced him to exhibit at the Liverpool Fair where he won a prize; so that the great World's Columbian Exposition—the Chicago World's Fair—would become a logical goal for this venturesome Norseman.

The Roknes had been advancing culturally. Lars Knutson Rokne married Martha Gjermo, whose forebears included doctors, teachers, and clergymen. Rockne was born in Voss, March 4, 1888, and baptized in the Lutheran faith in the village church which had begun as Catholic—as Rockne was to end—seven hundred years before.

IV

Lars Knutson Rokne came to the Chicago Fair in October 1893, won his prize, decided to settle in Chicago and got a job as a machinist, went to a night school to improve his language and to prepare for citizenship. When these fundamentals were taken care of, he sent for his wife and the three children, in chronological order, Anna, Knute, and Martha. Two other girls, Louise and Florence, were born in this country.

Knute Kenneth was a Gjermo in size, appearance, and inclination. His father called him *klureneve*, which is Norwegian for "all thumbs" and, in the manner of fathers, probably wondered how this one, and his only son, had wandered into a family of artisans. Rock was a healthy boy, small for his age; but it is hardly likely that anybody, noting the force in his eyes, tried to bully him; or if so, got away with it. Among other talents he was always handy with his fists. He had an obviously superior mind, with an excellent memory, got fine grade-school marks and liked to read. The family had a pleasant custom which permitted any member to delve into the purse for money that would be spent for gifts to some other member. Knute bought books for his sisters—and read them first.

Rockne had excellent home training. His father was a solid man, a firm disciplinarian; and not always in agreement with his son's passion for American sports. The mother, Martha, perhaps because of the clergymen in her lineage, was very religious. The family attended church services and Sunday school at Immanuel Norwegian Lutheran Church. They prayed together and played together; all were musical. The father played the cornet, the mother and daughters took to the piano, and Knute learned to play the flute, which would always be with him.

He was undoubtedly a proper pest to the four sisters, especially to the sensitive younger one whom he could make cry simply by pointing a finger and saying: "Cry." Baby-sitting never bothered him much; he would carry the little sister on his shoulder and deposit her on the curb for a grandstand seat at whatever sport was in season.

The Logan Square neighborhood in Chicago was an excellent polishing stone for this rough diamond. "It was not unpleasant going," he wrote, "in the new and spacious city, with its endless corner lots and tolerant police." The games were always between the Irish and the Scandinavians. (Chicago's broad ethnology lumped all Scandinavians together as "Swedes." As a coach Rock was sometimes —though never in his hearing—referred to as the Swede.) One of his stories told of a "copper named O'Goole who kept a paternal eye on us. When the Irish were pounding the Swedes, O'Goole grinned at such elegant sport. But once, when the Swedes imported two big Italians to give the Irishers a taste of the mud, O'Goole interfered, saying: 'The game is altogether too brutal and unfit for small boys.' So the Swedes appealed to the precinct captain to send us a Swede cop to balance up the mayhem.

"My first baptism of fire was received in one of these corner-lot games. I was an end on the Tricky Tigers—historic rivals of the Avondales—and we had a triple pass behind the line to impress onlookers. Our equipment wasn't elaborate: No helmets, one shin guard per player. We tied our ears with elastic tape to prevent spreading."

Rock graduated to the Barefoot Athletic Club, an Irish organization, which met the Hamburg Athletic Club for the district championship. "Trouble," he wrote, "came in handfuls. Crowds lined the gridiron and broke into the game. Things grew more pleasant for the players, however, when groups of spectators slipped away now and then to recharge their liquid batteries." Rock came out of the melee with physical evidence—and more trouble. His parents, "sharing the general belief that football was a system of modified massacre," banned him from further participation in what the lad himself thought only "pleasantly rough recreation."

Baseball was permissible. But, the next spring, an argument developed during a heroic struggle with the Maplewood boys. "Being

blessed or bothered by hidden strains of Irish ancestry, I found myself in the thick of it. Suddenly a bat bent the bridge of my nose. I
went home blinded; but uppermost in my mind was not sorrow but
logic. I said to my parents: 'I got this nose from baseball—and you
think football is rough.' So baseball was banned and football was restored to the sand-lot curriculum."

A Rockne friend wrote of this sand-lot period: "In one of the base-
ments of Cherry Place, the boxing, footwork, dodging, etc., of great
fighters were studied and practiced. Alongside one of the houses,
pole-vaulting was done with the aid of an old clothes pole, shot-
putting with an iron weight from an old kerosene lamp chandelier.
High-jumping and starting were practiced. The curves of the famous
Cub and Sox pitchers were rehearsed from newspaper articles and
hints in sporting guides. The boys had to make their own equipment.

"The spirit of adventure was inborn in these young men. The Norwegian poet, Björnson, puts it *'jev vil ud'*—'I will out.' Something new
in ventures, dares and stunts was always cropping out of these fertile
and imaginative Norse minds. Baseball and football teams, hiking
parties, fishing expeditions were being continually organized. Jaunts
way out in the country were common occurrences. Emissaries were
sent to other neighborhoods challenging to baseball and football
games. Uniforms or no uniforms, race or creed or color of opponents
—nothing made any difference. If your shirt were torn, play in your
undershirt—this was the spirit.

"By way of diversion stunts were in order. It is often recalled that
Knute would walk on his hands on the pickets of the wooden fence
in the rear of the church, an ideal (pole-vaulting) exercise for the
wrists. On Halloweens the neighborhood was in a state of anxiety
and expectancy. The boys were no respecter of persons. The wagon
of the alderman was conscientiously placed on top of his barn. A cow
and a horse were equitably exchanged. There was no roughness,
merely a delicious feast of folly."

(About 1938 I was one of a group of writers including Scott Fitzgerald, who would gather before a radio in an office at M-G-M, to
listen to Hitler whip himself and his followers into World War II.
At the time I would think how much better Rockne could have been
at this sort of thing than Hitler—and how fortunate for our country

that we followed Rockne's advice: "Hand them footballs instead of guns.")

Rockne lived near the White Sox baseball park and went through the phase of glorifying big-league baseball players. His favorites were Rube Waddell, the eccentric pitcher of the Philadelphia Athletics, and Three-Finger Brown of the Cubs. When he entered high school at the age of thirteen, he made the track team as a half-miler and, "with full parental approval," went out for football. "High school football in those days," he wrote, "had all the enthusiasm but none of the finesse of today. Coaches were few. Two professors, Peters and Ellis, volunteered to teach our squad. They did a good job of it, if only by holding me back and making me realize there was something more to football than the ball. The first big thrill of my life came when, at thirteen years of age and weighing one hundred and ten pounds, they put me on the scrubs of the North West Division High, now Tuley High. But it took me until my senior year to get on the team."

(After Warner Brothers made *Knute Rockne—All American,* following Rock's death, his widow gave Producer Bob Fellows a small picture of "Rockne's high school team" which the coach prized and carried about with him. Fellows later passed it on to me for safekeeping. There are eleven players in canvas jackets with nose guards and shin guards; a young manager in a derby hat; and a small boy mascot holding a round football labeled '99. The ball and uniforms have the initials M.T. for Murray Tuley. While the players are not identified by name, there is no mistaking the determined mouth and challenging eyes of the small one who would have weighed around 110 pounds. This boy has a lot of hair—maybe that added to its value to the early-bald K.K.R.)

Rock was not an outstanding high-school football player; he was just too small. But size was no handicap in track and with typical realism, he played to his strength. "Persistence at track meets won me a small reputation."

Persistence was indeed a word for Rockne. He joined the Y.M.C.A. for swimming and other body-building facilities; and became a member of Company F of the 132nd Infantry for the athletic work it afforded. He was good enough to make the Chicago A.A. junior team. And he was learning interesting things about people in the

catalysis of competition. "In minor meets the chance to win depended
as much on quick wits as stop watches and youngsters were quickly
initiated into the tricks of the trade. One official timer was noted
for his distaste for continuous Irish victories. Somebody on our side
would always stand near this official. If one of our opponents was
winning, our man would yell: 'Watch that O'Brien come.' But such
chickens come home to roost. Once, when I thought I had set a
record in the half-mile, a malicious opponent yelled: 'Come on,
Kelly.' The non-Hibernian official heard and the record was not
mine."

Alonzo Stagg, the patriarch of coaches, was then in his early prime
at the University of Chicago and supervised some of the city-wide
track meets. "With the fondness for coincidence that most of us
share," Rock wrote, "many have asked whether Stagg and I met in
those days. If we did, it must have occurred under the stands when
I dropped out of longer distance foot-races, as invariably occurred."
But young Rockne's football hero was one of Stagg's players; and the
way he tells of it, with one of the few glimpses of his private self,
indicates what a writer Rock *could* have made if he had ever allowed
his captive *jev* to vault the wall he had built around it.

"The first time I learned a football was something to think with,
and not merely something to kick, was when I saw a great football
player in action for the first time . . . The meeting of the Eastern
high school champions, Brooklyn Prep, and the Western champions,
Hyde Park, was a great event. Crashing the gate—a habit of mine
as a youngster—I sat spellbound before the brilliant, heady play of
Hyde Park's quarterback, a lad named Walter Eckersall. His keen,
handsome face, his sharp, staccato calling of signals, the smooth precision with which he drove and countered and drove again, handling
his players with the rhythm of an orchestra leader—all this gave football a new meaning to me. After the game was over and the Western
players went cheering from the field, shouting the name of Eckersall
like a slogan over the defeated Easterners, I tried to get close to the
hero of the day. But two or three thousand other youngsters were
trying to do the same thing, so I had to go home without a hand-
shake—yet, for the first time in a young and fairly crowded life, I
went home with a hero. Dreams of how, someday, I might shine as
Eckersall had shone that afternoon were my lonesome luxury. For

years they were nothing but dreams. Eckersall went on to greater glory as the sensational star of Chicago University. My path took me to nothing more athletic than being a mail dispatcher working nights, for years.

"But there came an afternoon when the Notre Dame squad ran on a field with the former sand-lot boy, ex-mail dispatcher, as captain. The referee was Walter Eckersall. In his smart, white togs he looked scarcely a day older than when he had led Hyde Park to its victory over Brooklyn. Grasping his hand I said:

"'I've been waiting years for this.'

"'For what?' said Eckersall.

"'To shake your hand,' and I began to tell him how his brilliant performance had turned my mind seriously to football.

"'Stop,' Eckersall said, 'or Notre Dame will be penalized five yards for speech-making.'"

Eckersall could have had no idea what a future speechmaker he was shutting off. Rock and his idol were to become great friends. In 1925, en route from the old Belmont Hotel in New York to the Yankee Stadium I rode with Rock and Eckersall in the first car of the cavalcade carrying the Notre Dame squad. We were just behind the motorcycle escort that whirled us through every red light from 42nd Street to the Bronx. As we got out Rock said: "I've had my thrill. I don't care who wins the ball game."

The passion for athletics led Rockne and several of his fellows to the disaster which has visited so many other high-school athletes. One day, the school principal, perhaps wondering what sudden illness had caused the absence of so many of his male pupils that day, was sauntering through Humboldt Park. Or perhaps it was because he had diagnosed the mass malaise; at any rate he saw the Tuley track team working out enthusiastically and noisily.

The track squad was thereupon desegregated and integrated among the other high schools. Rockne was allotted to Jefferson High where, perhaps by design, there was no track team. When he threatened to quit and go to work, nobody argued with him. His father practically insisted on it.

"It is my solemn duty," wrote the Rev. John W. Cavanaugh (who, as president, was later to admit Rockne to Notre Dame and, under some pressure, to appoint him head coach of football and track), "to record that Knute Rockne, afterward a stern disciplinarian of mental laggards, never got a high-school diploma from any institution in Chicago or anywhere else. It was necessary for him to face a worse than Spanish Inquisition on some of the entrance requirements for the Department of Pharmacy when he came to Notre Dame."

After drifting about for more than a year in the usual succession of odd jobs, and lacking the desire or talent to become a mechanic, he took the civil service examination for postal clerk. It was necessary to write an essay. His subject, in 1907, was: "The Advisability of Our Having a Larger Navy Is Becoming Greater Since Japan Whipped Russia."

V

KNUTE ROCKNE: Appointed substitute clerk March 21, 1907. Promoted to regular clerk same date—salary $600 per annum. Assignment, Stamper Mailing Division, Main Post Office. Transferred to Dispatcher Mailing Division, July 1, 1907. Salary advanced to $800 April 1, 1908; to $900, April 1, 1909; to $1000 April 1, 1910. Resigned November 28, 1910.

The Great American Tragedy may well be the unhappy fact that so few people are doing the work for which they are best fitted, at which they would be happiest and most successful. Rockne seemed to be well on his way to being buried alive, mentally and emotionally, in the Chicago post office. It was rough, dirty work, handling bags that averaged fifty pounds. It began at midnight and finished at eight-thirty each morning of the week, Sundays included.

He fought the boredom by choosing the harder job of dispatcher "to have something to do in this temple of loafing. Most of the old-timers called me a fool but there was excellent memory training in it. It was a good investment in mental energy; and if a coach needs one thing more than another, it's a memory for the swarming details of plays and combinations of plays—especially the personal styles of coaches and players in executing them . . . to remember what he himself has done that worked or failed in any given emergency."

Older workers liked him but smiled at the antics of this character who practiced wrestling, jumping, and foot racing in the lulls; who never missed his thirty minutes of swift running up and down the driveway each night; who rushed through work over which they had learned to relax; who was "a deep thinker, always reading books, even brought books to work with him."

This is what the Odd Ball himself thought: "Civil service taught me little save its unevenness and unfairness. You wondered why veterans smiled at youthful ardor and industry. I used to hustle letters into pouches as fast as I could grab them and think of train times. Older hands chatted and riffled. Merit meant nothing. The politicians got soft jobs for their favorites regardless of civil service. Enthusiasm could scarcely survive the discovery that a dispatcher who worked hard received nothing more than a henchman who did nothing more arduous than sit on a stool and sell stamps. I was on my way to becoming the smartest shirker of all, having reached a point of lethargy where it took me an hour to do what I had once done in ten minutes."

Lethargy is an antithetic word for Rockne. The superior mind requires fulfillment of its talents; and the better the mind the greater its need for expression; and the more furiously must it fly at prison bars. As a youth, he had thought of college as something beyond him; now in the unhappy stretches of the postal prison, he came to look forward to it as an escape. Always thrifty, he set $1000 as a target and the University of Illinois as his goal. Later he dismissed his success with characteristic terse modesty: "I was able to take advantage of the breaks when they came my way." Actually, as in all such cases, he was forcing his own breaks. He had several factors favoring him:

1. The Norwegian spirit of adventure and originality which had come alive in his great-grandfather and brought his own father to America.

2. The time for reading which was feeding his mind, making it stronger, more ambitious and rebellious.

3. The night work which gave him no time for girls; so that, when the green light came, he was neither married nor emotionally en-

tangled, as the average vital male is apt to be at age twenty-two, when Rockne entered Notre Dame.

4. The encouragement of one of his sisters, whom he did not identify by name. "The cold, unembellished fact is that a sister of mine was more ambitious for me than I was for myself. She insisted that a college education would mean more to me and the family than anything else. Also [and again the self-jibe] that I'd be able to waste my time better as a college track athlete than as a part-time wonder of the campus called the Loop." (The Loop, of course, is a synonym for Chicago as Broadway is for New York.)

5. Track (and proof that time-wasters sometimes pay off). His enthusiasm for track had been doubly served by the postal job: track provided relief from boredom; and without the postal job, he might have had neither the time, enthusiasm nor energy to expend in track. "I carried the colors of Irving Park A.C. and the Central Y.M.C.A., for which I managed to win the half-mile in 2:02 (two minutes, two seconds) a good mark then, and graduated to the Illinois Athletic Club. Here I ran against old-time stars like Lindberg, Harvey Blair, Ward, and Belot. Our coaches were Martin Delaney and Dad Butler; and we newcomers were able to touch shoulders with Olympic stars like Ralph Rose, Lightbody, Hogeson, and Irons—even the great Johnny Hayes, winner of the classic Olympic Marathon over Dorando; Hayes came to fraternize with us, not to compete, because he had turned pro."

The confidence that came from success in major-league track circles helped him vault the mental gap between college as a faraway dream; and college as a reality. When he had saved his thousand dollars he began to look downstate toward Champaign and the University of Illinois. Then came the big accident that was to mean so much to football; and to everybody whose life was to be touched by Rockne.

Two former teammates from the Illinois Athletic Club, Johnny Devine and Johnny Plant, suggested that Rock go with them to Notre Dame.

In his autobiography Rock has himself exclaiming: "Who ever heard of Notre Dame? They never won a football game in their lives." Actually Notre Dame had gone undefeated the previous year (1909), and one of its victories, over Fielding Yost and mighty

Michigan, had shocked the Midwest and begun an athletic quarrel which has never really ended and which Rockne himself was to keep at a stir.

"What swung me was that I could get a job and certainly get by cheaper than at Illinois. So I went down to South Bend with a suitcase and one thousand dollars . . . feeling the strangeness of being a lone Norse Protestant—if the word must be used—invader of a Catholic stronghold."

It may have been the most courageous step this bold young man ever took. Mrs. Rockne has said that he was never quite so sure about new things as his aggressive exterior indicated. After all, he was the lone son of a family in very modest circumstances; he was leaving the lifetime security of the postal service for what could be a chimeric and perhaps disastrous dream. At twenty-two, he was four years older than the average freshman; and because of his approaching baldness and the broken nose, he looked even older. He was going to have to work to stretch his thousand-dollar nest egg over four and perhaps more years of college. It is possible that he might have been influenced toward Notre Dame by the knowledge that, in Devine and Plant, he would have at least two friends in the new life.

Shortly after arriving he had been ready to call it a mistake and go back to the postal prison. The job they had given him was cleaning up the slops in the chemical lab; and he was in danger of being expelled when somebody stole some sacramental wine for which he was technically responsible. He packed his suitcase and was leaving the campus when word got to Devine, Plant and Fred Steers, another track star, who caught him in time and renewed their selling job. It will be noted in his service record that Rock did not actually resign from the post office until November 28, 1910; so it probably took him that long to definitely decide to be a college boy.

The person who discouraged him most was, of all people, the football coach, Frank "Shorty" Longman. Rock had gone out for the Brownson Hall team and had done well enough to be recommended for a varsity trial. But Longman, a power-minded coach, put the 145-pound, five-foot eight-inch rookie at fullback, possibly a derisive gesture. Rock was shipped back to Interhall. Rock never cared much for "Shorty" Longman, whose outlines were apparent in a stock coaching character Rockne later lampooned in his platform stories and in his boy's fiction book, *The Four Winners*.

The fact is, nobody at Notre Dame except Plant, Steers, Devine, and probably the track coach knew or cared whether a freshman named Rockne had entered; or if he stayed. Luck of the Irish? Undoubtedly; but Notre Dame was again cashing in on its hobby of taking care of poor boys. It fed a farm boy's horse one year, as well as the boy, and later got itself the present Morris Inn on the campus. It helped another boy and now it has the showcase O'Shaughnessy Hall of Liberal and Fine Arts. The LaFortune Student Center came from Joseph A. LaFortune, whose father had worked for the university; and so on.

Rockne could get very moody and depressed when his *jeu* beat futilely against whatever bars were balking him at that moment. But, from the Logan Square training, he knew his way around among the Irish and, as his writing many times indicated, felt kinship with them. They were, after all, his kind of people. And now for a better future understanding of the spirit of Notre Dame, let's take a closer look at the kind of people who had built the Irish stronghold into which the lone Norse had so oddly come.

VI

Back in 1836, Simon Bruté, Bishop of Vincennes, in the then Northwest Territory, had visited the seminary in Le Mans, France, looking for men who would preach the gospel and educate the Indians and white pioneers of his diocese. One of those who listened was Rev. Edward Frederick Sorin, C.S.C., a young man of comfortable background, who had the physique of a tackle, the zeal of a fanatic and the energy of an atom—and was going to need all of them in addition to considerable ingenuity and a very practical business sense.

He was a member of the religious Congregation of Holy Cross; and five years later, accompanied by six Brothers of the Order, he left Le Mans and headed for the great adventure in the Northwest Territory. As a priest, Father Sorin was the leader. The Brothers were modest men who devoted their lives to the more humble but very necessary duties of religious service.

Father Sorin's first problem was to remain with him for life—insufficient funds. The money given to him to get to the Northwest was not even enough to get him on the ship. So he did a job of persuasive talking; and landed his crew in the steerage where, for thirty-nine days, they shared space with such other adventurers as (noted in his report) "a company of French comedians and German Protestants." When he stepped off the ship he did the very thing which Americans returning to their native land often feel like doing —knelt and kissed the ground, as a sign of adoption.

None of the band could speak English; which was probably only a mild hindrance to such as these. The matter of further funds was taken care of by Father Sorin in New York. They headed west by canal, by boat, by horse and cart. They survived storms; and, when necessary, praised the Lord and manfully fought off robbers. On the night of the twenty-fourth day, when they knew they were approaching some sort of frontier protection, they stood "in the clear bright moonlight and sang all the hymns to the Blessed Virgin we knew."

There was a short stop at Vincennes, where they built a school in the wilderness; after which Father Sorin set off by oxcart, in bitter cold and snow, for a tract of nine hundred acres to the north. He now had a team of seven Brothers, of whom four were from Ireland. So early, the French had been integrated. After ten rugged days they arrived at the frontier village at the south bend of the St. Joseph's River, November 26, 1842. Alexis Coquillard, who had the trading post, gave them their first warm food, after which they went on to the site of Ste-Marie-des-Lacs, a missionary outpost already known as Notre Dame.

"Everything was frozen, yet it all appeared so beautiful," Father Sorin wrote to Father Moreau in France. "The lake, particularly, with its mantle of snow, resplendently white, was to us a symbol of the stainless purity of Our Lady. We hurried about looking at the various sites. Like little children, in spite of the cold, we ran from one end to the other, perfectly enchanted by the beauty of our new home."

There was a rude cabin shelter. Father Sorin and his Brothers knelt in the snow, dedicated their efforts to Our Lady, and went to work. They made bricks from marl beds found near the lake. Father Sorin talked the surrounding Catholics—and Protestants—into helping with the work. The building they put up, with some renovations, is now known as Old College. Nearby is a replica of the Grotto of Our Lady of Lourdes, where students can quietly be found at almost any hour. A New York sports writer, Bob Brumby, on the campus for a football game, once said to me after I had given him the "Fifty Cent Grand Tour": "Let's go by that outdoor cathedral again." He may have been feeling a sense of misty history; for at this point a television camera could, with artistic honesty, fade back through the years to find Indians squatting among the trees by the lake, listening to the words of the Black Robe. La Salle and Hennepin had passed this way in 1679, coming from Lake Michigan, making portage toward the headwaters of the Mississippi. Because of the waterways it was a favorite gathering spot and an outpost of religion.

Father Sorin built his school, and on January 15, 1844, through the kind offices of a Methodist friend, John B. Defrees, was granted, by a special act of the legislature of Indiana, a charter for the University of Notre Dame du Lac, with its meager endowment of flesh and blood. (Eight years later Knute Knutson Rokne, the coach's grandfather, would move his blacksmith shop from the farm into the village of Voss—the same year that Clem and Henry Studebaker would start the blacksmith shop in South Bend that was to become the Studebaker Corporation—with which Knute Kenneth Rockne would become closely involved, by a most circuitous route, just before his death.)

At the beginning Notre Dame lived by barter. For one hundred dollars a year it would feed a boy, wash and mend his clothes, give him medical attention and teach him, along with manners and cleanliness, "the complete English course—spelling, reading, grammar, history, surveying, astronomy." It would accept whatever dollars the parents could afford; but gladly take the balance in grain, produce, animals, furniture or other useful articles. Certain electives were extra. Latin brought an added hog; and something fancy, like the pianoforte—which the pioneers seemed to regard as the hallmark of culture—two big hogs.

The students were the advance guard of civilization, sons of plainsmen, farmers, trappers, storekeepers. Father Sorin's method was the

French device of keeping them busy from five-thirty in the morning, when they arose, until nine-thirty in the evening when they retired. Creditors were always at the door. The early days were a series of crises which required all the faith—and strong backs—of the valiant little group; and the help from South Bend and the countryside.

Fire, a constant hazard, destroyed the first ambitious college building which housed two hundred students. When the working capital was reduced to fifty cents, Father Sorin sold a valuable team of horses. Cholera became a serious menace during a national epidemic. He correctly diagnosed its local cause as a dam on a nearby property which caused swampland near the lakes. The owner would not raze the dam. "There are moments when vigorous action upsets the enemy," decided Father Sorin. So he sent his men-of-prayer-through-action, equipped with crowbars, to the scene. The dam was destroyed, the menace removed; and Father Sorin got away with it because he was supported by public opinion.

He was plagued, like other entrepreneurs, by currency fluctuations during the frequent financial panics. He was not above begging. During the gold rush of 1849 he financed a company which managed to get to California; but alas, no gold! This failure brought censure from his religious superiors in France. There were other difficulties from that quarter caused by the slowness of communication and the usual lack of comprehension by the home office of the swift problems, requiring swifter action, of the man in the field.

Father Sorin's drive was a complete faith, revealed in this testament: "If all men fail me there is one treasury that is always full, the treasury of Our Most Holy Lady . . . Never once has she failed me. I am compelled to go right ahead with this work, knowing that her power and kindness will not fail us in the days that lie ahead. And when this school has grown a bit more I will raise her aloft, so that men will know, without asking, why we have succeeded here. To that Lovely Lady, raised high on a dome, a golden dome, men may look and find the answer."

Father Sorin was adjusting his system to his personnel, shaping his offense to the opposing defense, to shifting weather; sometimes, as in the case of the cholera emergency, calling for daring measures. He founded St. Mary's, the school for girls, just across the Niles Road. Oddly enough, Notre Dame registration increased rapidly during the

Civil War; at its end there were nearly five hundred students, all housed and taught in a "huge" (Father Sorin never spared the hyperbole in his commercials) new five-story building—physical proof that Father Sorin had finally got his school solidly established.

The Congregation of Holy Cross thought so too, made him Superior General in 1868, the head of its activities throughout the world. He began the series of ocean crossings which were to total fifty.

He was in Montreal, on April 23, 1879, when the word came that every college building except the church had been destroyed by fire; that only $40,000 of the $200,000 loss was covered by insurance.

He returned at once, found the religious community assembled at the church, headed by the president, Rev. William Corby who, as an Army chaplain, had contributed to the Notre Dame tradition by giving mass absolution to the Fighting Irish Brigade at the Battle of Gettysburg. There was fear that the sight of his life's work in ashes might break the sixty-five-year-old Father Sorin. But he met them at the altar, prayed with them, gave them a fight talk Rockne would have envied. It ended: "If all were gone I would not give up."

He picked up the first wheelbarrow. That was in April. By September the nucleus of the present university was ready to receive students—a better Administration Building with a bigger statue of Our Lady looming higher in the sky from a wider golden dome so that all men might see and know the answer. It was this disastrous fire of '79 which first brought Notre Dame, its fighting leader, and its fighting spirit, to national attention. Help had come from many outside sources, including, as always, the original "synthetic alumni," Father Sorin's beloved Protestants.

On his way to becoming a patriarch, he exercised a firm but slowly decreasing supervision over the university. The new presidents, reflecting the faculty and student body, were all Irish. Father Sorin did not entirely approve of the Irish, found them "not too inclined to obedience" which is something the Irish never trouble to deny.

Father Sorin died October 31, 1893, from Bright's disease, at the age of seventy-nine. He would not have been pleased at the pageantry of his funeral, so expressly forbidden in his final instructions. The reason was contained in a line of the funeral sermon by Archbishop Elder of Cincinnati: "I do not think that in all our country, nor in any single country, there is a place where one single man has transformed a savage wilderness into such a city of splendor and culture as this University of Notre Dame."

Father Sorin still presides over Notre Dame; or at least his statue is firmly in command of the terrain from the Circle to the Administration Building. It is probable that few recognize it; nor would the founder see much similarity in the modern Notre Dame with the "tight little boarding school" which he thought could not hope to compete with state institutions and heavily endowed private schools.

He is not entirely forgotten. A few years ago another smaller statue of him disappeared from its place on the campus. Thereafter, for many months, postcards and other missives reached Notre Dame from far-flung corners of the earth with the usual message: *"Having a good time, wish you were here. Father Sorin."* It was a collegiate version of Kilroy's travels and nobody at Notre Dame, official or otherwise, seems to have been outraged. Father Sorin himself, with his close contact with masculine boys, might have been amused; and accepted it as an affectionate remembrance, a sort of student valentine to the old boy who had made all this possible.

Father Sorin was, after all, a traveling man. And he did return. The statue was found one day, peacefully intact, bobbing gently in a rowboat on the lake.

The thing Father Sorin would find most inexplicable about Notre Dame today is the football. He would like very much the money it has brought in, the publicity which attracted students and warmed the enthusiasm of alumni, especially those with fat purses. As an expert public relations man he would drool at the prestige it had helped to create.

But he wouldn't have understood it; nor have welcomed the problems it brought. As late as 1910, President John W. Cavanaugh was inclined to think the game was hardly worth the trouble it was stirring up. But football is an American institution which reflects American life; and thrives best in fertile masculine soil. It was already strong of stock at Notre Dame; and Rockne was already on the campus.

After Rockne's death a bishop would say: "Rockne was Sorin without a cassock and breviary."

VII

On a Friday in the early fall of 1949 I was in Detroit with fifteen
other authors on a book-selling junket. When I received an invitation to talk to the Michigan pep rally at Ann Arbor I thought I'd
better remind the student who called me that I was from Notre
Dame. "Oh no—" he cried. Then: "Okay."

There were five thousand voracious young Wolverines in Ferry
Field that evening. I was introduced as the author of the annual
Football Preview, which I had originated in *The Saturday Evening
Post* in 1937 and brought to *Collier's* in 1949. I told them my Preview
problems had been simplified: "I just pick Michigan first every year
and let the other predictions fall in place." This could have had me
expelled from the Notre Dame family but it was well received at
Michigan—until the next speaker, George Trevor of Yale and the
New York *Sun* (in that order), shouted to the multitude: "Don't
you know this guy Wallace has been kidding you? He's from Notre
Dame—"

"*Boooo—*"

"He's president of the Notre Dame Alumni Association."

"*Boooooooooo—*"

"And what he really does every year is pick Notre Dame first—"

Prolonged *BOOOOOO*. George then named Army to beat Michigan the next day—while they were boooo-ing George, I faded from
the platform and into the dark. Later that night the male students
raided sorority houses and indulged in other skylarking which might
just as well have included a whimsical apprehension of the Notre
Dame spy.

A Michigander would have aroused the same frenetic reaction at
an Irish pep rally because Notre Dame and Michigan, in a quiet way,
are the Hatfields and McCoys of the Midwest. "Why don't Michigan
and Notre Dame play football?" is enmeshed with another question:
"Why doesn't Notre Dame belong to the Western Conference?"
These are ancient quarrels about which the moderns know little, care

less, but still do not quite forget. I will merely hit the highlights:

Michigan was Notre Dame's first gridiron opponent, back in 1887, and won the first three games. But trouble began when, with the Irish primed and eager in new uniforms "that had the great advantage of being padded," Michigan, according to a Notre Dame student editor "backed squarely out, alleging various excuses." There were occasional later games which Michigan always won.

In 1896 the Western Conference was organized. Since Notre Dame was playing most of the state schools, it applied for membership but was shaken off as small fry, which, in terms of students, it definitely was. The Irish, under Coach Tom Barry, who had played for Brown and taken law at Harvard, put their house in order by meeting all Conference eligibility requirements. When Michigan withdrew in 1905, Notre Dame again applied, was rejected, didn't like it and, in the well-known Irish manner, let it be known. Schedule trouble immediately developed; and by 1909 there were no Conference games for Notre Dame.

But there was Michigan; and the Irish had served notice, by holding the Wolves to a 12–6 score in 1908, that a new power was rising. They went to Ann Arbor in 1909 under the previously mentioned Frank "Shorty" Longman who had been an end on one of Yost's famed "point-a-minute" teams.

The dressing-room speeches at Ann Arbor that day would be worth something today if they had been recorded on tape. Yost, a vigorous orator, no doubt called upon his champions to go out and put the bumptious upstarts in their places. Longman, a thespian thunderer whose idea of showing who was boss was to lick every man on his squad—or try to—was undoubtedly fired by the urge every pupil has to upset a famed master. His situation was psychologically ideal. Notre Dame was out to beat Michigan for the first time—after eight previous defeats; and to avenge the Conference snub by defeating the school which had snubbed the Conference. The juices were further stirred by rumblings about the eligibility of two Notre Dame linemen, Ralph Dimick of Hubbard, Oregon, and George Philbrook of Olympia, Washington.

It must have been quite a ball game. For years thereafter Rev. Matt Walsh indoctrinated incoming freshmen with an engaging and expanding tale of how fullback Pete Vaughn had hit the line so low

for the winning touchdown in the 12–3 Irish victory that the mark
of the goal post (then on the line) showed clearly on the back of his
jersey.

(Three members of the 1909 squad—Harry "Red" Miller, Pete
Vaughn, and Bill Schmitt—attended their fiftieth reunion in 1959.)

In 1910, again en route to Ann Arbor, Notre Dame got only as
far as Niles, six miles to the north, when they were called back by
news that Michigan had canceled the game. The specific point of dispute was whether an institution Dimick and Philbrook had attended
in Oregon had been a prep school or a college. Notre Dame, in turn,
raised similar doubts about Michigan players. Although neither
school belonged to the Conference, Notre Dame's failure to get into
that organization became part of the press debate. The Irish lost
and Rev. Tom Crumley, chairman of the Athletic Board, tartly observed that "the dispute seemed to have been settled on theological,
rather than athletic grounds."

Notre Dame was ostracized by the major powers in its own section. There were some who wanted to give up the effort to be a
major gridiron power. But Notre Dame was not a tired old man. It
was a vital youngster, sprouting in all directions. Its pride had been
wounded, its fighting spirit aroused. It said, as had Father Sorin after
the '79 fire, "If all were gone I would not give up." It faced to the
East.

Rockne was a freshman in 1910, living among the other athletes,
getting firsthand all the bitter frustration of those who had been
turned back at the Michigan border. It was then that this young
man with the low boiling point, fierce loyalty and blazing competitive spirit—and natural love of feuds—set up the personal antagonism
he was always to carry against Yost.

Notre Dame and Michigan have played only one series (two
games) in the last fifty years; but they seem to do very well without
each other. Notre Dame's position as a national school is much better
served by a national schedule; but it plays several Big Ten games
each year and subscribes to all the Conference regulations. The
Notre Dame of today is ample proof that it has not been seriously
affected by religious, racial, or social bigotry. But football is a smooth
ellipse with many submerged angles; and this one, like the hull of
a sunken ship in a long-forgotten wreck, has affected the course of

gridiron navigation for a half-century. It gave the Irish a forceful push toward their destiny as a national gridiron leader. It was indirectly responsible for the Army-Notre Dame series. It was a sort of gridiron growing pain.

VIII

Rockne was the ideal college man—a superior student who took an outstanding part in extracurricular activities, including major athletics; and was never a disciplinary problem. He was admitted in September 1910; was graduated June 15, 1914, with a Bachelor of Science degree in Pharmacy and a general average of 90.52 per cent. Here is the official transcript:

School Year	Dept. Title of Course	Spec. Title of Course	Sem. Hrs. of Credit	Per Cent Grade
1910	Pharmacy 1	Elements	6	94
1911	" 9	Phar. Arithmetics	6	94
	Microscopy 1	Lecture & Lab	2	98
	Science E	Chemistry	Credit	97
	Phonography		"	95
	Materia Medica		2	94
	Pharmacy 10	Pharmacognosy	3	97
	Bacteriology	Lecture & Lab	4	99
	Physiology 1		5	94
1911	Botany 1 & 2	Botany & Bot. Lab	10	90
1912	Pharmacy 3 & 4	Inorg. & General	8	93
	Chemistry 3	Qual've Analysis	4	93
	" 4	" "	4	87
	Materia Medica 8		4	94
	Chemistry 6	Elementary Org.	5	85
	Physiology 2		5	93
	Pharmacy 10	Pharmacognosy	6	94
	Compounding		5	92

School Year	Dept. Title of Course	Spec. Title of Course	Sem. Hrs. of Credit	Per Cent Grade
1912	Zoology		10	90
1913	Physics 2	General	6	84
	Chemistry 9	Advance Org.	2	89
	English 2	Essay: Oration	3	98
	" 2	Poetry & Poets	3	81
	" 1	Genung's Principles of Rhetoric	6	93
1913	Geology 3	Mineralogy	2	90
1914	" 1	Prin. of Geology	4	90
	Botany 3 & 4	Adv. Bot. & Lab	4.5	91
	Philosophy 5 & 6	Theodicy Rational Psych.	4	94
	Zoology 2		12	90
	Anatomy	Human Anatomy	8	98
	Chemistry	Electrochemistry	2	94

Rockne's academic record might well be displayed in every locker room for the scrutiny of those scholars who complain: "Arithmetics wasn't bad enough—they had to go hang letters on 'em." It might hang in the offices of deans who get complaints from coaches about the work load on their "pore little boys." It could well be studied by those coaches who try to switch serious students into snap courses so that "scholastics" will not interfere with football practice. And I hope this evidence will tend to disperse any thoughts the reader may have had about my exaggerating the qualities of this paragon coach.

The phenomenal freshman grades, all in the 90s, so contrary to the usual first-year performance, are easily understood. Here was no homesick seventeen-year-old but a twenty-two-year-old man who, in the frustrating coop of the postal service, had done a lot of serious thinking; whose demanding mind was finding the food it had craved. The only apparent slowdown was in the junior year when his father died and he thought of quitting school. The sister (he never identified her) who had been largely responsible for his going to college convinced him that he should remain. (It is probable that his consistent concern with money was aggravated by the fact, which I have on good evidence, that he also contributed to the support of his mother.)

The senior-year grades, also in the 90s, are the more impressive because Rock was then the captain of the football team, and good enough to make Walter Camp's third All-American eleven. There are certain accurate arrows to the future in these grades. It was hardly likely that the teacher of English 2: Essay Oration would expect a star football player majoring in science to become one of the great public speakers of his day; but that 98 was a tip. The 94 in philosophy, all the more surprising because he was not a Catholic at that time, revealed the future psychologist. And if you've ever been exposed to Genung you will appreciate that 93—and understand his ability to speak and write the language.

"I taught him physics in his sophomore year," Rev. Thomas Irving recently told me. "He had a very good mind and was an attentive student. That fellow would just sit there and look at you. There was no foolishness about him in class; and you would never make the mistake of taking him for a dumbbell. Out of class he was very jovial and funny. I was a prefect in Corby Hall one year when he was there. He was full of tricks but no real trouble. He took part in campus activities, played a squaw in a show; and played the flute in jam sessions with Mike and Art Carmody and some others." The old priest's young eyes twinkled; so did his voice as he went on: "One time he, Dorais, and some of the other football players had a baseball team. They came over to play the Seminarians and lost. Next time I saw him I said: 'The boys on the hill put it over on you.' He laughed. 'Their diamond wasn't square, Father.'"

Dr. Leo O'Donnell, now chief of staff at Mercy Hospital in Pittsburgh, was in school with Rock, and remained one of his close friends. "Rock came to Notre Dame to be a doctor. He had the best marks in biology and was the best man in chemistry in the school. Father Nieuwland [the late Rev. Julius A. Nieuwland, the Notre Dame priest-scientist] accepted him as an equal. He and Rock used to stand there and argue. It was because of his medical knowledge that Rock could act as his own trainer in the days when the squad could not afford one. He was probably far ahead of his field in what he called the 'heroic treatment' for sprains—making the boys use wet heat, then walk on them.

"Rock owned very little. He usually wore a monogram sweater for protection from the elements. If he wanted to go to town he would borrow Chief Tierney's overcoat. Chief was six feet one inch and weighed 250. You know Rock's size. He participated in all the theater plays that were given during his junior and senior years. He showed a tendency, even at that time, for dramatics. Rock, Ray Eichenlaub, and Rupe Mills loved to be in plays.

"It has always been interesting that some men who attended Notre Dame during Rock's period complained that he gave them very little recognition after he became prominent. The answer is that very few students knew Rockne as an undergraduate; and he knew very few, hence he couldn't know them well enough to make a fuss over them. The fact of the matter is such people were 'high hat' toward Rockne when he was an undergraduate."

Rockne in a high hat was a new and somewhat ridiculous thought to me, since I've never known any important person who was less inclined to toss his weight around. This is an old problem with celebrities but it might also throw another beam on Rock's essential character. He was very sensitive and inclined to be easily hurt. He might very well, in later years, have enjoyed ignoring the chap who had ignored the fellow who "owned little." He was probably not the easy person to know, as a student, that he later became. "Don't forget," his roommate Dorais told Grantland Rice, "he was about four years older than the rest of us in school. His thoughts tumbled out in such bursts that he was inclined to stammer. This was the reason for his machine-gun type of oratory later on; but he had trouble becoming a speaker. He seemed to have more problems than the rest of us. He was always threatening to quit school, for one reason or another, but, of course, never got around to it."

Without any doubt he was tongue-tied around girls. Here is incontrovertible evidence from a former FBI man and prosecuting attorney, who is now a member of the House of Representatives—Samuel L. Devine of Columbus, Ohio, a Republican serving the 12th Congressional District. Sam is the son of the same Johnny Devine who, along with Johnny Plant, steered Rockne to Notre Dame. He writes:

"My father, John F. Devine, Jr., and Johnny Plant both went to Touhy [high school] in Chicago. My mother [the former Kittie

Leeper], while dating my father, often double-dated with Rockne. She stated that he was so bashful and self-conscious that he would scarcely say a word all evening and hence rarely had a repeat date with the same girl . . . He was a frequent visitor at my parents' home after they were married. However, his shyness continued and every time he had an occasion to meet a girl he would blush clear to his hairline. My mother said that the amazing thing about him was his later ability to overcome this shyness, and to develop the ease, poise, and personality that drew people to him and made him a great speaker."

People who knew Rockne in this period invariably emphasized his shyness; the conflict in his moods; the force in his eyes; the voice that revealed power, guile, fury, charm, that could cut like a weapon or soothe like an orchestra. As late as 1921, when I began to know him, he was still uncertain about his ability to make a speech. But on-stage or off-, when his eyes and voice worked together, the rest of his face became unimportant; and might this be the secret of the charm of homely men—for women as well as other men?

The thing within Rock, the *jev* that wanted *ud*, must have been constantly agitating, gnawing, prowling. This could well explain his intensity. There was so much that wanted to be expressed; and which found release in so many activities.

IX

Rockne must have been a very good stage clown because all of his contemporaries remember his female impersonations. There is a fine picture of him as a squaw, with a heavy wig and long braids framing the flat face and spread nose. Psychiatrists might read into these performances, along with his shyness, a pleasure in ridiculing women. It is my guess that a psychiatrist who tried to quiz Rockne would have wound up on the couch himself—or run screaming from the barrage of grating, incisive questions, reinforced by the boring eyes and the jabbing finger.

Rockne was probably just having fun in his stage roles; as he did

in various other ad-lib campus performances. Notre Dame has neither fraternities, hazing, nor freshmen regulations prescribed by
upperclassmen. A man is treated as a man until he begins to act like
a boy; and then he becomes vulnerable, regardless of his class standing, to a psychological treatment known traditionally as "goofing."
It is deceptively devastating. All you have to do is admit you are
pretty good at something—anything—and soon you are surrounded
by flatterers who will espouse your cause and wind up building you
into a contender against the university champion in that field, be it
checkers, marbles, debating, foot racing, quarterbacking, dancing,
romancing, or physical fitness. You name it and they will dig up the
champion. The treatment goes on until the "goof" wises up.

Rockne, a fast ad-libber and excellent actor, was often the campus
"champion."

He is remembered by Father Cavanaugh as "a vigorous and in-
dustrious performer on the flute rather than a virtuoso"; but he was
good enough to make the college orchestra for which a "modest
honorarium was allowed against his college expenses." He and Dorais
lived in the Sorin "subway," where the rooms had windows on the
ground level. These were very useful for students who were "skiving"
(off-campus without permission). All you had to know was "whose
window was working" that night.

There is a story that Rockne and Dorais, when in financial emergencies, were not above exacting a slight fee for their window service
—until the night crawlers, operating quietly, loaded the room with
red lanterns, freshly painted signs, and other bric-a-brac accumu-
lated on a roistering journey home. The rector, on an early morning
call, came upon the mélange—and the taxpayers had had their revenge.

Rockne and Dorais were listed in the 1914 *Dome* (the college
yearbook) as Department Editors, with the departments unspecified.
Dorais later became a Detroit councilman. Rockne would have been
sensational as a political candidate; but he failed in his only political
effort on the campus—an attempt by the science men to have the
college yearbook dedicated to Rev. Julius A. Nieuwland. The lawyers, as usual, had the superior organization.

"Rockne's reputation as a student," Father Cavanaugh wrote, "still
lives in the memory of the men of his time. He never appeared un-

prepared in the classroom. He could sit in a room with three or four intimates discussing football or politics, follow the conversation accurately, participate in it occasionally with sapient remarks, while studying a textbook with seemingly complete concentration. His favorite method of study when alone was to place a book on a desk or table, and after reading a bit, march up and down, rolling a pencil between the palms of his hands and going over the matter he had read. Whoever interrupted would be invited to discuss the question Rock had been studying. That saved time and fixed the matter in his memory. Father Nieuwland, a very distinguished professor of chemistry, declares that Rockne was the most remarkable student he ever knew. He often audited classes in foreign courses to get a slant on other subjects as well as his own. In addition to his scientific studies he was deeply interested in cultural things and read broadly enough in general literature. His was a case of brain hunger. It remained so until the end of his life."

Rockne was an excellent boxer; and for years there was an unsubstantiated rumor that, along with his violin honorarium and cleaning up the slops in the chemical lab, he had picked up a little side money by appearing in neighborhood boxing matches under an assumed name. I had this confirmed by Joe Gargan, a student of positive character, who said he had served as Rock's manager.

(In after years Joe Gargan became associated with another well-known family of Americans, as brother-in-law to Joseph P. Kennedy, former Ambassador to the Court of St. James, and uncle of the present Senator. In his excellent book *Notre Dame One Hundred Years,* Rev. Arthur J. Hope tells of Notre Dame in 1917. "The campus, of course, was visited almost daily by Notre Dame students in khaki. Now and then the grimness was made tolerable by some lighter touch. For instance, when Joe Gargan came back in all his finery, lovable, swashbuckling, proud-as-punch, decked out in all the red and blue of a Marine, carrying a swagger stick, and accompanied by a Boston bull pup on a leash, it was the signal for fun. Butch Whipple, a mere private, got hold of a dog of doubtful ancestry, tied a huge rope around its neck, and then managed to show up in every spot visited by Gargan.")

Rockne's athletic record has as many surprises for the aficionado as the academic transcript. He was a regular end for three seasons and never knew defeat in his playing career which included twenty victories and two ties. He served under Jesse Harper as assistant football coach for the next four seasons which saw 26 wins, 5 losses, one tie. He never had a losing season as player or coach. His total record in both capacities: 151 victories, 17 defeats, 8 ties. He won nine out of every ten games in which he engaged. His twenty years saw seven perfect seasons and one other in which the team was undefeated but had one tie.

All of that spells *competitor*, which, more than any other one word spelled Rockne. He fought to live and he hated to lose, at anything, to anybody, under any conditions. The old dirt-floor gymnasium was used for basketball, indoor track, pep meetings—and sometimes for two sports simultaneously. When nothing else was happening it became a tennis court. I walked by there one day and happened to see Rock playing tennis with an Oriental student, of whom we had many, and all supposed to be filthy rich. Probably all this one had in the Occidental world was tennis and his measly millions. Yet, away from all the world, Rock was fighting to win that tennis match as he had fought against Army in football. From his purpling face it looked as if Rock might be losing; he would never have forgiven me for watching him lose, especially at a sissy game like tennis. So I went away.

Rockne's autobiography is almost barren of his real thoughts as a student and player. There was the same familiar refusal to uncover himself. He moved his characters around, including himself, to prove some valuable point; emphasize some lesson. Recently I read his juvenile novel *The Four Winners* in a detective-like fashion, hoping that he might, through the fictional characters, have become autobiographical. His hero was bashful and girl-shy, and he blushed; but the rest of it might just as well have been a lecture at a coaching school.

Rock was always coaching, teaching, and preaching. Humor was a stage prop. I doubt if any life was ever more brilliantly organized or controlled. Even when he seemed to disintegrate in emotion, he knew where he was going, how far to go. I believe he allowed himself to explode at times because his instinct told him he would get better results that way. With these qualifications, here are some examples of his literary style as they describe incidents in his playing career.

About his first practice: "They should have changed my position to drawback. Trying to spear my first punt I had frozen fingers . . . Finally I tried a punt. Nothing happened. I might have been a statue. Nothing was co-ordinated. I was half-paralyzed." Do you believe this could have been Rockne? Neither do I. But he was getting across all the things a neophyte should guard against. And there was this description of his first attempt at speech-making, at a pep rally: "There were natural hurdles in a social sense; a lone Norwegian, always mistakenly dubbed a Swede, had difficulties among so many Hibernians. These were largely dissipated when, blushing furiously, I was called on to talk at a football rally; and having heard somebody call somebody else a dumb Irishman, I had the good fortune to remark: 'There's only one thing dumber than a dumb Irishman.' Before the bricks could fly I explained: 'A smart Swede.'"

This story does reveal that in his early student days he may have been much more conscious of his *differentness* than his bold manner suggested. But the smart-Irishman dumb-Swede story is part of the apocrypha in the legend.

"Shorty" Longman, according to Rockne, was an oratorical coach, who would enter the dressing room dramatically, toss back his shock of black hair and burst into rhetoric. "Boys—today is *the* day. The honor of the old school is at stake. Now or never we must fight the battle of our lives. I don't want any man with a streak of yellow to move from this room. You've all got to be heroes—*heroes* or I never want to see you again. Go out and conquer. It's the crisis of your lives."

So the boys went out and barbecued Olivet. The next week it was Buchtel. Enter "Shorty," tossing back his shock of hair. "Boys—today is the *day*. The eyes of the world are upon you. Go out and *bleeeed* for the old school, and if anybody has a streak of *yellow*—" After which author Rockne has Bergman yawning to Dorais: "What do you think of the act today?" And Dorais yawning back: "He was much better last week."

This is one of the old-faithful stand-by stories which have different versions in different traditions. One has a very famous mentor at an Ivy League school sending the boys out, while he, weeping, shook hands with each at the door. The last one, the old pro, pauses to pat the suffering mentor: "Better get hold of yourself, Toots."

"If 'Shorty' Longman taught me the methods to avoid as a coach," Rockne wrote, "he impressed me with the value of perseverance. Mistaken as was his psychology—for boys will never do their best if they are bullied—he none the less pursued his players with a ruthless energy that got results."

The Master let a good-sized cat escape from the coaching bag with that final sentence. *Energy* is what a coach must have; he must *pursue* his men until they think as he thinks. There are times when it is necessary to be *ruthless;* when things must be done that the coach would rather not do. With Rockne it was his psychological tricks; his occasional verbal roughing-up. He always voluntarily repaired such damage; and for the common good, his boys could forgive him, even love him. There have been successful coaches who've been hated.

Longman left after the 1910 season and this was a pivotal occasion in the legend. Rockne and Longman were so far apart in thought and impulse that had "Shorty" remained, Rock might have left; or have been an unimportant factor. The new man, Jack Marks of Dartmouth, was quiet, imaginative, efficient. "He made us over," Rock wrote, "from a green, aggressive squad, into a slashing driving outfit; so that we gradually began to be noticed a little beyond the Midwest. I won a regular berth and almost imperceptibly, seemed established in football. One year practically abandoning the idea of continuing the game; and the next, being talked of—never mind by whom—as an All-American prospect."

Marks, whom Rockne obviously admired as much as he had disliked Longman, was another of those lucky accidents that combined to produce Rockne; and he might well qualify as the Unsung Hero of the long line of early coaches who, in those days, and for the most part, paused only long enough to pick up another degree. Marks made the first experiments with the forward pass; and in general had the situation in readiness for Jesse Harper, who was to sweep the way for Rockne—chiefly by the first expert use of the forward pass which changed football from the old push-and-pull brutality to the modern game of skill and speed.

X

In the same year—1887—that football began at Notre Dame, baseball was introduced by a student who was to become one of the diamond immortals—Adrian "Cap" Anson of the Chicago Cubs. The first contest with another school was not played until 1892 against—guess who?—Michigan. The Irish won 6–4. Players like Roger Bresnahan, Ed Ruelbach, Art Schaefer, Cy Williams, Frank Shaughnessy and a half-hundred others went to the big leagues as the diamond stars blazed the trail the footballers were to follow and pre-empt. From 1906 to 1908 the record was 60 victories against nine defeats; the 1908 squad, which won 20 and lost only one, had ventured eastward as far as Dartmouth and Vermont. In 1912 there was a ten-game Eastern junket; followed in the spring of 1913 with visits to Penn, Navy, Catholic U, Fordham—and Army.

The young baseball men who lost to Army 3–0, May 24, 1913, had not the slightest idea they had broken the ground in which a gridiron tablet would begin to be sunk the next fall. Jesse Harper came up from Wabash to succeed Marks, and, as he smilingly told me "sat down to write a few letters." Logically he followed the baseball trail. Army was ready to add a Midwestern team. The contract was signed by William Cotter, later a New York industrialist but then the Notre Dame Graduate Manager.

Harper had inherited a tough squad; and in Rockne and Dorais, who was an outstanding openfield runner and a cool quarterback who could also throw that ball, he saw the opportunity that was, despite a very short career, to make him a coaching immortal. From the beginning Harper seemed to have been smart enough to appreciate Rockne. Rockne and Dorais were to work the summer vacation at Cedar Point, as, at various times, night watchmen, night clerks, lifeguards, and restaurant checkers. Harper gave them a football and they spent their leisure periods on the beach tossing the ball. It was no doubt an odd sight to other bathers, since a football was something that had always been *kicked;* but one doubts the story Rockne threw in: "Once a bearded old gentleman took off his shoes to join the fun, seizing the ball and kicking it merrily, with bare feet, too, until a friendly keeper came along to take him back where he belonged."

The Army, even if it had known, would hardly have been impressed by what two welterweights were doing on the sands of Cedar Point; not even if they had been told, as Mrs. Rockne once told me: "Those devils said they were going to beat Army with the forward pass." Army could not have been expected to know that it was to serve as a springboard for genius, that it was to be engulfed by the gridiron wave of the future; that it would be facing a fanatical band of Young Lochinvars for whom this game would have social significance of a sort.

For what happened on the Plains of West Point, November 1, 1913, let's turn to the reporter who would seem to know most about it, with the customary allowance for his whimsical whirligigs; but in this account Rockne told us more about himself than was his practice.

"The morning we left for West Point the entire student body got up long before breakfast to see us to the day coach that carried the squad to Buffalo—a dreary, all-day trip. From Buffalo we enjoyed the luxury of sleeping-car accommodations—regulars in lowers, substitutes in uppers. There was no pampering in those days. We wanted none of it. While this game was not all-important to Army, to us it was the supreme test of our playing careers. We went out to play the Army like crusaders, believing that we represented not only our own school but the whole, aspiring Middle West.

"West Point, as always since our meetings have become famous, treated us most hospitably. We were housed in Cullum Hall and given the freedom of the Officers' Club. There was a fair crowd to see the game on the Plains and the New York newspapers were interested enough to send second-string football reporters. The Cadet body and most of the other spectators seemed to regard the engagement as a quiet, friendly workout for Army.

"For the first part of the first quarter it looked that way. An Army line outweighing ours by about fifteen pounds to the man pushed us all over the place before we overcame the tingling realization that we were actually playing Army. I recall Merrillat shouting 'Let's lick these Hoosiers.'

"So I asked him, in a lull, if he knew how the word Hoosier originated. 'We started it at South Bend,' I informed him, John Markoe, and whatever others of the Army team would listen. 'After every game the coach goes over the field, picks up whatever he can find and asks: 'Whose ear is this?' Hence Hoosier.

"The gag didn't work so well but something else did. After we had stood terrific pounding by the Army line, and a trio of backs that charged in like locomotives, we held them on downs. Dorais said: 'Let's open up.' It was amusing to see the Army boys huddle after a first, snappy eleven-yard pass had been completed for a first down. Their guards and tackles would come plunging into us to stop line bucks and plunges. Instead, Dorais, stepping neatly back, would flip the ball to an uncovered end or halfback. We marched up the field, gaining three first downs in as many minutes.

"Our attack had been well-rehearsed. After one fierce scrimmage I emerged limping as if hurt. On the next three plays Dorais threw three successful passes in a row to our right halfback, Pliska, for short gains. On each of these three plays I limped down the field acting as if the thing farthest from my mind was to receive a forward pass. After the third play the Army halfback covering me figured I wasn't worth watching. Even as a decoy he figured I was harmless.

"Finally Dorais called my number, meaning that he was to throw a long forward pass to me as I ran down the field and started out toward the side lines. I started limping down the field and the Army halfback covering me almost yawned in my face, he was so bored. Suddenly I put on full speed and left him there, flat-footed. I raced across the Army goal line as Dorais whipped the ball and the grandstand roared at the completion of a forty-yard pass. Everybody seemed astonished. There had been no hurdling, no tackling, no plunging, no crushing of fiber and sinew. Just a long-distance touchdown by rapid transit.

"At the moment when I touched the ball, life for me was *complete*.

"We proceeded to make it more complete. The Army resisted. They charged with devastating power and drove through us for two touchdowns. The score at the half was Notre Dame 14 Army 13. In the second half Army changed its defense to meet our open game. It didn't work. Dorais, always alert, reversed our tactics. We now reverted to the Army line-plunging game with Ray Eichenlaub as our spearhead. He ripped the Army line to pieces.

"In the last quarter Army closed up again to stop Eichenlaub. Dorais instantly switched tactics, opening up with a fresh barrage of passes that completely fooled the Cadets.

"Fitzgerald, a guard, took especial interest in McEwen, Army's great center. Their contest grew personal as Army lost ground and we gained it. Superheated between scrimmages, wild words flew. Fitzgerald closed in on McEwen. He socked McEwen on the jaw, then instantly yelled: 'Hey referee.'

"The referee turned around just in time to see McEwen crash home a right to Fitzgerald's nose. McEwen was promptly ordered from the game; but as captain of our team I had to stop and explain that both boys had been too boisterous and so the referee let them both stay in the game. From then on their decorum was more proper.

"Hard-fought to the end, this Army game with its score of 35–13 in favor of Notre Dame, does not quite represent the difference in playing quality between the two teams. The Army was much better than the score showed. It was, however, the first signal triumph of the new open game over the old, battering-ram Army game. And the Army was quick to learn. Press and football public hailed this new game, and Notre Dame received credit as the originator of a style of play that we had simply *systematized*. Our achievement was that we had demonstrated, by completing 14 of 17 passes, for some 220 yards, that the forward pass was an integral part of offense and not merely a threat. Recognizing this, Army, later in the year, went out itself and forward-passed to victory by 20–9 over one of the strongest Navy teams.

"Looking back to that match and its surprising revelation to Army players versed and skilled in the old-style game, it's no wonder that they could not solve the forward pass problem in a single hour. Indeed, after 20 years of making and directing forward pass attack, I know of only one genuinely effective way of stopping it, besides the obvious precaution of covering five eligible receivers—the two ends and other three backs—and that is to rush the passer: a tactic at once crude and unrefinable.

"Another new thing the Army learned was the Notre Dame experiment in 'boxing' the tackle. Philbrook, the gigantic Notre Dame tackle who weighed 220 pounds, gave me very good reason to be resourceful when I was a scrub and he was a regular. Philbrook had terrific hands. He made my life miserable until I practiced for hours the head bob and shoulder drop that Young Griffo used so successfully in the ring. It was a feint followed by instantly applied power and it worked. With this as a starting point I devised the Notre Dame style of 'boxing' a tackle. Other systems invariably use two men to block the big boys. By employing the smarter strategy of feinting with the head and shoulders we have made it practicable for one man to block one man, no matter what the discrepancy in weight.

"No varsity team was ever acclaimed as the crowd of us that returned by Pullman to Buffalo and by day coach from Buffalo to South Bend. The whole town turned out; brass bands, red fire, speeches; as if we had repulsed and conquered an attack on the West by the East. What particularly impressed everybody was the fresh appearance of the squad. A grueling game with Army was supposed to punish those on the receiving end so that they showed signs of wear and tear for weeks. We didn't find the Army so rough at all. Hardhitting, clean and fair as they have been ever since." (The phrase "life for me was complete" is trenchant. The big thing within Rockne was never satisfied except with a big reward—like that first touchdown against Army.)

Rockne told of another great moment near the end of his playing career. "This was, perhaps, a touch of vanity; but no boy wants his mother to see him try anything athletic unless or until he thinks he's pretty good at it." So he picked the game carefully and put on quite an individual show. When he came to his mother after the game she was still enthusiastic. "But not about me," Rock wrote. "She had been watching the cheerleader, thought he was wonderful."

The Irish were out of the Big Ten box.

XI

Rockne graduated from Notre Dame on June 15, 1914, and, like other ambitious young men, began to learn the true meaning of commencement. Notre Dame had no medical school (and still has none) so he went down to St. Louis, got himself a job coaching a high school and presented his ample credits to St. Louis University—where some unknown benefactor of Notre Dame decided Rockne could not carry the medical course while earning his living as a coach. He returned to Notre Dame and ran into what he probably considered another tough break.

A coaching job was open at St. Joseph's College (now Loras) in Dubuque, Iowa. Rockne and Dorais, the inseparables, were the final candidates. They tossed a coin. Rockne lost—or thought he did; and it was only then, after he had tried to flee her down the corridors of Missouri and Iowa, that he returned to the school of Our Lady to become head track coach, assistant football coach, and instructor in chemistry. The key item in the deal was the football job and it was arranged by Harper. "I had no trouble getting the job done," he told me recently, "and I don't think the university ever regretted it."

Rockne returned to Cedar Point where he did a very surprising thing for a bashful, blushing young man. The records of the parish church of Sts. Peter and Paul in Sandusky, Ohio, declare:

To Whom It May Concern: Knute Kenneth Rockne and Bonnie Gwendoline Skiles were married by Rev. William F. Murphy on July 15, 1914. Witnesses were Chas. Dorais and Marie Balzarina.

Father Murphy, a close friend of the Rocknes thereafter, wrote to Father Cavanaugh: "I can recall Miss Bonnie Gwendoline Skiles calling to see me about the first of July, 1914, to make arrangements for her marriage to Knute K. Rockne. Both were at the time employed at Cedar Point. The Catholic people employed there—and there were a goodly number of students from Notre Dame—were wont to come across Sandusky Bay to attend Divine Services in the church of Sts. Peter and Paul. Among the young Catholic ladies who came regularly to these services was Miss Bonnie G. Skiles, a pious and devout young lady, without ostentation, modest in her ways and manners, capable of winning the hand and heart of the staid and judicious Rockne. Her womanly qualities were of a superior kind. Certainly Miss Bonnie Skiles had no small part in forming the character, as well as sustaining the peerless Rockne in his upward climb to the pinnacle of fame."

Friends of Rock might question that "staid and judicious" charac-
terization. But this was a most serious expedition in which he was
again the "lone Norwegian Protestant" among Hibernians. (Bonnie
had become a Catholic only five months before; but it was to be
eleven years, despite his close associations, before Rock was to join
the Church.) He had known Bonnie for about two years and it is
my guess that she was his first and only girl. Certainly, once they
were married, that part of his life became a closed book, and there
was never the slightest hint of involvement with any other woman.
They had four children: William (1915), Knute, Jr. (1918), Mary
Jean (1920), and John Vincent (1926). Their home was always a
home to Rock's football boys to whom the youngsters were Bill, Junie,
Jeanie, and Jackie.

Rock was as right about romance as about most other things; and
their friends would enthusiastically agree with Father Murphy's estimate of the womanly qualities of Bonnie, "without ostentation, modest in her ways and manners . . . no small part in sustaining the
peerless Rockne in his upward climb . . ." She was small, dark,
piquant; always gracious, always friendly, always adequate, always
reserved. If you knew Rock well, you knew his family; for he had
them about him whenever possible. I was not an intimate of their
family life but was with them often through the years and Bonnie
always made me feel accepted, as she probably did with anybody
Rock brought around. I never heard her criticize him or try to throw
any rein about him. I never felt the slightest suggestion of strain between them.

Rockne, of course, never wrote about nor talked much of his home
life; but in the autobiography there was an editorial note by Bonnie:
"No one who knew Knute [she was one of the very few who ever
called him that; pronouncing it Kan-ute] could doubt that he was a
devoted home man. I have never seen him more pleased than when
friends spoke appreciatively of the home he and I had made together.
I do not see how any husband or father could be nobler or kinder.
He wanted us to have everything within his power to make the children and me happy and comfortable."

He liked to have friends visit the home, enjoyed singing with
them, even cooking for them. He wanted good food and plenty of
it, had a special liking for fresh fruit. He was a successful gardener

and won prizes for his lettuce, cauliflower, tomatoes, carrots, and cabbages.

He spent much time with the children. On the beach he tossed a football with his sons, organized races for which he gave prizes. He liked to take the family to the movies, practiced his jokes on the boys while giving them their baths. To the usual nursery rhymes and bedtime stories he added some of undisclosed authorship including this one which the children learned to sing in unruly chorus:

> There is a boardinghouse, far, far away
> Where they serve ham and eggs, three times a day
> Woe, woe! The boarders yell
> When they hear the dinner bell
> For they know the eggs will smell—far, far away.

It is my guess that he treated the children as equals. During a lecture period, young Bill, then about seven, wandered in. The players grinned but remained quiet. Rock said, "Bill, what did I give you that dime for?" Bill thought that over for a moment, left the room and the lecture resumed. Rock played jokes on the youngsters and they played jokes on him. When his trusty flute stopped a crying spell of his first-born, the father accepted the favorable criticism modestly: "He forgot the original irritation in the presence of a greater one."

Bonnie confirmed that "in many ways, he was extremely shy, not at all overconfident, even about his work"; and that he was a greedy reader of science, ancient history, detective stories, current fiction and, like most sports people, all the newspapers he could buy. During a vacation abroad in 1928 (one of his extracurricular projects, an Olympic tour), he lectured the members of his party on history, monuments, cathedrals, and other points of tourist interest. "In Germany," Bonnie wrote, "he pointed in the general direction of the west, said the Black Forest should be ahead. One of his friends, hoping to catch him in error, consulted the guidebook. But the father of the family was, as usual, right."

Rockne liked animals. The family owned a police dog called Noxie, which did duty as a butler in 1929 when the Master was ill. He would escort the visitor to the bedroom and, later, to the door. Rock was not supposed to even think about football during that period; but once, after Bonnie had left the room, he reached under his pillow, like a kid after forbidden candy, and showed me the diagram of a new play, a triple-spinner which could only have been compounded of dream and delirium.

XII

The most difficult coaching job is the first, especially when the fledgling attempts to teach boys with whom he had played the preceding season. When one of his old mates decided to test his authority, Rock barked: "Go to the showers and turn in your suit. We won't need you any more around here." Harper upheld him, the player apologized and returned to the squad. This incident, Rock wrote, "gave me the reputation of being a martinet—which is valuable to any coach provided he doesn't work too hard at it." He never threatened, thereby giving the sinner an excuse to think the first warning could be safely disregarded. He let the sinner have it; but off the field he was a friend. This split-level personality encouraged a certain amount of give-and-take. Here, from players of the '14–'17 era, are impressions of Rockne, the assistant.

"He was obliged to work with an extremely limited appropriation; and when we complained he would quote long passages from Franklin and Burke on the virtues of frugality. Ordinarily, at mealtime in a strange city, he would marshal the squad into a 'popular-priced' restaurant, select the menu and settle the account. But one morning in Buffalo, where our car was sidetracked for us to attend Mass, he gave each of us a half-dollar and said: 'Have a good breakfast, boys, but don't overeat.'

"After Mass, while in the process of 'case-ing' the restaurants, a group of about eight of us observed our good Maestro about to enter a substantial eating establishment a block ahead. Our decision was quick and unanimous. We followed him in. We ordered sumptuously and enjoyed our food magnificently. In due time our spokesman deposited our checks and the fifty-cent pieces with Rock, suggested the half-dollars as adequate tip money; and explained that, as simon-pure amateur athletes we felt that personal retention of such funds might be frowned upon by the Big Ten. We departed, as he spluttered.

"As a trainer, Rock was disposed to take the most optimistic view of any adversity on the field. During a rough scrimmage session in 1915 a young man named Ducky Holmes was on the ground obviously in agony. Rock's preliminary diagnosis disclosed little more than his own bewilderment. Then a new theory of orthopedics was born: 'If you can wiggle your toes, Ducky, the leg's not broken. Try it, Ducky.' Ducky wiggled his toes; and Rock summed up his masterful diagnosis. 'Okay, Ducky. Just a bad sprain. Hobble into the shower, give it some wet heat; after practice we'll tape it up.' But Ducky's leg was not so optimistic. An X ray disclosed a fractured shin bone."

En route to the Army game in 1916, Rock and some of the players got off the day coach for a bit of the brisk air at the Cleveland station. At the end of the train, in a private car, they recognized ex-President Teddy Roosevelt. They gave him a cheer, were invited into his car and much football was talked. One of the Notre Dame lads predicted in detail just what was going to happen to Army.

"That sounds bully, Coach," T.R. said to Rockne.

"Yes sir. Just plain bull, sir," Rockne replied, correctly, since the Saturday score was Army 30 Notre Dame 10.

In 1916 Harper came down with a heavy cold before the Wabash game and delegated Rock to handle the team. The game was not considered a big one; but Rock was taking no chances on blowing his first assignment as a head coach. "Previously," Walter (Cy) DeGree wrote me, "we had thought of Wabash merely as one of the many good Christian seats of learning which happened to be on our schedule that year; and though of a different denomination and of somewhat lesser athletic prowess, not too much unlike our own university. But through an unrevealed source, Rockne had discovered that some sinister and diabolical influence at Wabash had marked Notre Dame for oblivion. He confidentially intimated that if every man, including the cheerleaders, gave all he had, we might, through some perhaps providential intercession, possibly mitigate the smirch about to befall us by holding the imported mercenaries of the op-

position to a fairly low score. He concluded, in an eloquent, screaming blast of desperation: 'Now get out there and crucify 'em.'

"The records of the game indicate that Notre Dame scored a
point a minute. Rock's vocal efforts, though lacking in his later refinements and finesse, and slightly tainted with a demagoguery I
never knew him to employ again, uncovered for the first time the
forceful effect and inspirational quality of his prolific imagination
and dramatically electrifying personality. Since we had been expected to win by only two or three touchdowns, I am convinced
that the results encouraged him to develop that part of his coaching
equipment."

The Yale game in 1914 produced the biggest disaster on the
campus since the '79 fire. Ready to chew the Bulldog were Irish
mastiffs like Eichenlaub, Elward, Bergman, Jones, Pliska, Finnegan,
Fitzgerald, and Keefe. "Humility," Rockne later wrote, "is the lesson
every athlete must learn in secret commune with his soul—or he gets
it in big, sour doses on the field as thousands roar. Everybody but
Harper, and including myself, was suffering from a bad case of Char-
ley horse between the ears. Yale, captained by Bud Talbot and led
by crack halfback Harry Legore, lateral-passed us right out of the
park."

The score was 28–0 and Notre Dame had lost its first football game
in four seasons. Obviously this situation called for drastic changes;
so Harper installed the backfield shift he had learned under Stagg
at Chicago, and incorporated the "crow's hop" and other moves
Rockne had invented to help small ends box big tackles. The basics
of what was to become known as the Notre Dame system, the most
popular formation of the twenties, were thereby established. When
the squad went to West Point for the second game of this series, the
shift was new; but there was no Dorais-Rockne combination to make
the forward pass effective.

Army won 20–7; and invited the Irish back in '15 for the rubber
game. Notre Dame won that one 7–0. Army had to get even again,
which it did, 30–10, in '16. The Army kept on trying to win the
rubber game, which it was never able to do; and that's as good a
reason as any why little Notre Dame remained on the Cadet schedule until the game, from Army's standards, got too big.

From the beginning the Army was the Big One for Notre Dame;

and one of the reasons Army gave for terminating it after 1947 was that it was becoming bigger than the Navy game to the Cadets. It was the battle, in Notre Dame tradition, where "nobody quits and nobody cries." The roots were set in these early years as each contest developed its own incidents of thrills and sportsmanship. Rockne told this story worthy of enshrinement among tales of sportsmen: "Our center, Pepper O'Donnell, had a broken rib. Harry Tuttle, the Army trainer, heard of this injury and came into our dressing room with a special pad. As play began, John McEwen, the great Army center, asked O'Donnell: 'Which side is the broken rib on?' O'Donnell pointed to it. He played every minute of the game."

Rockne referred to Elmer Oliphant in the '16 game as a "one-man team phenomenon. If anybody asks me who was the greatest player Army ever had, my vote goes to Oliphant." George Gipp, then a freshman, was schooled to imitate Oliphant in the Notre Dame practice sessions. Rock said: "He gave a perfect imitation of Oliphant's veering style of ball-carrying, which arched his body so that he could spin or pivot at any fraction of an instant. The only drawback was that in the actual game with Army, Oliphant gave a perfect imitation of Gipp."

XIII

I suspect this is the favorite Rockne story among the Notre Dame faculty. Teaching a class in chemistry, he had demonstrated a formula, then jabbing a finger at a pupil he shouted: "Did you get that? Like heck you did—it bounced right off your dome." His customary attitude toward females tended to be Victorian; but he had, this once, forgotten he was talking to a summer class of teaching nuns.

Rock and Father Nieuwland had had an unusual student-teacher relationship which expanded when Rock became a teacher. The Belgian-born priest was an authentic genius in his own field. As far back as 1921 I remember the smell of an old raincoat he had made from chemical products. Vincent Sweeney, then his student secretary, but later National Public Relations Director of the United Steelworkers of America, told me this story: "We went out in the open

campus before old Science Hall. Father Nieuwland had a substance
he was going to test. The only trouble, he said, was that he didn't
know whether it would burn; but *if* it burned, the best place to be
would be away from there.

"So he lit it," Sweeney said, "and I established what must have
been a new Notre Dame record for the hundred-yard dash. Nieuwland was just behind me—the only reason I beat him was because
he was wearing a cassock. The substance did not explode. We
walked back slowly. Nieuwland inspected it and said, 'Vincent, this
is synthetic rubber.'" Specifically it was the base from which synthetic rubber would come.

The legend relates that, when Jesse Harper was leaving, Rockne
had to go out in the forest and commune with himself about the
great decision: football or chemistry? Father Nieuwland is depicted
as pleading with his brilliant disciple to choose chemistry.

It is all just a legend. Nobody now doubts that Rockne could
have been important in chemistry; but he was already head of a
family, with growing financial problems. The following, from a
source close to him at the time, reveals his state of mind—and perhaps, another of the lucky accidents that kept him at Notre Dame.

"Early in December 1917, during a farewell dinner and take-off
party he had given for a small group of Notre Dame varsity men
about to leave for Europe and the First World War, he revealed,
confidentially, that he had decided to leave Notre Dame the following spring and accept the head coaching job at Michigan Aggies
[now Michigan State]. He further said that after four years as
Harper's assistant he had become a bit weary of his various and
conglomerate assignments: assistant football coach, chemistry
teacher, head track coach, football scout, and a few others. He felt
there would be better opportunities elsewhere. We who were close
to him in those days agreed. But the unexpected death of a relative,
a short time later, removed Harper to his cattle ranch in Kansas and
narrowly prevented Rockne's departure."

In various archives at various colleges are various documents reputed to be various forms of contracts Rockne had signed to leave
Notre Dame and coach these various schools. There are various versions, some of which we will encounter later. The above testimony
would seem to indicate some validity to the document still reputed
to be in the files at Michigan State; but it is doubtful if Rockne at-

tempted to use this proffered job to pressure Notre Dame at the time of Harper's resignation. The fact is, Rock was hired as head football coach only after a letter-writing campaign by alumni; and a persistent insistence by Harper himself. He recently wrote me:

"When I resigned in 1918, Father Cavanaugh asked me if I had anyone in mind to take my place. I told him I had—it was Rock. He immediately said: 'He won't do at all—the boys will steal him blind.' I knew there was no need to really argue with Father Cavanaugh about it so I did not press the matter at that time. Every week or so he would come to my office and would suggest somebody. My stock answer was: 'He's a pretty good man but not as good a man as Rockne would be.' Finally he said: 'You insist on taking Rock?' I said, 'Yes, I promised him this job two years ago.' Father Cavanaugh said: 'Well, if you promised it to him, I will give it to him.'"

A motion picture, covering the significant additions to the Notre Dame schedule as Harper angled for new opponents, would flash a montage effect on the screen that would read like this:

1913	Notre Dame	35	Army 13
	" "	14	Penn State 7
	" "	30	Texas 7
1914	" "	0	Yale 28
	" "	7	Army 20
	" "	48	Carlisle 6
	" "	20	Syracuse 0
1915	" "	19	Nebraska 20
	" "	7	Army 0
	" "	36	Texas 7
	" "	55	Rice 2
1916	" "	10	Army 30
	" "	14	Michigan Aggies 0
	" "	20	Nebraska 0
1917	" "	0	Wisconsin 0
	" "	0	Nebraska 7
	" "	7	Army 2
	" "	23	Michigan Aggies 0
	" "	3	W & J 0

Jesse Harper was the Good Samaritan of Notre Dame football—and another Protestant to boot—who came along when the going was rough and friends were few. In five years, he won 33, lost 5, and tied one. He set up the Notre Dame system of football play, gave the schedule its Army keystone, broke the solid Conference front by scheduling Wisconsin in '17, and Nebraska, which was, for many years, to be the Western anchor. He resumed relations with Michigan Aggies and made the first Southwestern explorations. He developed Rockne, bequeathed him to the university as the first of a series of home-bred coaches continued through Hunk Anderson, Elmer Layden, Frank Leahy, Terry Brennan, and Joe Kuharich.

Harper was the transition between the old Notre Dame football and the new; and before we leave the old, let's bow briefly to some of the great names of that era which come to memory, with apologies to the innumerable others: the Cartiers for whom old Cartier Field was named; Jacob Rosenthal, three-year letterman; Rev. John "King" Farley; Rev. Dominick O'Malley; Frank Shaughnessy, later president of the International Baseball League; Nathan Silver, four-year letterman; Don Hamilton; Charles Crowley, later coach at Columbia; Jack Meagher; Luke Kelley; Charles Bachman; and Rock's close friend, Howard "Cap" Edwards.

The curtain was going up on Scott Fitzgerald's Flappers, Westbrook Pegler's Era of Wonderful Nonsense, Grantland Rice's Golden Age of Sports—and the Thirteen Exciting Years of Rockne.

XIV

Rockne's grave in Highland Cemetery, South Bend, is hard to find because the family plot is marked by one small headstone—at the request, I was told, of Bonnie, who now lies beside him. She may have been following Rockne's wish, or her interpretation of what he would have wished, for this modest man had not the slightest idea of the commotion his passing would cause.

There are, of course, monuments. There is the stadium, for which he fought the faculty and which he planned, stone by stone, to make the most modern of its day. There is the Rockne Memorial on the campus, erected by his friends. There is a nostalgic equity in other buildings, in teaching salaries and similar items in the days when football profits were more important than now. There is his large part in the development of football as a national institution; there is his place in the memories of people who never knew him; in the hearts and lives of the boys he coached. There is the record of the Rockne Victory Era, which falls naturally into six periods:

1918: The informal wartime year when three games were won, two tied, and one lost.

1919–21: The World War I returnees who won 28, lost one (by three points), and went undefeated in their first two seasons.

1922–24: The Four Horsemen and Seven Mules who won 27, lost two, tied one; and in 1924 concluded an undefeated National Championship year with a Rose Bowl victory over Stanford on New Year's Day 1925.

1925–27: The Forgotten Men who merely won 23, lost four, tied two.

1928: The Bad Year when his gallant cripples won five, lost four—and gave him his most dramatic victory.

1929–30: The National Champions who won 19 games in two perfect seasons against the absolute best from every section.

Here is the "suicide schedule" he built; and the way he built it, year by year, with the more important games listed; and the significant additions italicized:

1918: *Purdue*, Great Lakes, Nebraska. (Army out—war year.)
1919: *Indiana*, Purdue, Army, Nebraska.
1920: *Northwestern*, Army, Purdue, Indiana, Nebraska.
1921: *Iowa, Rutgers*, Army, Purdue, Indiana, Nebraska.
1922: *Georgia Tech, Carnegie Tech*, Army, Purdue, Indiana, Nebraska.
1923: *Princeton*, Army, Georgia Tech, Carnegie Tech, Purdue, Nebraska.
1924: *Stanford, Wisconsin*, Army, Princeton, Georgia Tech, Northwestern, Nebraska, Carnegie Tech.
1925: *Minnesota, Penn State*, Army, Georgia Tech, Nebraska, Northwestern, Carnegie Tech.

1926: *Southern Cal*, Army, Georgia Tech, Northwestern, Carnegie Tech, Indiana, Minnesota, Penn State.

1927: *Navy*, Army, Southern Cal, Minnesota, Georgia Tech, Indiana.

1928: Army, Navy, Southern Cal, Wisconsin, Georgia Tech, Carnegie Tech, Penn State.

1929: Army, Navy, Southern Cal, Wisconsin, Georgia Tech, Carnegie Tech, Northwestern, Indiana.

1930: *Southern Methodist, Pitt, Pennsylvania*, Army, Navy, Southern Cal, Northwestern, Indiana, Carnegie Tech.

Rockne had no grand design. He never sat down one day and figured all this out in advance; nor saw it in a vision. He did this matchless job on an ad-lib, day-by-day, year-by-year basis; by thinking faster and acting faster than his opponents; by getting there "fustest with the mostest"; by being, as always, phenomenally *right*.

His early handicap was the factor of prestige. Top Drawer U is content to win its fair share from Old Family; but it cannot afford to be upset by a Basement Tech or a Homeless Aggies. It was here that the Rockne charm, diplomacy, psychology and salesmanship operated. In his favor was the fact that major schools with big stadia like to play at home—especially against a guaranteed stadium-filler; a style-show champion led by the magical showman Rockne. His brand of football helped because his open, clean, nonbruising game took little physical toll. He never played "customer" football; he was out to win, as he almost invariably did; but once he had a safe lead, he took his regulars out and sent in substitutes for the experience they would need the next year. He never humiliated a proud school or threatened another coach's job.

Topping all this was his electric personality, his healing charm. He could beat them, leave them reasonably happy; and be invited back. It was an education in human relations to watch him handle athletic directors and coaches as he handled his players; and just as efficiently. For Stagg, whom Notre Dame did not regard as a professional friend in those days, he had a deference probably born in his youth when the Grand Old Man was already a towering figure. He met Zuppke of Illinois with matching wit—and the jousts of these two at coaches meetings became hilarious occasions. For Yost it was boxing gloves only.

There had always been at West Point a faction which questioned the wisdom of the Notre Dame game from the prestige point of view. Rockne's personal popularity had this opinion immobilized; but when a new coach, Bert Sasse, succeeded the friendly Biff Jones, word came that Sasse had been influenced by the anti-Notre Dame opinion; and that Sasse was then en route by train to Chicago. Rock canceled whatever business he had, met Sasse at the train, brought him down to Notre Dame—and that was that.

Rockne always had a fine press—which helped both him and Notre Dame—because he was personally popular with reporters. In 1928, on a train bound for South Bend, I met W. O. "Bill" McGheehan, the most incisive, and perhaps the best sports writer of them all. He usually took the hide off his "ponderous pachyderms" of wrestling, his "Three Dumb Dukes" of boxing; and the intriguing characters of his favorite, baseball. He was not a football man but he was going to Notre Dame. "I just wrote a column," he smiled, "saying I was going out to South Bend to investigate the rumor there was a university located there. So tell me about it."

I told him. And at South Bend, when there were no hotel rooms, Rock invited us into his home. I took "the Sheriff" to the noon lecture, the afternoon practice, gave him the Fifty-Cent Grand Tour. That evening, when Rock was with the team, we were sitting in the den of the modest home, attended by Noxie, the butler-dog. The starched cynic, rolling one of his cigarettes, said, almost to himself: "Gee, I hope we win tomorrow." We lost; but McGheehan was thereafter the attorney for the defense on Broadway.

It's quite a story, the Rockne story, from almost any angle you look at it—sporting, institutional, business, personal. Let's start watching him at work; and see if we can go beyond the usual treatment of sports figures in print and on film—the popping of colorful corn. Let's try to get into the laboratory where the human kernels are separated and analyzed.

XV

There are people who must have responsibility, authority, excitement. Rock was one of these. He complained about being overworked, about "inefficient student help," about being poorly paid, about faculty interference and many, many other irritations; but I think he enjoyed himself exorbitantly as he roared from scene to scene, dispensing advice, wisdom, philosophy, scorn, satire, humor, and all with the garnishing telltale quip.

He loved an audience, was always on-stage and the spotlight always found him. And still looks for him. Recently, at a conclave before the All-Star game in Chicago, where the elite of football were gathered, a veteran reporter asked: "Suppose Rock were to walk in here right now?"

It was said of Grantland Rice: "Wherever Granny sat—there was the head of the table." Rice wrote this: "Rockne was a man of great force, deep charm and an amazing personality. I have never known anyone quite his equal in this respect. Whenever there was a gathering of coaches in any city there was usually one question: 'Where's Rock staying?' That's where they all gathered. . . . I've sat through a lot of dinners through a lot of years. In my mind Jimmy Walker was the paragon of after-dinner entertainers, but Rock was the only man who could follow Jimmy Walker."

The Rockne of 1918 "drove an old white Lyons-Knight car. The campus roads were of gravel. He never came to a stop like an ordinary taxpayer. He'd jam on the brakes and slide the last fifteen feet." This was the man—intense, fast, brilliant, forceful, instinctively and intuitively right. He poured all of these qualities into his players. He wouldn't have a player around into whom such things could not be poured.

There are three things about football which are also true of almost any organization, from a business to an army: (1) Over a reasonable length of time, usually about three years, a football squad must inevitably reflect the personality of its coach. (2) The surest way to win a football game is to hit harder—and think better—than the other fellow on *every play*. (3) The most consistent winner among coaches is the one who can most consistently put his team on the field, hitting harder and thinking better than the opponents.

All of these things explain Rockne, as they explain almost any leader. In the heat of battle, he could be ruthless, even cruel. In the calm periods he could be petty, almost amusingly suspicious of an inoffensive subordinate. But he was never mean or malicious. In the after-quiet he would go around soothing whatever hurts he may have thought it necessary to inflict on an individual in order that the team might win.

I think that he permitted himself to be aroused to emotional surges —so that he might better arouse his charges. He honed himself to sharpness so that he might cut more swiftly and surely in combat. Even in what might look like a tantrum, I think he always knew what he was doing, how far it was wise to go. I have personal reasons for these opinions.

Shortly after I went to work for him we were having a dual track meet with Illinois. Notre Dame never had the well-rounded depth in track that Illini did, but usually had specialists who could score individual victories. One of these, in this 1921 indoor meet, was Johnny Murphy, the national champion high jumper; but Murphy was being defeated by *two* Illini jumpers, then unknown but later famous as Harold Osborne and Dewey Albert. They were doing it by using a new shoulder-roll device against Murphy's classic "split" jump.

Rock was purpling with frustration as he went about supervising events. As part of my job was to serve as official scorer at all varsity athletic events, I had to be in the thick of things. For no reason I heard myself being publicly dressed down by Rockne. I took it, as one of his athletes would have done. The next day was a holiday. I walked long through the forests that surround the two lakes. Then I came to the old office for my second crucial conference with Rockne.

"Rock," I said, "I need this job badly. But not badly enough to take what I took last night for no reason."

He said: "You're right, Frank. I have this unfortunate habit of sometimes blowing my top at whoever happens to be handy. You stay with me and it won't happen again." We talked, or he did, because I was on a cloud of relief. The thing I remember that he said that day was: "One thing nobody can ever take away from you is your own integrity." That was exactly what I was trying to protect that day when I came to him. I thought Rockne was passing his own credo on to me. I've passed it along to thousands of other young fellows since, in speeches and in print. I think Rockne had very high personal standards and that he tried to live by them.

Like everybody close to him I had to serve as a vocal sparring partner. I enjoyed it, was flattered by it, because if Rock didn't like you he wouldn't bother with you. I enjoyed, as did all the others, scoring against him occasionally; as, I believe, Rock also enjoyed it, because he was hungry for competition and respected anybody who gave it to him. But he never again humiliated me, either alone or before people. And there were times when I gave him plenty of real provocation.

The Drake Relays in Des Moines, Iowa, were always held the same day as the Penn Relays in Philadelphia. Though Drake was not a member, the Big Ten had chosen to uphold Midwestern prestige by supporting the games. In 1923 Rockne was referee of the Drake meet.

Monday afternoon I ran into a glowering storm. It seems that the referee of the Drake meet had been more than embarrassed when his needling Big Ten friends had shown him a one-paragraph story in the Chicago *Tribune*. It said that Rockne had brought four of his stars to Drake; but had sent his national champion high-jumper to Penn because there was *no competition at Drake*.

I had written that story. It was true—which was what had given all the more sting to the barbs sunk in the hide of the referee. I was still too naïve to know that Rock had been made referee so that he would bring *all* of his stars to Drake.

He spluttered and glared—and walked out of his own office. It was either that, I figured, or punch me in the nose.

My classmate, Frank Doriot, had a room in the gymnasium where his job was to look after equipment. He also saw—and heard—a lot of Rockne; and we often compared notes as to what he said to each of us about the other. In my time only two New York sports writers visited the campus—Lawrence Perry and Ray McCarthy. I considered it my job to see that they were indoctrinated, but Rock said to

Doriot: "Since he's been around with Lawrence Perry, Wallace walks like this." And he gave an imitation of how I walked—importantly.

Before graduation Doriot called me over to the gym and made a little speech: "Frank, we've always been friends. I want to give you something to remember me by." So he gave me a varsity sweater (a wonderful piece of material I still wear for winter golf). The next September I made the mistake of wearing the sweater when I reported to Rockne. "Where did you get that sweater?" he demanded.

I took the Fifth Amendment.

"I know where you got it—that Doriot gave it to you. He gave everything away but the Main Building." We were flattered by such attention. Doriot, as much under the guns as I, had a thicker hull and probably took more cannonading. Here, almost forty years later, is a letter from him which, I think, reflects the attitude of Rock's boys: "It is a pleasure to write about 'Rock.' To me, it is amazing how his fame has lived through the years, because he was really a very humble and sensitive man. We struggled with the limited means at our disposal from the fall of 1918 to the spring of 1923. And that struggling included a permanent financial stringency and the occasional jealousy of persons best left unnamed.

"His explosive temperament was a common spectacle. His outbursts left a lasting impression on the adolescent minds under his care and helped to mold their characters for the problems they were to meet later.

"Not only was he the football coach, he was the ticket seller, his coat pockets doubling as his office. Ducats were always available to all applicants. Until the appointment of Morris Starrett as Athletics Manager in 1922, we had no systematic method for handling tickets, finances, and necessary records. Succeeding him, Al Ryan moved Rock's office to the Administration Building. It was then that Rock whispered confidentially to me one day, 'That Ryan is trying to make an executive out of me.'

"I will never forget the time in 1922 when Rock made three speaking engagements in three different cities all for the same evening. He resolved this dilemma by canceling one, taking another for himself and sending the captain, Eddie Anderson, on the third.

"A lover of music, principally the popular tunes of his day, Rock was proud of his flute playing, his acquaintance with Paul Whiteman, Isham Jones, and many other of the name band leaders of that era. On many occasions at my room in the gymnasium, he could be found listening to dance tunes of the day on my hand-cranked victrola. Every so often he would exclaim, 'Just a minute, I'll tell you just who that sax player or trombone player is.' And he would invariably be right.

"As track coach he once said to me, 'That job is so easy it's a shame to take the money.' (Which wasn't much.) You may recall, 'Skip' Barber, the broad-jumper. Despite 'Skip's' contention that he was doing his best, Rock kept insisting that he jump another foot. It was so like Rock to inspire every one to do better than his best.

"Sarcasm and severe criticism were his constant tools in his coaching repertoire, his objective being to arouse such ire in his charges as to force them to do some thinking and self-analysis. His constant theme was 'mental co-ordination.' He tempered his stern methods with a keen wit and an understanding of human nature that left his men calm and without rancor. Though his methods were severely criticized at times by his athletes he never bore a grudge or took any punitive action.

"Much has been written about this man, but I personally think that his greatest asset was his thoughtfulness and kindness to fellow human beings."

XVI

Rockne, who in his last years, could cause an opponent's stadium to be enlarged merely by scheduling a game, was once hard put to fill even the 2500 wooden bleacher seats at his own Cartier Field. His indiscriminate acceptance of speaking dates was part of his ticket-selling campaign. "If you bought ten," chuckled Jimmy McGarraghty, "he would write you a letter." (McGarraghty, a Chicago businessman, bought so many that he finally came to Notre Dame as manager of the university cafeteria. At last count he had seen about 350 consecutive Notre Dame football games.)

Here is an illuminating letter, dated September 26, 1919—a year in which Rockne was to go undefeated and win the Midwestern title:

Mr. Frank Bilinski,
227 Laurel,
South Bend, Indiana.
Dear Friend:

A selected list of representative citizens of South Bend has been prepared, a list of live men who will promote any plan to boost South Bend. Your name is on the list.

The Notre Dame football team travels from coast to coast and they advertise the city of South Bend in a very effective manner. Notre Dame plays the best teams in the country—away from home. I know that the people of South Bend want to see these teams. The only difficulty in bringing them here is the payment of a reasonable guarantee. Our gate receipts have been too small to warrant bringing the best teams here to play.

We shall receive at Nebraska about six thousand dollars, at Indiana and Purdue about four thousand each, to support the other sports which do not pay. If, however, I receive a return which shows that South Bend is willing to back us I will guarantee to bring Purdue and Nebraska here for the fall of nineteen twenty. I will bring Indiana and some other strong team here for the fall of nineteen twenty-one. We already compete with the best teams in the West at home in track and baseball. It is our intention to bring basketball up to the plane of the other sports.

To secure this needed support I am enclosing a season ticket. Please return in the enclosed envelope your check for five dollars or the season ticket. This ticket is good for all athletic contests at Notre Dame and includes four football games, about eight basketball games, four track meets and ten baseball games. We believe that this co-operation will be of mutual benefit and will secure more firmly the pleasant ties which already bind our city and our university. We welcome any suggestions or any constructive criticism which enable us to further this project.

Very sincerely,
K. K. Rockne.

Rock was to do the selling job for football that Babe Ruth did for baseball, Jack Dempsey for boxing, Bobby Jones for golf, and Bill Tilden for tennis; but in those early days he was just another shavetail, scrounging around for the loose buck and accounting for the pennies to an administration whose top executives and best teachers—the priests—worked for their keep and the right to dip into the community cigar box. I am indebted to Herb Jones, now business manager of athletics who was one of Rock's early part-time secretaries, for some priceless "Financial Reports of the Notre Dame Athletic Association" which tell a stark tale of Notre Dame and Big Ten athletics just after World War I when the modern growth began. Here are some highlights:

A baseball trip to Iowa State and Iowa U. 1919: Hotel expenses for 13 men $13; Streetcar $2.70; Phone .75; Railroad $403.01. Total expenses $419.46. Receipts $190.68. Loss $228.78.

A football game, Notre Dame vs Morningside at Sioux City, Iowa, November 27, 1919: Hotel $36; Railroad $1039.20; Meals $258; Taxi to and from field $28; Baggage transfer $7; Tips to porters $6; Tips to waiters $12; Doctor for Bahan and Trafton $5; Iodine, Petrogen, and Sloan's Liniment $1.20. Total expenses $1392.40. Receipts $2500. Profit $1107.60. Received from Treasurer (beginning of trip) $1500. Returned to Father T. Burke $2607.60.

Baseball, Notre Dame vs Wisconsin at Madison, Wisconsin, June 7, 1919: Hotel (Planters) at $1.75 each, $24.50; Railroad 14 men at $6.99 each, $195.72; Meals, two on train at $1.25 each; one at .50, $42; Streetcar, (two Madison at 6 cents each; two at Chicago; one at South Bend) $4.48. Incidentals (work on Cartier Field) $2. Total expense $268.70. Guarantee $100. Paid out by Chas. E. Dorais $268.70; Loss $168.70.

Football, ND vs Purdue at Lafayette, Indiana, November 23, 1918: Railroad $163.20; Meals $60; Streetcar $4.80; Taxicab for Shanahan, Lockard, and Kirk $1.50. Total Expense $229.50. Receipts $587.60. Profit $358.10.

Football, ND vs Indiana at Indianapolis, November 1, 1919: Hotel $143.50; Railroad $357.56; Meals $237.80; Taxi to field $35; Doctor $8; Baggage $6; Cane $1; Ice pack $1; Tips to waiter $6; Fixing Bergman's shoes $1. Total Expense $796.86. Receipts $3335.34. Profit $2538.48.

Football, ND vs Purdue at Lafayette, November 22, 1919: Hotel $72; Railroad $241.40; Meals $270; Streetcar $4.32; Telephone for shoes .75; Message .50; Doctor for Madigan and Bergman $6; Taxi to field and return $2; Tips to waiters $6. Total expenses $602.97. Receipts $2182.05. Profit $1579.08.

Football; ND vs Nebraska at Lincoln October 18, 1919: Hotel $48; Railroad $1104.72; Meals $264; Streetcar to and from field $30; Taxi to school 1:30 A.M. $10; New suit for H. Anderson $34.60; Doctor for Gipp $4; Tips to waiters $10; Tips to porters $6; Total Expense $1511.32. Receipts $5027.18. Profit $3515.86.

It is assumed that a satisfactory reason was given to Father Burke about that $34.60 item for Hunk Anderson's suit. It will be noted that explanations were always in order for the use of taxicabs instead of streetcars. The sentiments of waiters regarding tips can best be left to the imagination. In one football game, against Mount Union on October 11, 1919, the receipts of $97 were not enough to pay the officials $101; the guarantee of $500 made the loss $504.

Basketball was almost a total loss; as was track. Baseball operated at a loss. It cost $73.50 to feed the athletes at the football banquet in 1918. In a scouting trip to Indianapolis, Gus Dorais reported: Five meals $5; plus .60 to get in the game. (Gus must have scouted that one from behind the goal posts.) When Alfred Bergman scouted Purdue at Lafayette, November 15, 1919, he charged up $4.50 for a "doctor in Peru" which was, I believe, his home town; so probably "Big Dutch" stopped off at home to cure a cold. A Michigan Aggies football game at East Lansing showed a profit of $627.36 which is a considerable gap from the probable $400,000 the two schools grossed there 40 years later.

A $15.12 Pullman charge sneaked into the Drake Relays report for 1919, along with .60 tape and $2 tips to waiters *and* porters. A Mrs. Gilfillan charged $24 for sewing pads on 36 jerseys. A trip to the Penn Relays showed $1.20 streetcar and $2.50 tips to waiters *and* porters. The receipts for a track meet at Ann Arbor in 1919 were $240, and the profit $13.45; but an Illinois meet at Champaign later that spring brought a $267.40 loss. Rock had to guarantee Michigan $360 to come to Notre Dame for track and showed a $360 loss.

The need for frugality, and Rock's reputation for parsimony as a coach can, perhaps, now be better understood. Nevertheless he was sometimes a problem to the faculty committee that was supposed to control him. As, for instance, the tarpaulin that he wanted to order for the football field. The Committee was sorry, but a tarpaulin was a luxury that could not be afforded. "Rock acquiesced," Father Tom Burke told me recently, "but a few days later we got the bill." When ordering the article some time previously, Rock had no doubt assumed the Committee would see the dire need of a tarpaulin.

There were other individualists in the picture in those early days. The athletes, many of whom had served in World War I, were as a group, valiant, witty, loquacious, physically tough, mentally bright, a little wild. That Rock could handle them was testimony to his strength; conversely they were perfect instruments for his genius. The fact that most of them became successful coaches later was no accident.

Edward "Slip" Madigan, who was to rival Rock in some respects as the coach and athletic director of St. Mary's in California, was a 160-pound center with a good part of the weight in his heart and his head. He told of an impetuous teammate in 1916, identified only as "Moralis, King of the Mexicans," who took off on such a flying tackle near the side lines that he missed the runner, hit a parked automobile—and broke his shoulder. Against Morningside at Sioux City on Thanksgiving Day, it was so bitter cold that the Morningside coach had equipped his players with cotton gloves. Rockne never went in for such pampering; but the resourceful Irish took care of that. On the first play, there was one of those mountainous pileups at the line of scrimmage—and Notre Dame came out of it with the gloves.

They were playing-field lawyers who also had their little diplomatic devices. The defensive center is always at a disadvantage because he has to concentrate on passing the ball while a vigorous opponent may be concentrating on the center's defenseless head. A husky Wisconsin guard had been giving the lightweight Madigan such a bad time that "Slip" decided to try psychological warfare. Before centering the ball he turned to quarterback Joe Brandy and pointed to the opposing guard. "Did you ever see such an ugly-looking, repulsive Simple Simon in your life?"

Brandy, a sharp-tongued gamecock, added his tribute to the troglodyte. The stratagem, which has changed the course of many an important game, was to incense the Ugly American into slugging his tormentor in view of the officials—and get thrown out of the game. But the anthropoid merely looked the more impassive; and remained in the game. "I thought maybe he was deaf," Madigan grinned, "until the whistle blew. Then he punched me on the nose."

Then there was Gipp.

If where Rice sat was the head of the table; and where Rock became the center of any group; where Gipp was, was always the story. His name was pronounced with a hard G as in give, which he did, but only when necessary; for this was a most peculiar athletic saint whose canonization was hurried, as was that of Rock, because he died at Glory Peak.

XVII

The legend has Gipp turning up at Notre Dame as a blob of unsuspected athletic clay which Rockne discovered and shaped into a flawless masterpiece called Gridiron Superman.

As always with a legend—yes and no.

George was born in Laurium, Michigan, high up in the iron peninsula, the son of a Congregationalist minister named Matthew Gipp. He had every natural gift of body, mind, and spirit except the one which more than anything else made Rockne—the driving ambition to be *best*. George just didn't seem to care much about anything—including fame when it came.

As a freshman I lived downtown, with a family named Poulon. The son, Clarence, about my age, sometimes invited me out socially. One of these parties was to a place called Eagle Lake where somebody had a key to a cottage. There were about five couples and some necking which impaired nobody's amateur standing, least of all Gipp's, whose attitude toward such goings-on was consistent with his attitude toward the other aspects of life: he could take it or leave it alone and in this case he obviously had left it alone.

The girls were all townies, nice girls, with cars—which is as nice as a girl can get in a town near a male boarding school where cars are not permitted. Coming back I was in the car with George. His date was driving; and one of her friends who obviously thought that he had not been sufficiently attentive, was pointing out that plenty of other young men were interested in a pretty girl with a car. She was not the least bit subtle nor was George's reply.

"When the competition gets too tough I just drop out." Period. A big silence; but it was also a big and obvious lie because George never really started to work, at least on the athletic field, until the competition got too tough for the rest of the team. He was a sleek and quiet machine which ordinarily ambled with most cylinders idling—but which could take off with speed and cleverness. The power was there but the spark had to be unusual to reach it.

The story that he never played football before coming to Notre Dame is, like so much of the Rockne legend, not quite true. My authority is the late Perce Wilcox, who came to Notre Dame with Gipp, Hunk Anderson, and Ojay Larson. George played Calumet High School football with Wilcox but never made first string. He liked basketball better and later played on the town Y.M.C.A. team. He was good enough in baseball to have been signed by the Chicago White Sox just before he died—but he never won either a baseball or a basketball monogram at Notre Dame; nor had he seriously tried for them.

Lazy? Superb indifference, more likely. Things came easy for George and he took things easy—until a challenge appealed to him; and it could be a mental or emotional challenge. After high school he was content to drive a taxicab; and the minister's son learned about the seamier side of his home town. He must also have played baseball with the town team because he came to Notre Dame on a baseball scholarship on the recommendation of Wilbur T. "Dolly" Gray, a former Irish diamond star who had gone up to the White Sox; and whose home was also in Calumet, near Laurium. So Gipp was at Notre Dame as a twenty-one-year-old freshman. Awaiting the baseball season he did what most healthy youngsters did for exercise during football season—he kicked a football.

He was drop-kicking, the forgotten art of today which has been abandoned for the greater accuracy and distance of place-kicking. Rockne, who always had an eye for the small miracle, happened to see him. Gipp was invited to come out for the freshman squad. He did. A few weeks later, in a freshman game, he kicked a 62-yard drop kick which you will still find in the record book as the second longest of all time. After that he forgot baseball; and from such little accidents, taxi drivers from places like the iron peninsula (which is about as far from the spotlight as you can get) become national heroes and gridiron immortals.

Gipp's career was one of relaxed valleys—and dramatically stormed peaks. He did what he had to do; or what appealed to him at the moment. Army appealed to him most, because Army was the biggest target, the toughest foe. The 1917 game at West Point was the first in which he had played much time. But he was in there at the finish, on defense, an unusual place for a sophomore to be in the waning minutes as his team protected a 7–2 lead against a strongly advancing foe. One play—one sophomoric mistake—could mean defeat.

Army, with fourth down on the Notre Dame eight-yard line, lined up for a place kick and three sure points. But that would make the score only 7–5 and Notre Dame would receive and run out the clock. A place kick would not help. Army was going to fake the kick and—

"Pass. Pass," Gipp yelled. "Look out for a pass."

Army did pass. Gipp, the twenty-two-year-old sophomore, the marvel of poise, knocked down the pass; saved the game. This, incidentally, was one of the *odd* games. If Army had won it, and gone ahead in the competition with the parvenu Hoosiers, the Army series might have ended.

The year 1918 was the informal war year with an abbreviated, informal football schedule that did not count against eligibility. The next year the war was over, all the big boys were back. In the opening game against Kalamazoo, Gipp made two long runs for touchdowns. When the first was called back, he took it in stride. When the second one was also canceled out by a penalty, George said to the official: "Next time give me one whistle to stop or two to keep going."

Later, against Nebraska, the Irish were leading 14–9 in the early part of the fourth period; but tiring rapidly after injuries to key personnel. Rockne put Gipp in command of what the military would probably call a successful Fabian retreat. The resourceful George used every legitimate time-waster in the book; and some which the officials seemed to think had a slight odor of illegality. The Cornhusker crowd booed; the Cornhusker players raged; but time was a-wasting and the tired warriors had more time to recuperate after each play. When it had ended, the Nebraska coach, Henry Schulte, accosted Gipp: "What course do you take at Notre Dame?"

"Plumbing," George laughed.

Three weeks later the situation again called for Gipp's talents. Army was leading 9–0; Notre Dame had first down on the Cadet one-yard line and was hurrying into position, because time seemed to be about up for the first half of the game. There were no clocks in those days. Time was kept by an official. Gipp saw him looking at his watch, saw the hand with the gun begin to slowly rise. Gipp yelled to the center: "Give me the ball. Hurry."

He got the ball, dove over the line for a touchdown—as the gun went off, ending the half. Since the ball was in play before the gun sounded, the score counted. It was one of the oddest touchdowns ever scored, without a line charge by either team. Notre Dame not only had six points but that incalculable lift which sometimes makes all the difference in the between-halves morale-building. It was a dingdong second half in which Notre Dame had just enough left to score the winning touchdown shortly before the game ended. The Irish had won two straight in the series and were out in front to stay.

After that 1919 Army game it was all downhill. Rockne had his first undefeated season, a claim on the Midwestern championship— and most of his squad returning, led by Gipp, who was now regarded as a sure-fire All-American for 1920. The picture was not so rosy when Gipp got scholastically careless and was declared ineligible. But I've told you of the day when Father Burns was kind to both George and me—and to gridiron tradition.

XVIII

Rockne football, reflecting the man, consistently beat brawn by nimble brilliance. His teams gave away weight and size, won by brains and personality. He smelled talent, attracted it, developed it. It is not surprising to find his players showing a high content of success in later life. And it was that way from the beginning. The key men of the 1919–21 group became doctors, judges, publishers, business

successes. They thought in terms of victory by mentality—as a telegram from Gipp to a South Bend friend just before the 1920 Nebraska game at Lincoln reveals:

NEBRASKA WILL BE TOUGH BUT BRAINS WILL WIN

Brains did—Gipp's brains—as he improvised a successful play on
the field. That isn't permitted now; and it was not common practice
under Rockne; but, since he emphasized brains, he was never one
to discourage such demonstrations, especially by his magnificent ex-
ception, Gipp, who was still the leader on the field even though the
whip of discipline had passed the captaincy on to tackle Frank
Coughlin.

There was an envelope of thought about every game; and Valparaiso, which followed Nebraska, was a typical example. It was a
small school, not too far from Notre Dame, and ordinarily would have
been considered a frank "breather." But these were postwar days
when notable collections of players might turn up at a small school.
The word was that George Keogan (later Irish basketball coach)
had salted such a mine at Valparaiso, and that he hoped to surprise
Rockne on the "down" Saturday between Nebraska and Army. Rock
decided to warn his men but not to "key" them. At the end of the
half "Valpo" had a 3–0 upset going; but Rock must have found the
right words in the dressing room. The final score was 28–3.

Then came *the* Army game without which George Gipp might
have been finally listed as just another exceptional halfback. Army,
after two straight defeats by the Irish, was primed with one of its
best teams, led by Walter French, who had previously starred for
Rutgers and later played baseball for Connie Mack. Jack Lavelle,
who scouted Army for Notre Dame, and was very close to the people
at the Point, told how Gipp might have won that game before it
started. "Gipp and Russ Reeder, the West Point kicking specialist,
were engaging in an impromptu field-goal match in the warmup
period. Reeder stopped at the 40-yard line; but Gipp lined up four
balls at midfield, sent the first two over the crossbar at which he had
been aiming—and nonchalantly turned and drop-kicked the other
two through the opposite posts."

Gipp and French staged one of the stirring star duels of all time in a major setting; and this *was* major because Notre Dame was no longer the little school from the Midwest but the rising power under the coming coach—and led by a potential All-American. The big-time writers at the Point that afternoon included McGheehan, Rice, and Ring Lardner.

At the half it was Army 17 Notre Dame 14; but in the second half the Irish scored 13 points for a 27–17 victory. It was in the last period that Gipp reached his competitive heights. Ordinarily his contributions were passing, punting, drop-kicking, open-field running; but this game had become a fight-to-the-finish and Gipp put the stamp on his greatness by winning it the hard way—as a line-plunger, by ripping the Army line with unstoppable blasts; and by great defensive play.

Many Irish stars have climbed the ladder of raw courage to greatness but none farther than George Gipp on this single day. Something had touched the deep well-spring of his being. He became a burst of rockets, so thoroughly ablaze that Joe Byrne reports, "he once took off his headgear, threw it to the ground and challenged the entire Army team." On this one afternoon Gipp had everything that Rockne had, including the blowtorch spirit. It was a show for immortality.

Back at South Bend the students sensed its importance. We marched through the streets, in and out of lobbies, across the stages of theaters, marched to the chant: "Gipp, Gipp—Gipp, Gipp, *GIPP*." Six weeks later we would march those same streets silently; but before that George had further peaks to hit en route to Glory Peak.

The next week, at home, he got the hero's welcome; and responded with a smooth style-show performance that included an 84-yard off-tackle touchdown run. It was one of those perfect plays where blocking and clever running kept the runner untouched. The final score was 28–0 and the victim was Purdue. The next week we were getting the Indiana game in the gymnasium by an interesting scoreboard called the Grid-Graph, where a little white light showed the progress of the ball.

The light failed for Notre Dame. After three periods Indiana led 10–0. Gipp had been hurt, and was on the bench. The "down day" had come, the inevitable reaction after top emotional performances against Nebraska and Army. It was not made easier because now the psychology had been reversed and Indiana was fighting for the prestige of the Big Ten against the upstart Irish. Indiana was getting the scent of a big upset—and there is no tougher situation for a team or a coach to face than the surging elation, translated into relentless, reckless physical fury, of an underdog that has begun to get the smell of Sunday-morning headlines.

The diamond tip of Rockne's greatness as a coach rested in this field. He could most consistently get his team "up"; and, conversely, he could most consistently sense that coming "down day" and do something adequate to meet it. Usually he did something in advance. In this case he certainly could not have anticipated Gipp's injury; but there was an internal situation on his own team which, in the emergency, he could utilize.

Just about the most difficult personnel problem any executive can face is to have to choose between two highly intelligent, fiercely spirited competitors of proven loyalty and effectiveness. Rockne was to meet this situation later with Crowley and Layden, with Thomas and Stuhldreher, with Flanagan and Niemiec, with Savoldi and Mullins. In 1920 his problem was at right halfback, between Johnny Mohardt and Norm Barry.

Mohardt was the junior, Barry the senior. Rock always liked to give the senior every opportunity; but on his own testimony, he favored Mohardt because he was a better blocker—and superior blocking in the right halfback position was necessary in order to help shake Gipp loose. (In Rock's system, each halfback supplied the key block for the other, against the opposing end.) But Norm Barry was not just an ordinary Notre Dame man. He was the only one in history, to my knowledge, who came up all the way through the educational system, from the "minims" (grade school) and prep school to the varsity football squad. Norm was a blue-eyed black Irishman with spirit and pride. Nothing was going to keep him from finishing as a varsity regular.

There had been, Rockne wrote, a natural sizzling situation between Mohardt and Barry. Now, in the emergency at Indiana, Rock sent Barry in for Gipp with (his own quotation): "Get in there and wake 'em up. Insult somebody if you have to."

"Starting with Mohardt," Barry yelled as he tore from the bench. It was a dangerous thing for a coach to do—invite dissension to explode in a backfield; but it was another case of Rockne knowing his men, of his precise application of individual as well as mass psychology.

It became not so much a running contest between them as a blocking contest. Barry was in there to prove that he could block as well as Mohardt. So, as each rode the opposing end like a broncobuster, each began to get away with gains, and, in the process, to so rouse their teammates that the spark of fury jumped from the Indiana side of the scrimmage line to that of Notre Dame.

It was Norm Barry's day—the one for which he had been priming since he had watched the early canvas-padded heroes on old Cartier Field. Here was the dream of every American boy. Rock probably hadn't figured it down that fine; but his dramatic instinct was right. Back in the old gym, watching the little light on the Grid-Graph begin to flicker *our* way, we couldn't see or know about the blocking contest; but we knew that again, as always, especially under Rockne, Notre Dame was putting on its copyrighted performance of coming up with the man for the emergency.

Barry scored after a sustained advance. It was now Indiana 10 Notre Dame 7. With only a few minutes remaining. Get that ball! They did. They came again. Barry—Mohardt—Barry. Then they stopped. On the five-yard line. Barry was hurt; or exhausted. He was taken from the game.

GIPP! Gipp was back.

Come on, George!

The electric light moved—wavered, stopped.

Gipp was stopped. That shoulder must really be bad.

Indiana was smelling those headlines: *INDIANA WINS FIRST GAME FROM NOTRE DAME IN 30 YEARS.*

The light moved—leaped—

GIPP SCORES. Notre Dame 13 Indiana 10.

There was no doctor on the bench in those days. Rock didn't know what had happened to Gipp—and Gipp wasn't telling.

The open-field runner, passer, punter, drop-kicker, defensive star had made himself into a battering ram to go that last five yards, protect a two-year winning streak, drive the final spike into his own banner, up there on Glory Peak—with a broken collarbone.

With only two more games to go, Gipp's playing career had ended;

or had it? The next week, before a sellout crowd at Northwestern, he was in uniform, with a great hump of padding on his left shoulder. Before the game, in the warmup period, he gave an informal exhibition of drop-kicking. I was in the stands that perfect football day with a friendly sun presiding.

Notre Dame was flawless, even without Gipp. Barry was back in there before his home-town people. Late in the fourth period the score was 26-0.

"Gipp . . . Gipp . . . Gipp . . ."

The crowd had taken up the Notre Dame student chant. The game was over, they wanted to see the player-of-the-year. The chant became louder; and louder still when Gipp, with the lumpy shoulder, edged from the bench out near the side lines and began talking to Rock—who was shaking his head vigorously.

"Gipp . . . Gipp . . . WE WANT GIPP."

Rock was very human. He was a dramatist. Here was his boy, his Barrymore, pleading for that last chance to face an audience. And the audience, a foreign audience, was commanding the appearance.

But it was a crazy idea. Rock shook Gipp off.

The crowd chant became a crowd roar.

Gipp ran out on the field. Notre Dame was on defense. George was playing the unaccustomed position of safety man. When the punt came his way he let it roll. It was very obvious that he had been sent in there to take it easy, to avoid contact. The crowd hummed with pleasant approval. It was not after blood.

The Rockne offense could still be modern today. Every play started as a running play, with the quarterback, from a tight-T, shifting with the others, and the ball going on a direct pass to the tailback, already in motion. When there was to be a pass, the left halfback, the triple-threat man, faded back, took a short pitchout from the man who had first received the ball, rolled out a few steps —and threw to the man who, by that time, had had time to get downfield. When Gipp threw the ball it was done with a noticeable wrist action. It had speed, was not a floater, but was a soft ball, easy to catch and control.

Gipp was still in there on offense. Barry was now at right half. On the first play Barry carried and Gipp, instead of the normal block, drifted back out of contact.

On the next play Gipp passed to Barry, the home-town boy, for 55 yards and a touchdown! I don't think Rock called that one. The boys have a way of figuring those things out for themselves—as they later did for Marty Brill at Penn.

Gipp stayed in to kickoff. And played safety, where there was no danger, because the Irish line was in control. The next punt came, Gipp moved toward it.

"Let it roll," everybody in that crowd was thinking or yelling.

Let it roll, hell. George picked it up, had running room as the Northwestern ends had slowed down, never expecting this fool play. It was now up to the Northwestern ends. I'm sorry I do not have their names because they did the finest thing I have ever seen on a football field. They met George, converged on him like two detectives in a crowd, softly, gently, sort of gave him a few extra yards as they slowed him down, then sat him down, as if he were little baby brother, seemed to be saying: "Now look, George, after all—"

Rockne was already on the field, getting George out of there, talking to him, shaking his finger. George was probably grinning, asking for a cigarette. (He's supposed to have lighted one surreptitiously during a Rockne pep speech in a dressing room—but this I would have to have seen.)

Rock was probably saying: "Suppose you'd have got hurt? What would they say about me, letting you go into a game with an injury?"

Which was exactly, people being so funny, what some of them did say when George died a few weeks later, on December 14, 1920. They said he had been hurt in the Northwestern game and had died from the injury.

It was a strep throat which got George. Penicillin would have saved him.

XIX

Gipp was no sought-after prep-school star but a sand-lot fellow who came to Notre Dame on about as skimpy a "ride" (as scholarships were called) as was available. He lived in the Siberia of Brownson

Hall, where the unsought Rockne also was first lodged; and his campus job was a "hasher" or table waiter. He later moved to Sorin Sub where, a favorite story has it, he was housed next door to the shower room, and declared himself, though a minister's son, as more moral than any of the Catholics because the Bible said "cleanliness was next to Godliness."

In his last two years he lived at the Oliver Hotel where, it is now generally accepted, he had his own private job plan. He paid his expenses by certain skills around the green tables, skills for which he was temperamentally suited and which he had probably first developed during his taxi days in the Michigan home town. It is not true that he educated students in such indoor sports. I once heard Hunk Anderson, his pal and fellow townsmen, say with some indignation: "George wouldn't play cards with the college boys." It is also probable that George might have had a few bucks going for him on some of the games in which he distinguished himself. There was, in those early days, a student pool that went to West Point where it was always covered by a similar Army pool.

Gipp was billiard champion of South Bend and definitely a "pool shark"; but he never played with students for much more than fun; and I qualify as an expert witness because I racked up the balls at the Oliver. It seems to be true that he matched his poker proficiency with town hotshots and hotel transients with reasonable success. Should the university have known that Gipp gambled? That would have taken a lot of detection. It was certainly not common knowledge. I worked in the hotel where he lived and where he presumably played cards. I worked on the *News-Times* during his big senior year. Yet I never heard that Gipp was a gambler until years later. I'm bringing this up because every so often the subject gets written about, and not always fairly nor kindly.

The truly great respect greatness, especially in moments of greatness. Rockne was always quiet after some notable achievement as if, for that little while, he didn't have to prove anything. Gipp had to be aware of his position; but he went to the extreme length of wearing his monogram sweater inside out, a fashion adopted by other athletes at the time. Two weeks after the end of the football season the annual football dinner was held at the Oliver. Nobody thought it too unusual when Gipp left early. We figured George thought he might have to make a speech—something nobody had ever heard him do. But two days later we knew it had not been a simple case of normal modesty. He was confined to his room with tonsillitis. Then he was taken to the hospital with pneumonia. Soon he was critical as poison from the streptococcus raced through him, tearing him down, eating him.

There was gloom, an impending doom, over the campus he had kept so brightly lighted. The lamp of the High Priest of Victory was flickering. Daily bulletins began to be printed throughout the country.

Every so often sports produces an off-field situation much more gripping than anything that could happen on the field. Gipp was making the front pages now. An athlete was dying young. People who didn't care about football prayed that his life be spared. The drama mounted when *Collier's* announced that George Gipp was the first Notre Dame man who had ever made Walter Camp's *first* All-America eleven. And it was learned that he had signed a professional baseball contract with the Chicago White Sox.

In the quiet hospital room two other things happened. Gipp made a request to Rockne: Someday when the going was particularly rough against Army, Rock was to ask the boys to go out and win for Gipp.

And, two days before he died, George Gipp, one of Our Lady's Tough Guys, became a Catholic.

(One of the finer things about the Notre Dame football tradition is the deep respect non-Catholic boys have for the spiritual faith of their teammates. Some became Catholics later on, as Gipp and Rockne did; others get something from it they never lose; something talked about only among close friends and on tender occasions. At our twenty-fifth class reunion, the first night had the customary alcoholic tinge. The next morning there was the "reunion in the sky" Mass for the deceased members. Everybody was there—including two Protestant ex-football players who were also Masons.)

Not so long ago I visited a funeral home which held the body of a seventeen-year-old high-school boy who had collapsed during a football workout. He was an only child, an exemplary student, son, and athlete. What does one say to the parents? I told them about

George Gipp; and the sermon preached by the then Prefect of Religion who is now John Cardinal O'Hara of Philadelphia:

"To the eyes of the world it is deep tragedy as we contemplate the abrupt and painful close of the life of a young man, energetic, skillful, alert, keen-minded and resourceful—a life full of promise—snapped off in the moment of highest glory.

"But to the eyes of faith it is a miracle; the passing from a life of transient joy and abiding sorrow to a life of happiness eternal. What wrought the miracle of this beautiful death? It was the reward of Notre Dame, the Blessed Mother, for a humble service which is dedicated to her honor; he strove in his own way to add lustre to its tradition; and although we did not think of George as a deeply religious man, his inmost thoughts came to the surface when he faced death.

"You offered a novena of communions for him and when informed of it he said: 'Tell them to keep it up.' On the day the novena ended he asked to become a member of your church and the following day was baptized. He lingered on, sustained only by prayer and offered his sufferings to God. On the afternoon before his death he became more his real self than he had been for two weeks; and he spoke, not of the honors he had received but of his death in the arms of God. He spent his time repeating the prayers the sisters at the hospital had taught him and was happy to die. May God grant us all the grace to view death in the same tranquil way. I commend him to your prayers."

I marched in his funeral procession; then went to the *News-Times* to write this story of the way the students surrendered their idol:

"Braving the rigors of a blinding snow, 1500 Notre Dame students marched in silent tribute Wednesday before the body of George Gipp, football sensation of the year, who died Tuesday. The line extended for blocks as the procession moved four abreast through the business district on its way to the New York Central station.

"Business stopped as the long escort filed through the streets with all the cheers of previous Notre Dame processions absent. A platoon of police led the procession which was immediately followed by the football team, lined up in signal formation, with the position of left half significantly vacant. The Monogram Club led the student body and faculty, moving reverently before the hearse carrying the body of the man who had been most intimately linked with the name of Notre Dame in the glorious victories of the fall.

"Heartley Anderson, Fred Larson, and Percy Wilcox, who had followed Gipp through other journeys in high school and in college, marched on one side of the hearse. On the other, Frank Coughlin, Joseph Brandy, and Norman Barry made the first steps of their last trip with the boy who had shared with them the trials and glories of three sensational campaigns. These six men will accompany the body to Calumet as pallbearers and will represent Notre Dame in the last act of the life of George Gipp.

"Following the hearse came three automobiles carrying the parents and relatives of the dead man. The feelings of priests, students and all of South Bend who witnessed the procession were in spirit with those in the first of these machines where the mother rode with bowed head.

"When the first of the escort reached the station, the lines separated and the students bared their heads to the snow as the body of their 'Gipper' went on to its appointed end. Here where Notre Dame could do no more for its wonder man the procession waited. As the Chicago train arrived the crowd moved forward toward the casket which was being prepared to enter the baggage car. A blanket of flowers on which the ND monogram was mounted, the last symbol of the love of the Notre Dame student body, will accompany the body to its final resting place.

"Telephone poles, baggage trucks and every point of vantage were utilized as the casket was elevated to the door of the car. As though by an unspoken command a hat came off here and there and in a flash the crowd was bareheaded. Silently, with almost defiant faces, the students gazed at their departing idol."

And, I add from this vantage point of years, the students, most of them meeting death for the first time, would never be quite so young again. I did not look upon Gipp dead. I did not want to remember this magnificent physical specimen as weighing just eighty pounds.

The last six miles of his journey to Laurium were covered by sled. The incident of this death, a thanatopsis of a sort, was not lost upon the editorial writers. Housman's *A Shropshire Lad* was quoted:

The time you won your town the race
We chaired you through the market-place;
Man and boy came cheering by,
And home we brought you shoulder-high.

Today the road all runners come
Shoulder-high we brought you home,
And set you at your threshold down,
Townsman of a stiller town.

Smart lad to slip betimes away
From fields where glory does not stay
And early though the laurel grows
It withers quicker than the rose.

Now you will not swell the rout
Of lads that wore their honours out
Runners whom renown outran
And the name died before the man.

The Scholastic, Notre Dame's weekly news magazine, carried a poem whose authorship was not credited; but which I have always thought came from the pen of Rev. Charles L. O'Donnell, the poet-priest who had been a World War I chaplain and was to become president of the university in 1928. It ended:

O Lady, you have taken of our best
To make a playmate for the Seraphim;
There on the wide, sweet campus of the blest,
Be good to him.

Rockne's statement included a facet few had suspected about Gipp (or about Rockne): "The outstanding feature of his character was a deep affection for his mother." In his athletic estimate, Rock said: "George Gipp was the greatest halfback who ever represented Notre Dame; and his unquestioned ability was surpassed by a grit which featured all his work on the gridiron and was the marvel of his attending physicians."

Ten years later, in a *Collier's* article, Rock said: "George Gipp was the greatest football player Notre Dame ever produced. He was unequaled in the game by anybody, save, perhaps, Jim Thorpe. Gipp had everything to make a man great—splendid physique, balanced temperament, a brilliant mind."

Just how good was George Gipp? What is his true stature in grid-iron history? There is no doubt but that his tragic death dramatized his memory. Nobody can honestly say who is the best player of *any* year; because nobody sees all of them under equal conditions. I've seen or been professionally studious of most of the publicized stars since 1919; I invented the Football Preview in 1937 and for the next twenty years probably gave more time than any other one person to the business of rating stars.

For what it may be worth, Gipp has as much right as any I've known to rank at the top. There just wasn't anything demanded of a player that George Gipp could not do, and do superlatively. He was the defensive captain, a sharp tackler and, Rock wrote, "the one player about whom it could truly be said that 'nobody ever completed a pass against him.'" Co-ordinating all these talents was an ideal playing temperament, mostly ice-cold but, when fanned to a flame, operated (as Rock always did) at highest efficiency. He was, on the football field, much like Rockne was in almost every field—a specialist at everything. In the modern day, he would have made a superb T-quarterback, in college or pro ball.

Football has not found, nor is ever likely to find, another pair like Rockne and Gipp. They had much in common. Each was three to four years older than the average college age. Each went out at the fame-insuring absolute top, dramatically, tragically. They differed in basic temperament; and the difference was expressed in their eyes. Rock's eyes always probed, blazed, attacked. Gipp had sad eyes, as if he knew and were waiting; and because of that was not too much concerned about the commonplace.

Cullen Cain, a Philadelphia columnist, recalled the epic lines of Omar:

> I sometimes think that never blooms so red
> A rose as where some buried Caesar bled.

The Gipp rose, carefully tended by Rockne, would bloom eight years later, on a gridiron grave of his favorite foe "the brave old Army team."

XX

During the summer of 1921 I had written Rockne seeking certain information. His answer, dated August 2, is a typical example of his terse writing style. He had typed it himself in slapdash fashion.

My dear Wallace: Very glad to get your letter. Regarding Champs winner of first in Conference meet is Conference champ, regardless of whether or not he is from Conference school. Winner at Nat Collegiate Meet is National College Champ, winner at Pasadena is rated Nat AAU Champ. The East may not recognize Nat Collegiate meet but they will have to.

If you get here the 14th it will be all right. So far as you are concerned for publicity we begin the 15th. I will write you a lineup with prospects later so you can send them on to your papers. I am sorry that Fr Davis cannot put you in Sorin Sub as he has already filled up every available room in every hall. Possibly there will be a vacancy after a few weeks and he will fix you up then.

Murphy and Alberts tied at 6 4 but AAU rules make them keep on jumping at different heights until one or the other is the victor. Hayes was left at the mark in the 100 on account of quick gun. Will write you again in a few weeks. Sincerely K. K. Rockne.

My first football news release, which appeared in the Sunday Chicago papers and had wide circulation, was an optimistic view based upon the fact that Notre Dame had 17 lettermen returning. I was called in and Professor Rockne lectured me on the basic difference between news and publicity. His opening remark is still the model for college sports publicity—at least, as the coach would have it written: "Never tell 'em how many you've got coming back. Tell 'em how many you lost." This aspect of coaching philosophy explains why the mentors spend so much time during the season before the Wailing Wall, wringing out tears from the Crying Towel.

Football is a game of brawn, brain, and speed; but these are usually so evenly distributed among the major competitors that the winner on any given day is he who makes best use of his equipment; and he who does is the one who is most emotionally aroused—emotion being the ethyl in the gas which powers the human engine. An overconfident team has a cold motor, operates at low efficiency, and may well be upset by an inferior opponent who feels he must fight for his life. So coaches try to give their young men a healthy dose of fear as a form of psychological insurance. A pleasant by-product of this policy is the fact that, if a team exceeds expectations, the coach is apt to be regarded as a superior workman by alumni, press—and perhaps other schools which might pay higher salaries.

You can observe the operation of such psychology as we proceed. DePauw, for instance, was not the type of school to make Notre Dame quake; or residents of South Bend to come to the box office in unusual numbers. But Rockne, in briefing me, divulged some disturbing facts: (1) DePauw's coach, Fred Walker, had always been a sort of mystery man. (2) He had assembled one of those surprise teams which could suddenly materialize at a school which played freshmen, especially following a war when experienced players were available. (3) He was lying in the woods down at Greencastle, Indiana, preparing a deadfall for the unsuspecting Irish, fat-headed with pride. (4) As proof that something was in the wind, DePauw was bringing its own drinking water.

I duly reported all this startling information; and when DePauw canceled its first game, it began to look as if there might be real fire behind all this smoke. There probably was, since DePauw proved to be very tough in the first half. The final score was 57–10. Had Rockne been kidding the public, through me, to build up the gate? Or, remembering the Valparaiso scare of the preceding year, had he been taking no chances of being upset?

The next game was against Iowa at Iowa City. Rock gave me no briefing on this, other than the warnings he gave his players at the daily lectures. Here the simple truth seemed sufficient to bring the boys "up." Iowa, a contender for the Conference title, was coached by Howard Jones, a proven mentor. It had a solid cast headed by quarterback Aubrey Devine, fullback Gordon Locke and Duke Slater, a giant Negro tackle. The boys were made aware of what faced them at the usual pep meeting. We made the eight-hour daylight trip by day coach. There were songs, horseplay, card games.

At Iowa City we were received as heroes. Small boys wanted to know which was Mohardt, which was Hunk Anderson. I had been entrusted with $125 of student money—in small bills—to bet; but the Hawkeye students proved to be very practical people who did not think their squad had much of a chance against the great Notre Dame team which had won 20 straight.

I walked to the field with the players, said I would see them after the game, good luck, just like that. A job of work to be done, heigh-ho. There had been more real worry about DePauw. I went to the press box to send the play-by-play back to the students in the gymnasium.

Iowa scored 10 points in the first period, mostly by twisting sorties through our great line by Aubrey Devine—and probably behind blocking by Slater. Notre Dame finally got the fat out of its head, arose from the carefully prepared bed of flattery, and went to work. Mohardt passed to Kiley for a touchdown. Later another pass to Eddie Anderson gave us first down on the five-yard line. That seemed to be it—except that we could only make four yards in four downs and lost the ball on the one-yard line. At the half it was Iowa 10 Notre Dame 7; but I sent a message back to the lads in the gym not to worry.

In the third period Iowa flurried offensively but gave most of its energy to protecting the 10–7 lead. The final quarter was almost all Notre Dame. Four times we were within their ten-yard line. Once Kiley blocked a punt and seemed about to score. Again, Castner was loose with a pass. Two of Mohardt's passes, intended for Kiley, were intercepted by Belding, the Iowa end. Nothing in life is more final than the final whistle of a losing football game. And the score, 10–7.

I hurried to the dressing room. Nobody was there but the players. Some of our tough guys were crying.

Rockne came in, said: "There will be no alibi." Then he began going among his young men, testing for injuries, applying bandages. He was the trainer, too.

Duke Slater, still there at the finish, had no doubt been responsible for considerable of the final frustration. He had also done one of the fine things in my football memories. Chet Grant, our quarterback, weighing 138 pounds, recklessly caught a punt with big Slater bearing down on him. Grant could have been annihilated, in his defenseless position, but Slater sat him down almost as gently as the Northwestern ends had handled Gipp the preceding season. Slater won Notre Dame's lasting respect that day.

Years later I was back in Iowa City as one of the telecasters (with Jack Drees) of a CBS-TV Regional Big Ten game. I told Al Coupee what Judge Roger Kiley had recently said: "I passed Duke Slater in the Hall of Records the other day and instinctively stepped aside."

"I'll tell him that tonight," Coupee said. "I'm interviewing him on my TV show in Des Moines. It might warm him up—he doesn't talk easily."

Next day, at the game, Coupee came grinning: "I told Duke—and he was so pleased I had trouble shutting him off."

Just a year ago I saw an interesting picture sent out from Chicago by AP Wirephoto. The caption read: "The installation of Superior Court Judge Fred W. (Duke) Slater in Chicago resembled a football reunion. The former football men are, left to right: Appellate Court Judge Roger Kiley, Notre Dame; Slater; Superior Court Judge Norman C. Barry, Notre Dame, and former star of the Green Bay Packers; and Probate Court Judge Robert Jerome Dunne, Michigan."

Rockne, ever learning, may have wondered if he had not made a mistake in stimulating the boys for the DePauw game—instead of saving the battery charge for Iowa. An interesting development came out of this historically important battle. Notre Dame's colors are blue and gold; it wore dark blue jerseys. Iowa's jerseys were black. It was getting dark in the final period and Notre Dame blamed Belding's two crucial interceptions on the gloom, the similarity of jerseys—and the fact that Belding somewhat resembled Kiley. A likely story, you may say; but Rockne ordered another color of jerseys—to be worn when contrast was needed. That's how Notre Dame began wearing green jerseys. Now all squads have contrasting jerseys.

XXI

Somebody loses—somebody wins. Iowa had won and this was Iowa City. They hadn't expected it but here it was and it was wonderful, ecstatic. It was a small town and every stranger was automatically a Notre Damer. We were not scheduled to leave until midnight. There was no place to go. It was a long evening.

The squad was going back in style—in a Pullman. There were about thirty in the official party; about fifty got on that special Pullman car waiting at a siding. None got off. Rock had the drawing room and had shut himself in early to ponder the first defeat in three years —and one he should have won. Somebody knocked on his door, told him he'd better come and get—let's call him Clarence.

"Where is he?"

"The cops have him."

Rock got "Clarence." Later, after the Pullman car had been joined to a train and we were moving away from Deadfall Gulch (Iowa City), "Clarence" was sitting in the smoker, explaining. It had been a long, long evening. Guys had been making cracks. "Clarence" had stopped at the lunchroom near the station for some coffee. More guys had made more cracks. "I didn't mind it when they called me an Irish Catholic so-and-so, but when they called me an Irish Catholic such-and-such, that was too much. So I cleaned out the joint," said Clarence, who was neither Irish, Catholic, a so-and-so, nor a such-and-such.

When there was nobody left but "Clarence" and me, I began to feel conspicuous and climbed into an upper berth with Pete Smith, a Texan. For a while there was only the rumble of the car and the snores of boys who had labored hard, if not victoriously. Then came a sinister new sound. Some stinker at the station had reported contraband aboard—or we had a very nosy conductor. He had awakened Rock, who was giving a fine imitation of an indignant coach learning for the first time that college boys without tickets sometimes traveled with football teams.

Trapped, I waited. My roommate had the old college spirit. He rolled over to the edge of the berth, tried to make a barrier behind which I could hide; but he was a small quarterback rather than a big tackle and the conductor was a tall man. "Two in upper seven," he droned.

"Wallace—" Rock spluttered, probably in genuine surprise. "What the hell are you doing up there?"

That separated the goat from the lamb in upper seven.

"Got a ticket?" the conductor asked.

"No. How much is it?"

"Nine sixty-five."

"I'll see you in the morning."

"You'll see me now—nine sixty-five."

I got my carefully folded pants, took out the large roll of student money I hadn't been able to get placed, peeled off ten bucks. The conductor gave me the thirty-five cents change and a dirty look which said plainly what he thought of a heel who would try to cheat the railroad while carrying all that money.

Sleep comes even to the vanquished and harassed, when they're young. The next morning, as I piled off one end of the car in Chicago, Rock got off the other end. I was ahead of him and moved rapidly to stay ahead. I could hear him stepping up his pace. It was like a spy movie. Finally he called: "Frank."

I waited. Now I would get it but *good*.

"Next time," he said calmly, "not upstairs."

He told me how to do it next time. Rock surely knew all there was to know about football.

(For the rest of my tenure I followed his wise counsel with such success that in three seasons I negotiated over ten thousand miles as the guest of the railroads and some of the best hotels in America. In my senior year I became president of the exclusive campus organization called the Road Scholars. We even had our picture in *The Dome*, the student yearbook.)

We were going to walk to an eight o'clock Mass. We decided to split up into small groups. We didn't want to be identified as that Notre Dame team which had lost a football game.

We were free to spend the day as we pleased. A few took earlier trains but the main body was on the New York Central that was due in South Bend at one in the morning. I was alone in the smoking car. Rock joined me.

He was depressed, had things on his mind, wanted a listener. He could no longer carry on as coach, trainer, athletic director, business manager, track coach, and all of his other duties. He was going to have to have more help. This was going to have to be done and that was going to have to be done.

He had, you see, after 20 straight victories, lost a football game to a team that was to become Big Ten Champions—and a team he had outgained three yards to one. But he had lost and that was intolerable. I was not conscious we were pulling into South Bend until the train began to slow up and I heard the familiar yell known as the Skyrocket—an afternoon sound of victory at one o'clock on a morning of defeat. The student body had marched three miles into town to meet the team.

They were looking for Rock. He had sneaked out on the other side of the train. I told them where he was. He fought them with his fists. People didn't do things like this to Rockne. Rockne had dignity. When he wanted to go hide nobody was going to drag him, lift him to a baggage truck.

But these kids did. A thousand males stood there and cheered. Rock stood there and cried. And said: "After this I will never leave Notre Dame as long as they want me."

I've often wondered, during the contract negotiations with other schools, how much Rock remembered of this night; and if it was the same truck which held his body after he finally did leave Notre Dame.

Nobody smiled on the campus the next week. The pressure of the long winning streak had been broken; and the psychological processes which had victimized Notre Dame at Iowa City made a living sacrifice of Purdue. The raging Irish line forced fumbles, blocked punts, disrupted any semblance of Boilermaker poise. Hunk Anderson may have set a record for a guard by scoring two touchdowns in three minutes after blocking punts. End Mike Seyfrit blocked another kick with his face. The halftime score was 30–0. I've never seen a team with more fever in the blood.

Following that game I was given another lesson in publicity, this time by a delegation of players. Newspaper people had begun to ask: "Who will succeed Gipp?" Rock had answered that by moving Mohardt to left halfback, the triple-threat position. What the reporters really wanted to know was: "Who is your All-American candidate this season?" Today there are certain guide lines and routines to follow in the tricky business of making an All-American. But back in 1921 this was an uncharted field. I had been hired as a newspaper correspondent; and while every reporter who follows a team closely eventually becomes a sort of agent for that team, I did not feel qualified to take the responsibility of deliberately picking certain players and slanting publicity in their direction.

I got no help from Rockne, who, apart from giving the senior a break in case of reasonable doubt, leaned over backward to avoid any suspicion of favoritism. This is a delicate area where clumsy action can wreck squad morale. Players do not resent publicity going to the man who earns it; and they understand that publicity automatically goes to the man who, for the good of the team, has been cast in the role of the star. That man in '21 was Mohardt; so I went along with him and there was no objection. The line was a different problem entirely. We had at least four men—Roger Kiley, Eddie Anderson, Hunk Anderson, and Buck Shaw—who were legitimate All-American candidates. But we also had a flamboyant sophomore tackle who had caught the eye of reporters and was getting more publicity than any of the six seniors. I had evidently drifted along with this wind.

So a delegation of senior backs came to me and their spokesman said, very nicely: "We don't want to tell you how to do your job; but we do ask you to do one thing: Take a closer look at the *other* tackle."

I began watching the senior tackle, a quiet fellow named Buck Shaw who is still operating efficiently as coach of the Philadelphia Eagles. I noted particularly how he blocked on offense to open the holes for the backs. I switched the emphasis, not just in my newspaper stories but in word-of-mouth opinions to influential outside reporters; and I was in excellent position to do this because these were the days before players were numbered, and, in a press box on the road, I was usually the one person who knew the Notre Dame players. As such I had access to the ears of reporters who are always anxious to get the "inside" on every story.

A publicity man cannot *make* an All-American who does not have it; but he can give a better chance to the man who does have it. The thing I learned from this incident was: in case of doubt about the merits of certain players, go to the men who play with them and against them. The most-prized honor in football should be an All-Opponent team. I once saw Rockne go to a freshman center, George "Chunky" Murrin (now a Houston attorney), for such information. After all, it was Murrin who was getting hit.

The team was righting itself nicely after the Iowa debacle. They knew, now, that the surest way of winning a football game is to *hit harder and think better than the other fellow—on every play*. If they hadn't learned that at Iowa City they might have had to learn it in the two games that would have hurt even more—Nebraska and Army. As it was, they put their nose against the stone against the Cornhuskers and were much more convincing than the 7–0 score. They took a tough Hoosier rival, the University of Indiana 28–7, in the rain at Indianapolis. Army, with most of the players who had forced Gipp to heroics, was undefeated and confidently waiting.

The Army game that year was to have a trailer—on Tuesday, November 8, Election Day, at the Polo Grounds in New York against a Rutgers team aspiring to major-league status. The following home game—third in eight days—was to be against Haskell Institute. Rockne, regardless of his motive in the matter of DePauw's mystery men, was a shameless Barnum as, with a straight face, he briefed me on the Indians. Fullback John Levi was a grandson of Sitting Bull, the famous Sioux chief. Other Haskell players were traced to various other Indian celebrities who have since been better immortalized on TV Westerns. I listened, also with a straight face but wayward ears.

A big pep meeting in Washington Hall notified the boys of the student desires against Army. The message was received, especially by their favorite pin-up, Hunk Anderson, whose brief speech "You do the best you can and I'll do the best *we* can" thenceforth became part of the tradition.

When the train had passed Elkhart, and the conductor had made the first ticket check, I turned up on the special Pullman. Rock was outraged. "I thought I told you to stay back home and build up the Haskell gate—" he stormed; then turned and left me, thereby setting a pattern for all the future trips. *Going* to the game I was always an interloper, a bum, a guy who was shirking his duty back home, an added starter without status, to be welcomed by the players if they chose but to be ignored by the coach.

Coming back was something else, especially after a victory, which was almost always. Rock was always very curious as to what the boys in the press box had to say about this and that. He would listen very attentively. Sometimes he would ask about the reaction to some new wrinkle of play which neither the experts nor myself had noticed;

but I always tried to give him an honest answer, even when slightly fictional. He was so pleased by praise. And it made my presence on the train more socially tolerable.

Actually he probably liked such demonstrations of loyalty. One of the things he understandably didn't like about bums was their habit of bunking in with the star players at night. He finally solved that by (a) putting up a list of those entitled to bum; and (b) assigning those of us who rated this second-class citizenship to sleeping partners. Once, when I climbed into an upper berth in the still of the night, my good friend, Big Jack Flynn, then a sub-tackle, bellowed:

"You big cow—what are you doing up here?"

"Rock sent me."

"Heck—that means I won't get to play tomorrow."

XXII

Rock had a severely scientific mind which left no place, in his gridiron planning, for playing of hunches or praying for breaks. Plays were planned and breaks were made. He seems (from other sources) to have had his share of the normal athlete's obeisance to such items as the lucky flute, a lucky shirt, a lucky overcoat. But I never thought of him as superstitious. I've read that the first Notre Dame football squad to play Army (1913) had entered the Army mess hall via the kitchen; and since the Irish won, Rock insisted on that lucky entrance thereafter. This pretty story doesn't explain the second and fourth games, which were lost; and I can't imagine Rock wasting time on discredited charms.

I was there for the eighth game and I have no recollection of how we entered—perhaps because of the great thrill which ran through me like a zinging current as I listened to the greeting of the Cadet Corps as we filed to our places in the great mess hall. Army has had a special place with me since; as it must have for every boy who has ever gone to the Academy with a visiting team. We were given the freedom of the post, including the Officers' Club where we played billiards (I wonder if Gipp beat them at that, too) and wrote letters to all the girl friends we could think of, using the Officers' Club stationery. We were well fed, smiled-at, respected for the deeds of other days; but as for the game—nothing to it but to count the score. It was Army's year and, at the piercing pep meeting that night, the trim Cadets spoke much of Navy. It was the Iowa script in reverse.

There was no big hotel at the Point then and the squad was quartered at something called the Annex. There were four beds in our room, two against each wall, which left just enough space for me to lie on the floor between them, though I was comfortable enough in four monogram sweaters. A bellboy who made several nonscheduled calls may have been just a hero-worshiper but he gave me a lot of exercise rolling under the beds. I didn't sleep much but neither did Paul Castner, one of my four roommates, who spent much time watching the lights of the boats on the Hudson. But he played a great game the next day which seemed to prove Rock right (again) in his claim that the important sleep was *two* nights before the game.

West Point is located on a flat expanse of high ground overlooking the Hudson. Near the parade ground in those days was the football field. There were bleachers on either side seating a few thousand people. Admission was free—the reason Army could only offer a $1000 guarantee to Notre Dame until 1923 when the game, because of the demand for tickets, was moved to the New York baseball parks, where there was an even bigger demand for tickets. (I have never "bought" the claim that the games in New York brought out a "rabble" of "subway alumni." It was rather, a blue-chip crowd. You almost had to be a "somebody" to snare a ticket.)

Against Army our team was functioning with all the smooth efficiency claimed by TV commercials for their various mechanical devices. At the end of the first half we led 14–0, our goal had never been threatened and Army had made just one first down.

When something unusual turns up, in or out of sport, people try to explain it with unusual reasons. Rockne's teams were becoming unusual; and one of the reasons for their success was the backfield shift which, a growing number of other coaches said, gave Notre Dame an unfair advantage because the backs were in motion when the ball was passed. Between halves of this 1921 Army game, Charles Daly, the Cadet coach, registered an objection.

"I'll relieve you of embarrassment," Rock said to Ed Thorp, the referee. "For the rest of the game we will not use the shift."

In the second half Notre Dame, running from stationary punt formation, scored two more touchdowns and won 28–0. Johnny Mohardt ran—and passed to Roger Kiley and Eddie Anderson. Wynne displayed exceptional running ability, Castner took his first starring honors, Buck Shaw kicked four points and stood out defensively, along with Hector Garvey, Harry Mehre, Hunk Anderson, and Jim Dooley. Ten of the Notre Dame players that day earned later first place choices on various All-American teams.

The agitation against the shift, with following legislation, was to continue throughout Rockne's career; but he always had the answers; and when they finally forced him to a full second's stop—which seemed to pull all the teeth—he went to heavier backs—Carideo, Schwartz, Brill, and Savoldi—and finished with two national championships! But of all that, later.

The $1000 guarantee did not take care of the actual expenses, especially when we traveled Pullman; but Rockne had a secret weapon in New York; two of them, in fact, bearing the same name, Joseph M. Byrne. Senior had been a catcher on the baseball team way, way back. Junior graduated from Notre Dame but as I have often told him, never really got out of the sophomore class. "My college, right or wrong but always right" was Joe's motto; and in addition to this wonderful loyalty he had been a classmate and friend of Rock's—and had a substantial bankroll from which the bands were easily removed. There were no second-class citizens on Joe Byrne's horizon. That night, when the team went to see *The Ziegfeld Follies of 1921*, I was among those present.

Joe had an operating vice-president named Danny Sullivan who knew his way around Broadway; so the audience was not left ignorant of the fact that Notre Dame, the new toast of the town, was in the house. A comedienne made a pass at Hunk, who had been strategically placed in a stage box. Will Rogers, in the course of his rope-twirling act, had a few well-chosen words to say about Notre Dame, after which his lasso just happened to circle the shiny bald target of Rockne, who was pulled to the stage—and that's how Rock and Will Rogers first began a friendship that ended with the beautiful tribute Rogers wrote on the day Rock died.

There is a fraternity of the elite. The top-echelon celebrities have a way of recognizing and admitting one another. Rock, because he had so many facets, had a wide circle of such friends—Jimmy Walker, Grantland Rice, Paul Whiteman and such. Many of them had started, as had Rogers and Rockne, in the By Gum We Gotta fraternity. Rock was probably around with some of them that night after the '21 Army game because when he got back to the Pennsylvania Hotel he was in good humor, which was just as well.

I had come in shortly before, had seen a clean, unoccupied bed in one of the big dormitory-type rooms. I had been asleep only minutes, or so it seemed, when I heard that familiar voice: "Wallace—get to heck out of my bed. Get over there with Mayl."

Gene Mayl was a rangy sophomore end. It was a single bed but we both slept well. The wonders continued the next morning when, after Mass at St. Patrick's Cathedral, we returned to the hotel for breakfast. Food was so immediate and sumptuous that we thought it a Joe Byrne production. Another group of huskies who had been there ahead of us were still waiting as we left. This was the Harvard team, losers to Princeton the day before and to Notre Dame that morning. It had been their breakfast, probably ordered months before.

Sunday and Monday were spent at the Coleman House in Asbury Park, New Jersey. Since this was November, we had the resort hotel to ourselves, a most delightful interlude for a big and very happy family on an unexpected vacation. Papa Rockne sat at the head of the table, twirled his cigar and wise-cracked. Next to me Roger Kiley gave a judicial decision: "Look at that sonofagun. He can make you so mad you want to kill him—he smiles and you wonder what it was you were mad about." This was Rockne's way with players, and his way with people.

The Rutgers game on November 8, the first appearance of Notre Dame in the big city, was a 48–0 style show such as a big-league baseball club might put on in a minor-league town. The weather was crisp, the crowd surprisingly large, the team mechanically perfect. The game got so "gaily vigorous" that Rock reported this dialogue between himself and Foster Sanford, the Rutgers coach:

Sanford: "I insist that, after the shift, your backs remain rigid."

Rockne: "Too many of them are already rigid—on *their* backs in the dressing room."

The three remaining games were almost an afterthought. The second team took Haskell 42–7. Marquette was beaten 21–7 in a let's-get-it-over-with struggle at the ice-cold baseball park in Milwaukee. The Thanksgiving Day 48–0 victory over Michigan Aggies was a farewell party to the last of the 1919–21 group which had cemented the place the 1913 team had first made for Notre Dame in the national gridiron. Rockne was definitely building the better mousetrap; representatives of Yale, Princeton, and probably most of the Midwestern schools, were in the stands at the final game.

Roger Kiley, Eddie Anderson, Hunk Anderson, Buck Shaw, and Johnny Mohardt had been three-year regulars and the nucleus around which the three postwar squads had been built. The 1920 backfield—Gipp (185), Mohardt (165), Wynne (180), Brandy (150) —suffers by no comparison. Mohardt was lighter than Gipp and did not punt; otherwise he was a good carbon copy of George, an even better runner, almost as good a passer—and another Rockne in the classroom where he also took pre-med science, with philosophy for an elective! Wynne was a Layden-type fullback; and Brandy, though small, was the model for the Rockne gamecock quarterback. All were blockers, had flaming spirit, were mentally bright and physically tough.

The 1919–21 linemen are still better known as individuals than the Seven Mules or the undefeated 1929–30 linemen. They played together longer; and most of them have remained in the public eye chiefly as coaches. The efficiency of the 1921 team can be traced largely to the fact that the linemen were expert offensive blockers. It is the hardest gridiron knowledge to acquire and to put into execution.

Here is what the sports editor of *The Dome* wrote about Rockne after the '21 season: "Rockne is what the psycho-analysts might call a 'football complex,' a bundle of instincts and conscious states governed by a predominant idea of turning out football players and football teams. He lives and thinks football in terms of his everyday life and applies the smallest lesson of his experience to his football theory. He knows psychology and he uses it in his theory and practice. He has a healthy interest in a great number of subjects not concerned with athletics, but he extracts from these extrinsic pursuits, germs of human action and tendency and applies them to his athletic theory. He has a natural drive and a dynamic personality that is ideally adapted to handling a squad of athletes. Rock is boss of the field—there is never any doubt of that—but his men recognize that Rock utilizes his authority always with the one object in view toward which they are all working—their own perfection and the superiority of the team.

"Rockne loves his boys and he labors to turn them out as men. He believes that athletics are a valuable preparation for future life, and his theory is that physical contact gives an athlete the moral confidence to 'go out and crack 'em' after the school days are over. He is as proud of his men's scholastic standing as of their All-American rating. He is strong, courageous and determined; he is also lovable, delightful, and witty. He is stern but he is considerate. When a game is on he 'cracks 'em'; when it is over he binds their injuries. The whole school is behind Rock."

If this seems to be what I have been saying right along, you are right. I wrote it in 1921 and am including it here to let you know what we knew about Rockne even that early. The most accurate part of that analysis was his emphasis on athletics as a preparation for life. Rock's coaching never stopped with graduation. He was always there for consultation; he liked to have his boys bring their problems to him, expected them to, was disappointed when they did not.

He took a very strong position against professional football for his graduates. His reasoning was based on his own experience in the pro game, which was then a haphazard sport. The danger, he pointed out, was that it paid just enough money for a few months' work to tempt a player to hang around and do little else until the next season began. Such a life tended to develop a postcollege football bum; and he would cite examples. He advised his boys to go into coaching; to use the money and prestige thereby gained to get themselves established in their own profession or business in the off-season; so that when they tired of coaching—or it tired of them—they would be solidly grounded in their life's work.

He implemented this advice by making it easy for them to go into coaching, usually in the college ranks. Other schools wanted his graduates on their staffs to get the Rockne secrets and routines. (He had such a waiting list that he once, seriously, offered to get me a high-school coaching job.) Most of his boys went into coaching. Some, like Eddie Anderson and Roger Kiley, used it to help with postgraduate professional work. Johnny Mohardt played pro football with the Bears to finance his education at the nearby Rush Medical School of Northwestern. Most of the other 1919–21 group became successful coaches. Dr. Eddie Anderson of Holy Cross (still combining coaching and medical practice) is the dean of present college coaches. Buck Shaw is still in pro ball. Hunk Anderson profitably combined college and pro coaching with his engineering profession. Frank Thomas became one of the top college coaches at Alabama. Mehre, Wynne, Tom Lieb, Clipper Smith, Arthur "Little Dutch" Bergman, and others were important in the field.

These men paved the way for the flood of other Rockne-trained coaches who were to follow in such numbers that the Notre Dame system was to dominate national gridiron play long after Rockne's death. They were not selling Rockne's mechanical routines—these were common knowledge—but what they had absorbed, each according to his personality and ability, of Rockne's knowledge of the secret paths into the hearts of boys and men; and the practical methods of using such knowledge. They were selling certain fundamental human values that came out of their Notre Dame experiences; they were selling the least appreciated but most important quality any football player can have (assuming requisite physical and mental ability): character.

As, for example, a lightweight substitute end, not mentioned in the starring exploits of the 1919–21 group but dubbed by them, "the typical Notre Dame man." The story, and it's true, has Dave Hayes arriving at Notre Dame on a freight train from Manchester, Connecticut, back in 1916; working at whatever he could, playing whatever football he could—including a very valuable block against Army in '17; going off to war, returning with a sniper's bullet that shortened one leg a little; but playing back of Kiley or Anderson just the same; in '21, after graduation, going to the university's president, Father Burns, and handing him $250 to be applied to a building fund, saying: "I came here broke, on a freight, Father. I'm leaving the same way." Dave did all right in business, too; but there was a sad little sequel.

Dave's young son died, clutching the bright bauble of Dave's gold football—the last thing which held his attention. Hunk Anderson, while serving as head coach at Notre Dame, heard about this; and the toughest of Our Lady's tough guys sent his own prized gold football to Dave as a replacement.

XXIII

Championship teams often give their leaders a going-away present: the coxswain gets dunked, the baseball manager is doused with beer in the dressing-room celebration, the football coach is pulled under the showers. There was no established ceremony or tradition at Notre Dame; and no person dared take liberties with Rockne's person. But the coach himself issued the invitation, provided the opportunity for the departing '21 stars.

Already one of the pioneers of spring football practice, Rockne added an innovation in 1922 which was to become very popular and profitable. It was the annual Spring Game in which graduating seniors oppose those who will comprise the next varsity squad. The coach gets a look at his new group under game conditions; as do the students, alumni, and other supporters. Receipts, increasing every year, go to some deserving charity—often to scholarship funds.

This was a typical Rockne celebration. The opportunity was lying around loose. He saw it first, put it into operation fast—and had another long leap on competitors.

In 1922 the Spring Game idea was new. There had been no buildup, there were no gate receipts; the "crowd" included myself and whatever other insiders would normally attend final practice. Rockne, then thirty-four and beginning to develop a Santa Claus spread, decided to grace the occasion with his own presence at quarterback—on the Old-Timer eleven, where he felt reasonably safe behind that senior line.

On the first play Rock called signals in that stentorian, commanding, penetrating voice—demonstrating, as always, how it should be done. It was to be a quarterback sneak. But his trouble was—there were 21 other sneaks around him.

Every hole in the line opened and 11 eager varsity beavers piled on, forming a human triangle with the pudgy coach as its base.

Nobody laughed. The Old-Timers implied disgust with their inept quarterback. The varsity men returned to their positions.

Rockne, reclining, glared, snorted: "Wise guys." He called another play, in a louder, more abrasive voice. This time Mohardt threw a short pass to Rockne, who caught it. Then he took himself out of the game—but only *after* he had looked good. Rock always had to have the last word.

The departing seniors had graphically reminded their coach just how far his genius would have brought him without their help. They had delivered him into the hands of the new group with a challenge to beat their record of 28 victories against the Iowa defeat, and that by only three points. At the time it looked to be a fairly safe challenge. There was no promise of greatness in what was to be the 1922 squad.

During the 1921 season I had been as close to the situation as anybody, but I had no idea anything special was coming up from the freshmen. I knew there was a cocky little quarterback named Harry Stuhldreher who had prepared at Kiski Prep and, according to rumor, had been headed for Princeton. There was a kid named Jimmy Crowley who jumped around niftily on occasions. There was Elmer Layden, a track man with a rubber bandage on his knee. There were the last two of the Miller brothers; but the better one, Gerry, a scat back, was very small. There was a handsome blond center named Adam Walsh who probably owed his escape from freshman anonymity to the fact that he came from a town of interesting blondes—Hollywood, California.

There have been through the years, garish tales of Notre Dame's recruiting methods—chiefly of battalions of parish priests, obviously endowed with miraculous prescience, picking out the absolutely best prep-school stars and pressuring them to go to Notre Dame. It's a lot of nonsense. Even professional coaches cannot definitely pick the best players from college ranks. Priests had no reason to prefer Notre Dame over other Catholic football colleges until Notre Dame became successful.

Neither Rockne nor Gipp was recruited for football. And now let's look at how the Four Horsemen were assembled.

Don Miller's oldest brother, Red, was star of the 1909 team which beat Michigan. Ray Miller (later mayor of Cleveland and still a political power in Ohio) was Rock's substitute at end. Walter Miller played regular fullback in the 1919 backfield with Gipp. Don came to Notre Dame as a matter of course; even in the shadow of his brother Gerry. Don told me recently: "It took me three weeks to get a uniform as a freshman. I offered up Daily Communion during that time to get a uniform."

Stuhldreher's brother Walter was a nonathletic upperclassman at Notre Dame when Harry entered. Crowley had been coached at East Green Bay, Wisconsin, by Curley Lambeau (later coach of the Packers, the Green Bay pro team) who had played with Gipp; and Jimmy had been saturated with tales of the Gipp prowess. Layden had been coached at Davenport, Iowa, by Walter Halas, who coached baseball and track at Notre Dame. Halas wanted Elmer for both these sports. Rock had demurred because of the trick knee.

Leo Ward, a Los Angeles attorney and one of Rock's close friends, recommended Adam Walsh. When the boy's mother worried about his going so far away to school, Rock wrote Ward: "Send him on. Tell Mrs. Walsh I'll treat him like a father."

Next time he visited Ward's law office Rock found the letter framed with his picture. "He didn't see any humor in it," Ward wrote, "when I suggested that what he meant to say was—he would treat Adam like a son." This jab from one of his favorite sparring partners probably penetrated deeply because it reflected on Rockne the Writer. Adam had his arm broken as a freshman and Rock did treat him like a son; and continued the treatment. Had he lived, as we shall later see, Walsh might have become his successor.

Walsh became captain and center of the '24 team. It was he who named the Seven Mules who plowed ahead of the Four Horsemen. How did the Mules arrive at Notre Dame? Guard John Weibel and end Ed Hunsinger both came up from the discard of Interhall. Noble Kizer came on a basketball scholarship and was a football surprise. Tackle Joe Bach transferred from St. Thomas Military; end George Vergara, a regular in '22 and '23, had played freshman football at Fordham, though Rock did not learn this until later. Vergara, Bach, tackle Rip Miller, and end Chuck Collins were probably results of the Rockne recruiting system which was as casual as this: an ex-player, friend, or alumnus would recommend a boy. If Rock trusted the judgment of the sponsor, he would say: "Send him on."

And he did treat them like a father—a stern father who never spoiled them; a father who taught them to win honorably; who would apologize if he got too rough. He was director of athletics and interested in all sports; but football was his pet; and track, his first love, became something of an orphan. Frankie Doriot did an imitation of Rock coaching track while spring training was also in session on the field inside the running track. Frankie would put a finger on his button nose to make it resemble Rock's broken nose. He would, in the loud, stentorian, penetrating voice, with the rising inflections, talk something like this: "Oh, Paul Kennedy, do a little jogging to-day—that's all, a little jogging, protect that ankle—NICE GOING, DON MILLER—*only cut back quicker next time*—Oh, Gus Desch, about twice around tonight, Gus—and you sprinters, I want you to work on getting off those starting blocks better—OH CARBERRY—ARE YOU PLAYING END OR OFFICIATING AS HEAD LINESMAN—all right, you quarter-milers—THE LINE WAS ABOUT AS MUCH HELP ON THAT PLAY AS THE NATIONAL GUARD IN THE WORLD WAR—all right, quarter-milers—Paul, you know what to do—"

Rock had eyes in the back of his head, or so the hapless laggards had reason to believe. Once, he broke up the sideliners—but not the linemen—with this musical question, in an operatic baritone heard for miles around:

> Oh *where* was the line?
> Oh *where* was the line?

During the '22 spring practice, Rock, and the rest of us, began to get better acquainted with the freshmen. Individuals began to emerge as featured players instead of supernumeraries. Layden, no longer a track man with a trick knee, was now a potential Gipp, though 15 pounds lighter, who could run, pass, and kick. There was worry in inner circles when the report got around, perhaps from Walter Halas, that Elmer was pining for a high-school sweetheart who was a freshman at the University of Wisconsin. I did not ordinarily travel to track meets; but when the "thinly-clads" went to Madison that spring, Elmer and I were Road Scholars. I was a private eye with a tailing job to do. But while I was worrying about the sinister girl freshman, Rockne was more interested in the young Wisconsin men who walked about with monogram sweaters. "Strapping big fellows up here," he would marvel, "strapping big fellows." The mind of the track coach would stray to football, even on road trips.

After spring practice sessions I would sit in the coaches room alert for priceless pearls for my public. I remember the evening when Rock, as he dressed after his shower, erupted. "Did you see that Don Miller go out there today?" I had also been impressed; and I think this was the first time Rock really saw Don Miller, who had had to pray for a uniform, as varsity material. Don was a very earnest, reticent boy; it is quite possible that, had there been no spring training, which is the period for such experimentation and discovery, he might have been sloughed over in the hurly-burly of the fall; in which case there would have been no Four Horsemen. Nor, perhaps, if Jimmy Crowley had been less devout.

Crowley had been caught in a nickel crap game and was bounced out for the spring semester. Instead of going home, he went to Indianapolis, worked on a soda fountain, wrote letters to his mother, sent them to his ex-roommate, Rex Enright, who mailed them from the campus. He came back to summer school, made up the spring work, became eligible—and his family never knew at that time he had been out of school. This sort of faith, devotion, and loyalty, coming out in big games, made big men of little fellows.

Rockne wrote: "How it came to pass that four young men so eminently qualified by temperament, physique, and instinctive pacing, complement one another perfectly and thus produce the best coordinated and most picturesque backfield in the recent history of football—how that came about is one of the inscrutable achievements of coincidence of which I know nothing save that it's a rather satisfying mouthful of words." The coincidence is ordinarily held about equal to that of quads turning up in a family. I don't quite agree. Rockne had a backfield in '29 and '30 that missed the perfection of the Horsemen only because the fullback job was divided. The 1920 quartet wasn't bad, either. Pitt had its Dream Backfield and there have been other exceptional foursomes.

Much of gridiron fame is accidental. The great units all had the advantage of playing together for two or three years; of playing on well-publicized teams. The fact that Rockne had three such groups in his thirteen years of coaching is high tribute to his coaching; and adds support to my claim that he was a gridiron Vulcan who could weld invincible units from material other coaches would develop into mere adequacy. The Four Horsemen, however are, after thirty-six years, and probably will always remain the nonpareil because they resulted from a series of accidents, involving many creative people, not likely to be repeated. Now let's watch it work out.

Even though he was the last of the four to develop a face of his own for Rockne, Don Miller was the first to win a regular job; for the simple reason that he had less opposition. Danny Coughlin, the regular right halfback of the preceding year, had graduated; Castner, who had divided the position with Coughlin in the late going, had been moved to fullback in '22; and Tom Lieb, a backfield swing man, was being moved to tackle. Remaining was Red Maher, always a fine back, but a lightweight. Don Miller had sharpened his speed in indoor track; he was ready—and made the most of the door which had suddenly swung open during spring practice.

Stuhldreher had first caught Rock's eye. "He was a good and fearless blocker, sounded like a leader on the field and, as he gained in football knowledge, showed signs of smartness in emergencies." But Frank Thomas was an experienced senior, a deceptive runner and, as his coaching career revealed, had a big football brain. Rock always gave the edge to the senior in case of reasonable doubt; so Thomas was the starter while Stuhldreher literally sat at the coach's feet in the early parts of the early games, receiving the schooling he needed. There was no doubt in my mind that Stuhldreher would become first string before the season got too far along; but Rockne the diplomat had a fine talent for playing such situations. He was particularly careful in this instance because the quarterback was his vicar on the field. He wanted his quarterback to be respected at all times. The quarterback was never a target for Rockne's public sarcasm.

Crowley and Layden were destined to be rivals as players, as coaches, as candidates for the head coaching job at Notre Dame and as Commissioners of the two professional groups—the National Football League and the All-American Conference. The left halfback under Rockne was key man of the attack, the triple-threater who ran, kicked, and passed. Layden had greater speed and was a longer punter. Crowley was a truly great open-field runner, a shade better passer; and probably the best blocker of the quartet.

The friendship of the Four Horsemen has become legendary but there must have been a touch of nobility in their relationship from the beginning. Throughout their three years together they seemed to take turns, like a stage quartet, in sharing the spotlight. And that couldn't have happened if there had been any individual shirking or jealousy. Miller was first to take off as a sophomore with a running day against St. Louis. Layden and Crowley were sharing the left-half job; but Jimmy jumped out with a quite remarkable performance against Purdue. Rockne wrote: "Crowley astonished Purdue a great deal and me a great deal more with the liveliest exhibition of cutting, jumping, side-stepping, change of pace and determined ball-toting that I had seen in many a day."

The coach was being restrained. This is what I wrote after the 34–7 victory over DePauw the next week: "Coach Knute Rockne knew what to do when his charges were threatened by DePauw Saturday—he sent in James Crowley. Crowley did to DePauw what he did to Purdue a week ago.

"He is hailed as the 'wonder boy' of Notre Dame. Only a sophomore, he handles himself on the gridiron with all the ease and ability of the best of veterans. He is a lad born to the football purple. He is a Rockne product.

"Physically, just a boy and not a big boy, either; mentally just an average college student; more than an average sense of humor; emotionally—there it is. Emotion is the being which knits physical and psychological faculties; it is different in different men and accounts for their varying personalities. In Jimmy Crowley it has developed an unusual, paradoxical complex.

"Watch him stand in the backfield, seemingly asleep—his eyelids add the illusion. Listen to the quarterback call signals—no sign from Jimmy. The backfield *heps* into the first step of the shift—Jimmy reluctantly moves with them. The ball is snapped—whzz! The emotional switch has been pulled. Off around end quicker than thought. When a tackle hits—Jimmy hits too—and let the tackle worry. When a man obstructs his pathway—Jimmy plows into him and does a swan dive through space for a touchdown—if the play is within five yards of the goal. If it is in the open field he lifts one leg about six feet in the air and keeps the other on the ground—without losing speed. How he does it we don't know—doubt if he knows.

"He just has football instinct. He has a fearless drive, an angelic courage. He knows no more of fear than an angel does of sin. He was born to the football purple and he can't help what he does. When the Army scouts saw this boy, and saw Don Miller and Harry Stuhldreher and the other Irish kids, there must have been a run on colic medicine at the canteen. Three more years of Rockne and a gang of kids like this—getting better every day! Crowley, Miller, Castner, and Stuhldreher may accomplish wonders next Saturday at Atlanta when they take on the veteran and cunning Georgia Tech players. This outfit has not tasted defeat on its home ground for years and it remains to the Irish to do the trick."

XXIV

Rockne had lost 14 of 22 lettermen on the 1921 squad, including his entire starting eleven and, in some cases, the first substitute. There are always reserves with some experience but a reserve may have missed making a letter merely because he lacked talent. There is the further menace of injury—and a new man is always more susceptible to injury because he lacks the "savvy" (wisdom) to look out for himself. It was fortunate for Rockne that he did have an exceptional sophomore group. He was to need all of them.

When the squad left for Georgia Tech, Tom Lieb, the line stalwart, was already through for the year. Fod Cotton and Ed Degree, linemen of experience, had missed two or more games with early injuries. Captain Carberry, at end, was to be hurt at Georgia Tech and be an uncertain quantity thereafter. Bob Regan, a lightweight center, and Harvey Brown, a "watch-charm guard" had held up but sophomores were already becoming the mainstays in the line as well as the backfield. The coaching job Rockne did in '22 had to be one of his best.

Lieb, on crutches and wearing a flannel shirt, came to the station to see the team leave. When the train left, Tom was aboard—with Rockne's consent and probably for morale because Tom was good-natured and popular. It was a hazardous journey for Road Scholars because our car was to go over four different railroad lines en route to Atlanta, which meant frequent checking by new conductors, several of whom were inclined to be downright inhospitable. But Road Scholars also improve with experience and the trip was made without undue incident—except for a shoe I caught in the face when a freshman Scholar, Joe Bach, made a precipitous slide into my space without first scouting the position. But he was, fortunately, wearing dancing pumps; an unusual footwear for northern Indiana in late October; but wardrobes were not always complete in our set.

Otherwise the trip was enjoyable, as junkets by healthy young males usually are. It developed that Jimmy Crowley was running for President on the Pro-hy-bition ticket (this was in '22) and Mickey Kane became his manager. Kane was baseball captain and just a fair halfback; but he was a clown and Rockne always liked to have one along on trips. Our porter was a kindred soul. They called him Siki, from the colored fighter who was popular at that time, and, since he lived in Chicago, elected him a member of the Chicago Club of Notre Dame. At the end of the trip he was also made an honorary Road Scholar for honorable service to the Brothers in Distress—who had also distressed him. "Every time I reach for a shoe," he complained, "I grabs a leg."

High jinks were usually geared to the situation. This was a high-spirited, young squad, undefeated, going toward its first crucial battle. Rock had been keying them for two weeks (taking the DePauw game in stride) at the noon lectures and on the field. My news stories rose and fell with his thermometer. Except for an occasional stunt story, he never told me what to write; or, except when I was way off-base, did he criticize my writing. It is only now that I suspect that, when keying his squad, he also keyed me in the casual conversations we had each day. I was like a pup who plays with kids and thinks he's a kid. I thought as the squad thought; felt as they did. In my last season we worked so smoothly on these things that I began to consider myself the psychological coach. Rock must have approved; if I had been off-beam I could have done damage to his scheme.

There was an uncertain fillip to this Georgia Tech trip. This was the heyday of the Ku Klux Klan, whose headquarters were then in Atlanta. By this time I was doing a campus column called "Quad Wrangles"—mostly campus gags and light material. I kidded around about the CooCooClan. We were kidding but we couldn't be absolutely sure the Klan would be. We were a Catholic school heading into Klan territory. Rock made no reference at any time to the Klan; but he was disturbed about the possible effect the Rebel Yell of the Tech students might have on the squad. He warned them in advance about it. (After the first few minutes, the boys reported, it became another crowd noise.)

Before this game Rock gave one of his most publicized theatrical pep talks. With tears on his cheeks he read a telegram to the squad: "I want my Daddy's team to win . . . Bill." (One recent distorted account of the incident had Jackie, supposed sender of the telegram, greeting the team on the side lines when the game ended. Jackie had not been born at that time.) The incident got smiles from the old heads when it was heard around the campus. It is still recounted as a masterful stroke. But this time the coach had also been fooled. The tears he had shed were real. He had received the telegram from South Bend. A year later I had a date with the young lady, a friend of the Rockne family, who had thought up and sent the telegram.

The young squad played almost perfect football to win 13-3. In the press box that day I first met the grand old-timers, Obie Keeler, Ed Danforth, and Morgan Blake. This was the day Stuhldreher began to move front and center. One of the reporters, tired of trying to spell the name, said to the operator who was sending his play-by-play: "Give Miller credit for all his plays." They were all to learn how to spell Stuhldreher.

The return trip was even more enjoyable. The train stopped about 3 A.M. in Danville, Kentucky. Siki had been so well indoctrinated that he began bragging to a station employee that he was carrying the famous Notre Dame team which had beat Georgia Tech that day. The Danville man said: "You got nuthin'. We got the team right here in Danville. Centre College."

"Centre College? Who ever heard of that?"

"Harvard did. We beat Harvard. We've got Bo McMillan, Red Roberts and—"

"Okay," Siki challenged. "You go get your team. I'll get my team up—and we'll play right here."

(One of the stanch Notre Dame "Pullman Alumni" was Urban Turnquist, the first president of the Pullman Porters and Maids Protective Association. He made his maiden trip with the 1926 squad, was nicknamed Tom, and from that time until his death in 1937 was the personal porter for the squad, a friend of a generation of Notre Dame players. In his Notre Dame sweatshirt he became a familiar figure and a most successful mascot, on Notre Dame side lines from coast to coast.)

The Tech game of 1922 was one of the significant Rockne victories. It meant that the 1919–21 group had been no lucky accident of the postwar era but the creation of a master coach who could take raw material and begin to win immediately—instead of requiring the usual year or two of rebuilding. The Notre Dame students knew it. Fifteen hundred of them met the team when it returned. Again they caught a retreating Rockne, carried him for a block. I wrote this at the time:

"From amid the gloom that surrounded Atlanta following the first licking any Northern team had ever administered to the pride of the South in its own territory, there came the uniform opinion that superior coaching had turned the trick for Notre Dame. The lads who returned to glory today deserved it. No Notre Dame team ever went into a contest with finer spirit or determination. No Notre Dame team ever came through better, in individual contacts and team play, than did this crew of kids in their first big game before a hostile audience in strange territory. The game was rough and tough but remarkably clean. The crowd was not a rowdy crowd but the typical college crowd. The South made an impression upon Notre Dame and Notre Dame made an impression upon the South."

The next week was Homecoming and the opponent was the traditional state rival, Indiana. Castner was the star, and though the score was a convincing 27–0 the Hoosiers seemed to have done such an excellent scouting job that rumor spread there was a traitor on the campus—a student who had taken notes during practice, or a player on one of the Interhall teams which were coached by varsity players who had been careless (or lazy) enough to use varsity plays and signals.

Nobody in authority took this rumor seriously; there probably had been a natural letdown of spirit between the major peaks of Georgia Tech—and Army. But it was a good gimmick for morale purposes; and Rock took full advantage of it. That week there was secret practice for the first time in my memory; and a sign on the gates, in angry red print: SECRET PRACTICE—COME AND BRING YOUR NOTEBOOKS. K. K. ROCKNE.

XXV

The Army game again held the national spotlight. The Irish had won the last four games of the series, and Army, with an undefeated veteran team, was waiting to take on Rockne's youngsters—who were getting younger each week as injuries steadily eliminated the veterans who had begun the season as regulars. In the following list of 31 who made the Army trip, the 14 sophomores are in italics:

Ends: *McNulty, Vergara,* Murphy, Mayl, *Hunsinger.* Tackles: Cotton, *Rip Miller,* Stange, Flynn, Oberst. Guards: Brown, *Kizer, Weibel,* Flinn, Degree. Centers: Regan, *Walsh,* Voss. Quarterbacks: *Stuhldreher,* Thomas, Logan. Left Halfbacks: *Crowley, Layden,* Bergman, Kane. Right Halfbacks: *Don Miller, Connell,* Maher. Fullbacks: Castner, *Enright, Cerney.*

The changing complexion of the squad is indicated from my news story of that day: "It is peculiar that the injury jinx has picked upon the seasoned men of the squad. Of the regular eleven for Saturday only Brown, Cotton, Degree, and Castner are experienced holdovers. The sophomores are Vergara and McNulty at ends; E. (Rip) Miller will probably see more service at tackle than Oberst, who is not in good physical condition. Adam Walsh will play part of the game be-

hind Regan at center. In the backfield are the slippery trio of Stuhldreher, Don Miller, and Crowley."

The above was written after the list was posted; but there would
be an added sophomore; and a substitution in the starting sophomore
at one backfield position. These changes, which tell much of Rockne's
human relations with his players, and of his coaching psychology,
are explained in letters to me at the time of the 25th reunion of the
"Hosses and Mules" in 1949.

Bernie Livergood wrote: "The Army game of 1922 is the one I
most remember. Coach Rockne had made me a member of the traveling squad for the Georgia Tech game; but when listing the players
for the Army game he made room for one of the other sophomore
fullbacks by leaving me off the traveling squad. After scanning the
posted traveling list Thursday afternoon prior to the game, I passed
the door of Rockne's office with my chin on my chest and no doubt a
very dejected look otherwise. Coach Rockne happened to see me
going by and called to me, asking what was wrong and if I felt
badly because I wasn't making the trip to New York. I told him no
but evidently my disappointment was apparent, and he told me to
go back and pack my equipment and be at the train that evening.
Incidentally that was the closest I ever came to missing a trip during
my three years of competition at the university and it certainly ex-
emplified Rockne's stature.

"Paul Castner, senior and regular fullback, played three and one-
half quarters of the game without relief; and much to my surprise,
when Castner was battered and exhausted in the middle of the
fourth quarter, Rockne shouted for me. But I was so intensely concentrating on the game, and since I assumed I had been taken along
only for the ride, I didn't hear Rockne's call. Rip Miller nudged me
so hard on Rockne's second call I fell off the bench. The shock of
taking Castner's place was terrific; and this was the first big game
I was ever in. The first play after I entered the game, Army passed
to their halfback on the strong side—and only a flying, head-high
tackle over the interference near the goal line by our safety man
saved the game. I saw the Army back coming, I knew he was my
man to cover and I knew it was a pass; but I froze and couldn't
move. The game ended 0–0. This game I remember most because I
almost missed it and because I almost lost it."

The big play is long remembered. Here, received at the same time, is a recollection from that safety man: "My greatest thrill playing for Notre Dame was not one in which I had run for a touchdown, completed a pass for a score or anything of that nature. My greatest experience came in the 1922 Army game at West Point, the last, you will remember, played there. On the whole, Notre Dame was a sophomore group while Army had a great, experienced team. We had marched, late in the game, for what seemed to be a touchdown, with the score 0–0, only to lose the ball right on the Army's goal line by a fumble. Later on Army put on a march of its own. From about midfield Army's right halfback, Timberlake, got loose somehow or other and came all the way back to me in the safety position. By a stroke of luck I cornered him on the side line and with eyes closed made the tackle. The final score was 0–0." The safety man was, as you've probably guessed, Stuhldreher.

Rockne's gesture of taking the dejected Livergood to Army might have cost him the game. When he sent this sensitive sophomore into the game at such a critical moment he was probably gambling on the boy taking advantage of his second chance by coming up with a superlative performance; but he must also have known he was risking exactly what did happen—the mental freezing of a sophomore in his first big game. It has happened to the best of them. Rock said that it had happened to him against Ohio Northern. Stuhldreher's spectacular tackle probably saved Livergood, a serious-minded youth, from a lifetime of self-accusation (players do those things—one, from another Midwestern school, shot himself thirty years after a notable failure), but Bernie more than made it up in 1924 when, with Layden hurt, he went in against Carnegie Tech and put on a performance that may have kept the Horsemen record clear—and without a clear slate they probably wouldn't have gone to the Rose Bowl game which put the seal on their unique place in gridiron history.

There was another notable error that day; and it is involved in the change of the starting sophomores. Crowley's sensational play against Purdue and later opponents had given him the starting nod over Layden. Elmer thought himself a good football player, too good to sit on the bench behind Crowley for the next three seasons. "After I had played only a few minutes in the Indiana game," Elmer wrote me, "I went to Rock's office and told him I was quitting school. He told me I was going to start the Army game."

This had been a typical Rockne exhibition of skating around a difficult situation; or he may have deliberately set it up, figuring that Layden would be so full of fury that he would explode against the Cadets who would have prepared for Crowley. Actually it was no great gamble, even if he were merely soothing Layden, because both were Phi Beta Kappa in the gridiron fraternity. It was, as has been indicated, a vigorous, grueling game; but the Horsemen seemed to be winning, as Stuhldreher noted, in that final march. Crowley was in there at the time and he was the fellow who fumbled.

"When this occurred," Stuhldreher wrote me, "we all feared it might affect Jim and all of us immediately went up and said, 'Don't worry about that, Jim.' His quick comeback was: 'Worry! That could happen to anyone.'" The sophomore actually had been victimized by a wise old senior Army tackle named Breidster, who had knocked the ball out of Crowley's arms in the mixup of a scrimmage. In football it is perfectly legitimate to steal the ball or tackle the ball.

Ten years later Crowley and I and my niece got out of a taxicab on Madison Avenue at 51st Street. We were going to the baptism of my son. Another cab was coming our way. I looked at Crowley, carrying the baby as if he were a pumpkin, and said: "Hey there, Crowley —don't you fumble now."

Jimmy, with typical quick wit, grinned: "Suppose Breidster is driving that cab?"

Rockne, the multiple man, sometimes overlooked a detail; so the evening of the '22 Army game found all of his hungry young men in an open-topped bus at the corner of Broadway and 46th Street. Joe Byrne had gone down to the old Moulin Rouge Club to see what he could do about dinner for forty. Mickey Kane, who was to do well in Massachusetts politics later on, thought this an excellent time and place to introduce his candidate for President on the Pro-hy-bition ticket. So Jimmy Crowley, with the fumble far behind him, gave his sure-fire political speech which promised all things to all people; and at seven o'clock on Saturday evening there were quite a few people at this upper end of Times Square. A mammoth traffic cop came over to deliver a speech of his own. But, fortunately, Joe Byrne came up about that time to tell us we had to move on to another restaurant.

To Rockne, who hated defeat, the tie game with Army had been a bitter loss. The next day, on the train, he sulked in his drawing room like a modern Achilles. But younger spirits are more resilient, and late in the afternoon, a few of us were harmonizing. Rockne came out of his room and walked soberly down the aisle. We hadn't won; and when you didn't win under Rockne you were supposed to do penance until you redeemed yourselves; you definitely did not sing the day after a tie game. These were the things we expected to hear; but we continued the song. Rock waited until we had finished.

He sat down. "I don't know that one. Let's sing 'Darling Nelly Gray.'"

The next week we were to lose our All-American candidate and siege gun—Paul Castner.

The gridiron fates were shuffling in a most peculiar way to come up with the Four Aces of gridiron history.

XXVI

Butler University had one of those strong postwar groups, a "married man's team," mature, tough, and conscious of the short cut to fame a victory over the up-state Irish would bring. The field at Indianapolis was muddy and it was close for the first half. Notre Dame pulled safely away for a 34-7 victory but left its major star, Paul Castner, in an Indianapolis hospital with a broken pelvis. Right or wrong, the boys who had played in the game thought Castner had been a victim of viciousness.

The star is always a target, which is a reason the star is entitled to the extra plaudits. All of life pays off on victory—and the man who can score is the man of any hour. Football games go to the team which hits hardest, but there is a point where "hard, clean play" crosses a line to muckerism, even sadism. Rockne taught his boys that dirty football was stupid football; that the player who had his mind on inflicting personal punishment could not have his mind on the assignment he was to carry out. His general rule for handling such situations was: *Protect yourselves in the clinches but keep your mind on your work until the game is well in hand; then—if your adversary persists in the delusion that he is Jack Dempsey, disillusion him.*

Castner was clearly the star of the still-undefeated team. Always a superior punter, drop-kicker, and an excellent passer, his open-field running in the mud against Butler had been sensational. The injury, which closed out his career, may have cost him an All-American selection—and a rare triple-crown of college athletics, top recognition in three sports. In baseball he had pitched one no-hit game— and won another with a home run. He was good enough to have played big-league professional hockey—as I saw it played while covering it in New York for several years. He was intelligent, articulate, and personally impressive. After graduation he passed up all professional sport to go with the Studebaker Corporation where he would later tour with Rockne on sales promotion work.

Castner's injury may have cost the team an undefeated season; but it posed an immediate coaching problem to test the talents of Rockne—who solved it brilliantly; and in so doing, affected football history. Available were three sophomore fullbacks, each of whom was to later have his great moments; each of whom would have been capable and adequate enough as a substitute for Castner. Almost any other coach would have allowed these three to compete for the prize. But Rockne was not just any other coach; he was in the process of creating something; and neither of the three sophomores had the speed, savvy, or experience of the moving part the coach needed for the precision unit he had been building.

Rockne's concept of football, based on his personal necessity as a small man, was to equalize the power of the bigger man by superior use of speed, imagination, and intelligence. He emphasized that "before you can defeat an opponent you've got to outthink him." He had been using the backfield shift to permit his entire backfield to get the jump on bigger opponents. Castner, fast and quick for a big man, had been adequate; but it must have occurred to Rockne, as his brain whirred in relaxed moments, that a lighter, faster fullback might operate even more effectively.

That man was available. And moving Layden to fullback would solve that other problem which had begun to seem chronic—and might explode at any time—the necessity of choosing between Crowley and Layden at left halfback.

"Rock asked me in the Claypool Hotel, Indianapolis, following the Butler game when Paul Castner was hurt," Elmer Layden wrote me, "how I would like to play fullback and I told him I didn't care where I played just so I played . . . I told him he had three good fullbacks in Cerney, Livergood, and Enright. Then I told him I would like to talk with them, which I did. They stated that if that's what Rock wanted, we would battle it out for the position; and as it turned out, it was probably my kicking that gave me the edge."

Stuhldreher added this follow-up: "Remember those were the days when they had the big, battering-ram type in that position. On the train [home] Elmer raised the objection that he might be too small. Rock came right back with the statement that he was going to put into football for the first time a quick opening attack of full-back play; that Elmer, being a track man, was just the man to do the trick. Elmer was sold immediately. Sometime later Rock admitted to all of us that he hadn't thought of that until Elmer raised his objection. The handling of that situation was a pretty good example of Rock's quick mind and use of psychology."

In his autobiography Rock, with the customary blind spot in his view of his own historical importance, passed it off, thus: "I moved Layden from left halfback, where he had been alternating with Crowley, to fullback." And now, for the record, he professed to be amazed at what happened: "Layden amazed me by his terrific speed at fullback. He adopted a straight-line that made him one of the most unusual fullbacks in football. He pierced a line through sheer speed-cutting it like a knife, although each man in the opposing line outweighed him by twenty pounds. His power was not wasted in plunging. Compared with the orthodox fullback, he was a saber instead of a club."

Layden resumes: "That week I had dinner with Rock twice at the old restaurant that was near the JMS Building. He went over the signals and discussed the fullback position. The next Saturday in Pittsburgh in the Carnegie Tech game the ball had been taken to the five-yard line. Rock called Stuhldreher and myself to go into the game and gave us a pass play; Stuhldreher to pass to me off the T-formation. At that time [before the huddle] the quarterback called from his position and it was tough on me because you had to think. When we got into the game we found it was third down instead of the fourth; so instead of the pass, a buck over the center was called. I had shifted into position when the signal finally struck me; but before I could get adjusted, Bob Regan, the center, passed the ball back. It hit me on the knee and George Vergara took it for a touchdown. Carnegie thought it was a pretty good play [since it scored on them], but Rock put it back in the bag and we didn't use it any more that year. That was my first play at fullback."

Note how patently the pupil copied the master in the self-deprecation; the bland reference to the fumble "play" which Rock "did not use the rest of year." His players absorbed his psychological devices, his use of humor, his tone of voice, his theatrical methods of arousing a team. And these, more than plays, are important items in coaching.

The creation of the Four Horsemen was another demonstration of the way Rockne's mind worked. He saw the advantage of the knifing fullback in his "boxer" offense. He dared use it—and moved leagues ahead of his field. It was probably another natural development. Wynne, in 1920–21, was of the speed, rather than the burly type. Twice later Rockne was to attempt equally daring experiments at fullback. The first, with Savoldi, was originally disastrous but later most successful. The second, with Bucky O'Connor, was probably Rock's most dramatic achievement.

Rockne had sprung the Layden development, of course, as a surprise against Carnegie. My stories from practice during the week emphasized that Cerney, Livergood, and Enright were being worked in Castner's place with Livergood a probable favorite because of his line-plunging ability. Livergood did start the game, but with the shock troops, along with Thomas, Bergman, and Maher. After Layden's entry the newspaper account read:

"Regan intercepted a pass in midfield. Crowley got 13 yards, Miller turned the other flank for 21, Crowley came back with eight, Layden added seven and Miller nicked the final nine yards for a touchdown . . . The last score came early in the final period. Crowley blazed the way with a sensational dash through the Tech team for 22 yards. Stuhldreher, Miller, and Layden punched for short gains to the 12-yard line where Stuhldreher cleverly passed to Layden for the last touchdown."

That was to be the pattern for the Four Horsemen—the way they were going to operate for the next twenty-two games, getting better, more confident, more polished, more aware of one another, more complementary to one another; and more exasperating to opponents who tried to defense four backs, each of whom could run, pass, receive passes, punt if necessary, and block. Stuhldreher had a four-jet backfield and he knew when to touch what buttons.

After two days' practice they took off for Nebraska and what was expected to be a very happy Thanksgiving Day and a finish to an undefeated, if once-tied season. When we got to Lincoln I made a quick investigation and decided to violate the constitution of the Road Scholars.

"Rock," I said, "I've only slept in a bed twice in the last week. I'm all in. It's costing you two bucks for each player. Sign me up for a bed and I'll give you the two bucks."

The great coach pondered that, then made a notable decision and concession. "Well, Frank, I wouldn't like to see you do that. I've got a double bed in my room. You can sleep with me."

I established a new world's record, especially for Thanksgiving Eve, by being in bed that night at nine o'clock. At nine-thirty Rock came in with the Nebraska track coaches. They played cards until five in the morning. I didn't get much sleep but learned a few things about penny ante.

Later I would have known better. Rock got so keyed for every game that he couldn't sleep and liked to have people about him. There were friends in each town; opposing coaches, as in Lincoln that night; old teammates like Al Feeney or Cap Edwards; old schoolmates and close friends like Joe Byrne, Dr. O'Donnell, and Leo Ward. Eventually he became a traveling monarch with a trailing circus; and the Friday nights before a game on the road got so big that there had to be two and then three rooms, in which the various categories of guests were segregated. This is as good a place as any to state that, though I've met many people who professed to have got drunk with Rockne, I seldom saw him with a glass in his hand; and only once did I ever suspect him of being even tipsy. He never needed liquor to excite him, and never used it to escape from any problem. Yet even some of his good friends, in careless moments, have gone so far as to suggest that Rock might have signed some of those disputed contracts under the influence of liquor. He had a rule for this, too: "Drink the first, sip the second, skip the third." It is next best to the other practice of sipping straight ginger ale which looks like a highball.

It is possible that the football players were also tired after three games in 13 days; and too many nights in Pullmans and strange hotel beds. Or perhaps Nebraska, then at the height of its gridiron power, was just too tough. Too big they certainly were—especially in the first half.

"The 1922 Cornhuskers," Rockne wrote, "had one of the heaviest teams in their history—and they are known for very active heft. They pushed the relatively little Four Horsemen all over the field. At the half the score was 14 to 0 and it would have been another touchdown if the lightweight boys from South Bend hadn't held the Nebraska heavies on their one-yard line for four straight downs . . . But they came out fighting mad for the second half, whacked across a touchdown in the third quarter and carried to Nebraska's one-yard line toward the end of the final period. Stuhldreher called for a pass and Layden spurted to a corner of the field where he was all set to receive and down the ball for six more points. Stuhldreher was alert, but Weller, the huge 250-pound Nebraska tackle, crashed through the line and smeared the 150-pound Notre Dame quarterback. Our college alumni had a banquet ready for that night. Crowley said: 'We need a thermometer more than a feed.'"

It had been a thrilling thing to me to see these proud youngsters fighting for their lives on guts, intelligence, and will long after their bodies must have been in shock. After the game Rock did something I had never seen him do before or after (though it could have happened on a day I wasn't there). He came around the hotel rooms and congratulated the boys after a defeat. He told them they had never played, nor would play, a game of which they could feel more proud, because they had given everything they had. Rock that afternoon walked among his young players like a fan. There were other squads of which he would be proud; but only one other—the crippled heroes of the '28 Army game—about which he would feel so keenly, man-fashion.

Out of this Nebraska game may have come Rock's famous battle cry. I remember, during its progress, how the scarlet horde of

Nebraska beef would seem to sweep, like a wave, the Notre Dame line backward. I remember Bob Regan, a 158-pound center, literally crawling, like a gamecock, back to toe the scrimmage line again. Rock remembered it too, at the lecture which he always gave, reviewing the game. He said that Regan was so light that, stripped, he looked like "Spark Plug with his blanket off." (Spark Plug was the race horse in the *Barney Google* comic strip popular at that time.)

Rock then yelled—and it was the first time I had heard it: "I don't want a team to go in there to die gamely. I want a team to go in there—like Regan—fighting to live."

Regan coached with Frank Thomas and then Stuhldreher; and when last seen, was getting rich manufacturing women's dresses; a fact which would have amused Rockne, for reasons we will now explain.

XXVII

As a junior I lived in Sorin Hall, and about three one morning I was writing for *The Scholastic*, our weekly news magazine, a review of the '21 season, in the form of a grandfather of perhaps 1960 telling the story to his small fry. Searching for a snappy tag line I glanced to the upper-deck bed where my roommate had been sleeping through the clatter of my ancient triple-deck Corona typewriter. Then I had it.

"But Grandfather, where did Rockne get his shift?"

"From watching Bruce Holmberg at the Junior Prom."

Years later I read that Rockne had first got the idea for his shift from watching the dancing girls at *The Ziegfeld Follies*. This is a typical example of the literary weeds that have grown around this legend—like George Gipp never having played football; Rock getting his idea for deceptive ball-handling from watching a magician; the many versions of the Junior Prom, the Dumb Swede, and other gags.

When properly executed, the shift had the elements of a ballet movement; so much so that I once wrote a song (never published) called "The Shift," for a musical comedy (never finished). My room-mate Bruce Holmberg did have a copyrighted sort of dance movement. He was a popular campus character, and the reference to him at the prom became a popular campus gag. From that, perhaps, came the later tenuous connection with *The Ziegfeld Follies*.

There is another famous misquote about the time Rock, Hunk Anderson, and I were riding through the Maryland countryside with Scrappy Kessing, assistant athletic director at the Naval Academy. A truck driver was hogging the narrow road. When we finally found passing room, Rock leaned out the car window and let go at the truck driver. The latter waved for him to come back and say that.

"Stop the car, Scrappy," Rock ordered. Scrappy stopped the car. The truck pulled up, parked off the side of the road. As the driver got out, he seemed to grow taller and wider, like the heavy who always fights Popeye the Sailorman.

"Go get him, Hunk," Rock said. Hunk obediently started to open the door; but Scrappy laughed, pulled away, leaving the truck driver in the company of his own frustration.

Notre Dame has always been a coach's dream—a campus without coeds or fraternities; with automatic suspension for the use of alcohol; with tight disciplinary regulations that made it almost impossible for an athlete to get out of condition; with a religious program designed to produce spiritual health and peace of mind. That's the way Notre Dame was (what it still pretty much is) and the way Rockne intended to keep it. He fought any intrusion against masculine habits and outlook. When a debating coach suggested monograms for his vocal athletes, Rock called me in for a story conference and we knocked out a column describing a Debating Big Game with Northwestern, in which the gladiators wore cashmere sweaters with appropriate finery. His basic speech for outside dinner groups was the danger of our young people softening up, and of the wholesome influence of athletics on a sane American life.

Rockne's best story in the early twenties was (if the refining influences continued to have their way) a description of the Notre Dame-Northwestern football game in the then-distant 1930. He chose Northwestern because that school, adjacent to Chicago, was then being more publicized for its coeds than its athletes. Using all his talents as an actor—and he had the power of a Barrymore to hold an audience—Rockne would look into the future:

"Receiving at fullback for Northwestern was M. Bickerdash Pix III, of the famous North Shore family. The entire Northwestern team was gaily clad in purple-mauvette tunics, and about the waist was a white girdle with a Louis XIV buckle. The shoes were by Hanan and Son and the hosiery specially designed with beige tasseled garters by Patou—perfume by Houbigant.

"Kicking off for Notre Dame was T. Fitzpatrick Murphy, who is better known to his cronies as Two Lump, as he always asks for two lumps of sugar in his orange pekoe. The Notre Dame team also presented a striking appearance with their green shirt waists and their headgear resembling a woodsman's toque—giving a very neat appearance without being at all gaudy, although their hip pads were trimmed with georgette. Hanging from the necks were pendants, lavaliere type on which was engraved the motto of the university: 'Fight fairly but furiously.'

"Precisely at two-thirty the referee, dressed in regulation costume of plus fours and crepe de Chine blouse, blew his whistle. Two Lump met the ball squarely and sent it soaring down the field right into the arms of Bickerdash, who, catching it, brought it back five, ten, fifteen yards before he was tagged by a deft tap on the shoulder by Nouveauriche Gilhooey, the Irish left end. Northwestern lined up and tried three running plays to no avail. Notre Dame's tagging defense was impregnable. So, on fourth down, old Bickerdash dropped back from a kick formation and sent a long spiral soaring sixty yards down the field to old Two Lump, who was tagged right in his tracks. He couldn't move.

"Then, as Notre Dame took the offensive with the ball, they found to their dismay, that Northwestern was just as clever at defensive tagging as they were. As a result neither team could gain at all so all throughout the first half a punting duel resulted between old Two Lump and Bickerdash, neither gaining any advantage. Between halves both teams had tea. Refreshed therefrom, and inspired by words of wisdom from their respective professors of psychology, both teams went back into the second half with renewed determination to do or die. But, lackaday, nothing startling happened all during the third quarter as both teams continued their rare defense of superb tagging!

"Up until within about five minutes of the end of the fourth quarter, it looked as though it were destined to be a tie game, which, you know, is so unsatisfactory.

"Suddenly out of a rhythmical gavotte, a sort of hidden-ball evolution, old Bickerdash broke loose and went streaking up the side lines with a clear field to the goal posts. The Northwestern stands were mad with pandemonium; but in the Irish stands a deathly stillness because it looked like sure defeat for Notre Dame. But they failed to reckon on the resourcefulness and resiliency of mind of old Two Lump. Now when Two Lump, who was back playing safety, the last man on defense, saw Bickerdash streaking toward the goal line and no one there to stop him, did he give up and become panicky? Not old Two Lump. With a savoire-faire for which he was justly famous, he cupped his hands and he called in a loud clear voice that could be heard all over the amphitheater:

"'I say, Bickerdash, old thing, there's a terrible run in your stocking.'

"Imagine the intense embarrassment and mortification of poor old Bickerdash. What could he do to hide his discomfiture but drop the ball and sneak away to the clubhouse. So the game was saved."

(When the 1930 Northwestern game was actually played, the Wildcats were undefeated Conference champions and the Irish about to win their second consecutive national championship. Late in the fourth period a Northwestern tackle was detected taking a healthy tag at a meek, inoffensive Irisher [for the eyes of the official at least] named Marty Brill. The resultant penalty helped Notre Dame to its 17th straight victory.)

I had promoted myself a column on the South Bend *Tribune* whose title "Quad Wrangles" describes its coverage of the lighter side of campus activities. Rockne had no supervision over this part of my writing; but he thoroughly approved as long as I celebrated He-Manhood in such forms as high jinks on the football trips; the Monogram Club Minstrels in which Harry Stuhldreher and Roger Kiley were soloists—and Knute K. Rockne played the flute in the orchestra; a University Theatre production of *The Merchant of Venice* in which athletes revealed the thespian facet of their talents; and the initiation ceremonies of the "Black Cat Frat."

Notre Dame had no fraternities but it did have the custom of goofing. So when a certain naïve freshman footballer introduced himself to Frank Thomas and said: "I have the black cat," Tommy smelled a mouse. Demonstrating the quick thinking of a quarterback he told Mr. Freshman that he would also need a maltese cat. Then he inquired as to what was going on. He learned that Mike Seyfrit, in a routine conversation, had informed Mr. Freshman that the athletes had a secret fraternity into which they admitted only one freshman each year and that Mr. Freshman had been elected. He should get a black cat and report to—Frank Thomas. That figured to be the end of this off-the-cuff conversational goofing; but now that Mr. Freshman had demonstrated he was of the proper cut for it, a goofing was in order.

As the Walter Winchell of the campus I was invited. The initiation was held in the furnace room of Sorin Sub. Thomas was the Grand Cat's Ankle, Stuhldreher the Little Cat's Ankle, and so on. Mr. Frosh showed up with his two cats, which he was to carry (and he blindfolded and naked as the cats) one in each hand. If somebody nudged the cats into combat now and then, he was not to let either of them go under pain of expulsion. There were other rigid tests, some of which were ad-libbed on the spot. Mr. Frosh later earned final approval of the Black Cat Frat by appearing at the Hard Times Ball, in tails and white tie, where everybody else wore patches.

Rockne, as a former campus champion in goofing matches, probably enjoyed such stories in "Quad Wrangles." But he frowned when I began to intrude dances and downtown girls into the column. And he fumed when he read that I was going to conduct a search for the Grand Sheik of Notre Dame.

Sheik was then the synonym for what we now call a wolf; and Sheba was current for babe, chick, or whatever the present appellation. Both came into the language from the 1921 novel *The Sheik* by Edith M. Hull, and the silent motion picture of the same name which starred Rudolph Valentino.

The Maestro of Masculinity must have felt that he had grown a viper when he read this announcement in "Quad Wrangles": "The sheik business is getting out of control on the campus. There was a time when a reference to the Sheik of Notre Dame was generally recognized as a page for Mr. Kiley. But now if you yell 'Hey Sheik' it is probable that all the black-haired and most of the light-haired nomads of this particular desert will turn around. So in order to get back to normalcy we have decided to look into the qualifications of the various Arabs and after due deliberation and advice from those who should know—including the Shebas—pick an all-Sheik team— and a Grand Sheik. Each Hall will have its recognized Sheik—after which counterfeits will please lay off the title." Followed a list of candidates from each Hall, including the best-known campus characters, mostly athletes, of course.

Each day I would run a fictitious list of the "standing of the teams" with votes. I began to get real letters from students nominating roommates, from girls nominating guys, from roommates nominating the roommates who had nominated them. My good patron McCready Huston, editor of the *Tribune*, obligingly wrote a mildly deploring editorial. The contest was one of those solid hits; and when it had ended, I wrote a column which concluded:

"Our sheik who dies today was a symbol of the lad who is beloved by the ladies—and no man hates that—which is exactly why none of the 200 or more boys whose names we used in the 'contest' threatened to annihilate us. Our team is a nice clean crowd of boys; good-looking; well-dressed when they want to be well-dressed. Is it dishonor to look well, dance well, talk well? Is it unnatural to love and be loved? Today he was a sheik; seven years ago he was something else. Each generation has its language but man remains just man—the same old bozo—dumb, lovable, and eternally willing to believe that the women think him 'not bad.' . . . So welcome, everybody, and if sometimes we jar please remember that we speak the language of the group which is essentially our readers—the gang at Notre Dame—average age 21; inclined sometimes to be foolish; but don't you occasionally like to look back?"

During the contest, the apostle of Masculinity had registered every emotion from noble patience to grim disapproval; but when it was all over he gave me a big smile. All was forgiven; and now he would give me an idea for another contest; a He-Man contest.

I turned him down. I was being smart-alecky; I was saying no to the boss; I was rebelling against a dominant personality; I was doing what so many of Rock's favorite sparring partners did—letting him have it when he was vulnerable.

Professionally I was very wrong. Rock was entitled to equal time. A contest sponsored by him would have been a natural—a reverse angle on the Sheik theme. He would probably have come up with some ideas; there would probably have been opposition from the downtown Shebas. But I was facing the necessity of following a success; and I made the mistake of so many writers, editors, motion picture and television producers—I repeated myself. I started a contest to discover the Hobohemians of the campus. It didn't go because Notre Dame was not then, and is not now, beatnik.

Rockne sniped at me vocally. And one day in the mail I received a letter from Inferiority Complex which expressed his favorite theme: People who scorn strength are weak people who fear strength. It contained so many of his shibboleths that, though it was typewritten, I knew it had come from him. I printed it. Then answered it.

"Our conscientious objector—who so earnestly disapproved of the sheik—has already visited withering scorn upon the Bohemians. We gave them a lilywhite character but C.O. maintains that nevertheless, our Villagers will be inferior complexes, degenerates, advocates of free love. Poor little fellows—original sins hanging over and detected only by the keen eye of a superior complex." I administered another absolving baptism, then: "If they still excite the animosity of the conscientious objector then we acknowledge our failure—because we are not superiorly complexive; but who wants to be? A superior complex evidently discerns the future keenly. Dante encountered people with that gift who had ridden Charon's bark across the Styx. They had one bad fault however—the future was so clear that the present was dark."

That appeared on a Saturday. That night, as usual, we congregated at the Oliver Cafeteria. I was at one end with a group of student friends. Rockne came in, sat with people at the other end, regarded me steadily as if trying to make up his mind whether or not I really knew who Superior Complex was. What might have happened I do not know. But a few weeks later, when the contest had been concluded, we were in the old office talking about things in general, with several other people. Rock dragged in a reference to Superior

Complex; then he gave me a direct, forgiving smile, as if to say, okay, that's over, we'll forget it.

I've never been too proud of that final answer I had written. It wasn't sporting. There had been no way for him to fight back. You might ask: If he were such a big man, why should he concern himself so violently with such trivia? To Rockne, nothing concerning him was trivia. That's what made him the big man.

XXVIII

Each day during football season, and spring practice Rockne held a half-hour lecture in a classroom in the Main Building where everybody then ate. The boys gave up this half-hour of their own time, as did I. It was the most interesting class I had at Notre Dame. And Rock was one of my three best teachers.

His method was simple. First time around he didn't expect too much; but after repeating the lesson he expected reasonably good answers; he repeated once more—and whomsoever hadn't got it this third time was out. In the main he was a serious lecturer, but he would toss in a laugh when he thought one would help. He had favorite patsies, who bore the brunt of his gags; usually they were campus characters who could take it or didn't seem to mind. After the lecture series was over he would hold a written examination. Once I was second only to Stuhldreher. I hope it wasn't rigged. Rock wanted us both respected by the squad.

During the lecture he would lay out, with blackboard examples, the things to be done on the field. The boys began to gather on the field about three-thirty; and the early arrivals worked on their specialties. By four o'clock everybody was supposed to be there and organized squad work began. By five-thirty the practice ended, so the boys could shower and be ready to eat at six o'clock—and they always were—*ready*. Critics who think of football as a time-waster forget that the time given to it is mostly taken from what would ordinarily be leisure time; they forget that athletics is really an added course. Personally, I think that any boy who has engaged in competitive athletics has gotten much more from college than the boy who did not. There are things to be learned from physical contact that cannot be learned from books.

The field is a laboratory where players practice the theory they received in the class room. Each weekend, in the game they are examined, the hard way, by the opposing players and coaches, sometimes by the weather. Lady Luck gets in her licks. On the Monday after the game, at the noon lecture, Rockne always replayed the game of the preceding Saturday, pointing out where things went well, where they went wrong and why. In these days they have motion pictures which show missed tackles, missed blocks and other mistakes; they have student managers who take down the notes the coaches make during the game and practice sessions; they have statisticians who keep track of tackles and all sorts of other things. Rock had to keep all that in his remarkable memory—and seemed to do a good job of it.

Rockne seldom sent in plays from the bench. The other players were encouraged to give information to the quarterback; but the quarterback was always to be boss, the coach on the field, responsible to the coach. Rockne quarterbacks got special training in small meetings. He sought to have all of his players *think* like quarterbacks. One of his favorite devices during the lecture periods would be to pose a situation facing the quarterback—and then ask perhaps a third-string guard to call the play. Sometimes the answers were amusing; but everybody was influenced to think like a quarterback and improve the general IQ of the squad. This type of training, of course, was conducive to the training of future coaches—another field in which Rockne led by a wide margin.

We were to play Princeton, coached by Bill Roper, in '23—and this was a pelt Rockne wanted. So he began what today might be called subliminal coaching. He automatically made Princeton *the* game to win the next fall by a new device he introduced into the spring lectures. He projected his occasional questions of a tactical nature into a full-fledged game between Notre Dame and Princeton.

Notre Dame kicked off.

Rockne then decided how far back the Princeton receiver brought the ball. Before each play, he would name the conditions a quarterback would have to consider: Where the ball was, the down, yards to be gained, the weather, wind, the type of defense and so on. He would then ask a member of his class to call the play.

Rockne would decide, depending on how good or bad he thought the call, how many yards were gained or lost. In this way he complimented intelligence, scoffed at stupidity; called attention to notable weaknesses and penalized them. The weak blockers were hung up to view as the culprits behind the failure of a play which the press box would blame on a ball-carrier. Conversely, the flashy back was cut down by the proof that he would have got nowhere without the block of the unsung fellow who never got his picture in the paper. Rockne had a way of doing these things that made a boy mad at himself; at his own weaknesses, rather than at the coach.

He knew the Princeton players and some of their idiosyncrasies; the Princeton system and its strong plays. During the "game" he was acquainting his men with the people and conditions they were apt to face on the field at Palmer Stadium on that afternoon next October.

In this performance were utilized the combined talents of Rockne the coach; Rockne the teacher; Rockne the writer; Rockne the actor; Rockne the humorist, the psychologist, the propagandist, and the salesman.

The normal crowd was there when the "first quarter" of the Princeton game was played. The next day the stragglers were all present. The third day athletes from other sports crowded the lecture room. It was, of course, a highly exciting, dramatic game. The score at the end of the third period was conveniently tied.

After each lecture Rock and I would go to his office around the corner. Here again, I was the Press Box. He wanted to know how this had gone, how that play had been received. He was interested in the news that the "game" had spread around the campus.

Who was going to win? He wouldn't tell me, said he didn't know, the game hadn't been finished. Rock was unpredictable, perfectly capable of having us lose, for the chastening effect; to give the boys something to think and worry about during the summer. When the "fourth quarter" began, the hallways outside the classroom were crowded by students. And the campus awaited the result.

He stretched it in Hollywood fashion until the final minute when all eleven members of the team united with perfect teamwork—each executing his assignment on every play—to give Notre Dame a glorious victory. Cheers! Later, in his office, he said it would have been bad psychology for us to have lost. He wanted to have the boys go away with the idea that they could beat Princeton—but only after a terrific struggle, with tremendous concentration on every detail.

That old office was really something in those days. It was at the rear of the second floor of the Main (Administration) Building, looking out on the bakery. It was never locked; nor was the ancient roll-top desk which Father Sorin might possibly have used. A table against the wall was usually piled high with a leaning tower of correspondence. People were usually walking in or out, there were no secrets, the business was conducted with garnishments of humor. There were a few chairs; and a closet at the back where records were stacked—the archives, such as they were, since this was the Athletic Department.

Every so often, when the tower of letters was about to fall down, Rock would borrow a secretary—I remember Red Heffernan and Frank Dufficy—and sail through the mail. The accompanying dialogue, which never got in, would have made better, though not always flattering, reading.

Nobody ever disturbed anything—including the roll of currency that rested in one of the desk cubbyholes for months; and there was nobody who came in there who could not have found use for the money—probably receipts from some of the tickets Rock had placed in the cigar stores.

In 1913, when Rock was a senior, there were two freshmen on the campus who were to do well in politics—Harry Kelly as Governor of Michigan and John E. Cassidy as Attorney General and Acting Governor of Illinois. The hero-worshiping frosh became intimates of the coach and members of the celebrity circus which attended him. In the late twenties Cassidy invited Rockne to speak at an annual meeting of a business group in Peoria, Illinois, and sent a long letter detailing the importance of the occasion. A few weeks later he received a cable from Rockne, somewhere in Europe: I'LL BE THERE ON MAY TWENTY-SIXTH. REGARDS. ROCK.

Rock arrived, months later, wearing a brown suit and carrying a bag which might possibly have held pajamas, a shirt, and a razor. That evening, when everybody gathered for the occasion, Rock, still in the brown suit, gazed at all the other dignitaries in formal attire and blasted Cassidy: "Why didn't you tell me about this? I can't talk to these people. What will I talk about? I thought this was a football dinner. Why didn't you tell me?"

"Rock, I did. I wrote you a four-page letter."

Rock grinned. "Next time write me four paragraphs and I might read it." What did he do for a speech? He found one—and stole the show from the other speaker who was properly attired in a dinner coat.

That old office, from whence blasted the missiles which made Notre Dame a national sensation, should be a shrine. I stop there at every opportunity to sneer at the latest desecration. Once it was occupied by a tennis coach; again by somebody in economics; now a professor of education. All nice people, of course.

XXIX

Rockne began to experiment with the two-team system as early as 1920. In 1921 he sometimes started the second unit in minor games. In 1922 this became a definite tactic in most games. By 1923 the system was in full flower. Thereafter its use depended on the material available and the caliber of the opposition. Sometimes he would start a second-string backfield and a first-string line. He was years ahead of his opposition in this device which was the forerunner of modern platoon football. In view of the present fashion of experimenting with several teams, it is worth noting that Rockne also used three units.

This is the way it worked: He would start his second team, a rugged, defensive unit equipped with a superior punter. Since the rules then permitted a player to appear only once in each quarter, the starting team would play the entire quarter, if possible. Its job was to absorb the first heavy *shock* of the opposition attack, without, if possible, giving up any score. The defensive starters were logically called shock troops.

During the first period the lighter, faster eleven—the boxers—

would be grouped about the coach, who would be analyzing the other team, and setting up an attack and defense for the regulars to use. They would go in at the beginning of the second period and their job was to score. With the rest period between halves, they would go back and play the third period; or as much of it as was needed. The shock troops would then return to mop up, perhaps to score on their own. When things were well in hand, usually midway in the fourth period, a third team, composed mostly of sophomores, would go in to get experience.

The first team was predominantly senior; the shock troops, mostly junior. When one group graduated, another seasoned unit was always available. The system distributed the physical burden. It never humiliated an opponent. It emphasized defense as well as offense. It was a natural outgrowth of Rockne's fundamental concept of the fast, intelligent boxer as superior to the slower slugger. His players had to be well-rounded, well-grounded in every department. The speed and intelligence, and remarkable physical toughness of the Four Horsemen made them as valuable on defense as on offense.

Rockne never had much coaching help. But his assistants were thoroughly grounded in Rockne fundamentals—to block, tackle, think—and *give the best at all times*. The practices were well organized, simply conducted. The big offensive maneuver every day was the off-tackle play upon which the whole offense was geared. The linemen worked in groups, often with the seniors as supervisors. Rock was an Argus-eyed overseer who kept everybody on his toes. Until the phlebitis forced him to the side lines, he actively coached the ends and tackles. And his interpretation of *active* was to get into the pit with a big young tackle and taunt him in a voice carrying the field: "Come on, hit me—hit me—I won't hurt you, honest I won't."

The goading would occasionally get under the skin of a spirited youngster. If he really got hit, Rock would orate to those about: "There's power. *Power*. *POWER*." He would also probably, though privately, declare that young man graduated; and issue no more personal challenges.

"He was always challenging me," said my fellow townsman, tackle John Poliski, who had been called Bull from high-school days with very good reason. "So I thought—okay. We were supposed to charge on the count of three. It seemed to me he was charging on two. So I charged on one and put him down. He came up, ready to annihilate me." Poliski, a natural cynic, is one of the few of Rock's players who claims never to have been captivated by "the Swede." But recently, in Bull's office at the Catholic Community Center in Steubenville, Ohio, I saw a picture of Rock under the glass top of his desk. Bull claims that "somebody else" put it there.

The way Rock went at the tackles in practice was probably the way he had gone after opponents as a player—eyes blazing, face distorted, movements quick. I knew the pose would make a sensational publicity shot but also knew he would mow me down if I even suggested it. So one afternoon, when a photographer for the Chicago *American* was there, I arranged for him to shoot behind the protection of my circling arm. The next day the *American* used three-quarters of a page of Rockne's contorted face. The Chicago *Tribune*, well-scooped, sent a man down and now Rockne had to pose the shot. He knew I must have been responsible but he never asked how it had been done. Also, he might just have liked it. The picture was used in his autobiography.

When the 1923 training season began Rock was in the position, careerwise, of a director at a dress rehearsal. The fundamentals of his system had been set up, there remained the never-completed task of shoring-up details, of constantly adding refinements, of tightening up parts, of adding oil here and there, of listening, with the ear of the engineer, for discordant murmurs—and then giving the over-all operation what Boris Pasternak calls "the presence of art."

An off-stage noise developed during the fall practice. He probably had assumed that his growing publicity problem was in reasonably competent hands. But after a week or so I told him I was leaving to enter the Harvard Law School. He did not explode—as he had every reason to do—at this prospect of having to train another student in a sensitive area as the season was about to begin. He surprised me by saying: "We'll miss you around here but okay—if that's what you feel you should do." He offered to give me letters to Boston sports editors, since I would need a job. He made only one threat: "Just one thing. Come back here with a broad A and I'll kick you in the *derrière!*"

I decided, almost immediately, to forswear both Harvard and the law, to finish the season as a full-fledged graduate publicity man and then go to New York and enter the newspaper business.

The first game was a 74–0 romp over Kalamazoo; but the next, against equally small Lombard developed into a 14–0 contest as an unsung back named Lamb looked better than any of our scintillating sensations. Which may have been very fortuitous because Army was coming up, very early this year, and Army had every muzzle loaded to stop this silly business of constantly losing to the Indiana upstarts. To appreciate the full blaze of this Army frustration, it is necessary to know, as old-timers will remember, that these were the days when Army played graduates from other schools.

(It was not unusual for the Cadets to have a few men who might be completing their seventh year of college football. This gave them a definite advantage over the average school, including Navy, whose younger age limit for entrance practically ruled out the use of graduates from other colleges. The situation was to lead, in a few years, to a break between the service schools which made Notre Dame the big game for each—and put Rockne in an embarrassing position from which he was rescued, in 1929, by, believe it or not, the Black Friday break in the stock market. But that, in due time.)

The Army game, too big for the Plains, and much too exciting to be given away any longer, was to be played at Ebbets Field in Brooklyn because the Yankees and Giants were in the World Series. The Princeton game at Palmer Field was to follow. I found Rock in a surprisingly receptive mood when I went to him with a proposition: If he would pay my train fare to New York and back, I would, at my own expense, spend the intervening week in New York, visiting the newspapers, telling them about Notre Dame (and assumedly Rockne) and helping build up the gate for the Princeton game. This was not entirely altruistic on my part, since I was planning to attack New York on my own. He agreed.

Tuesday afternoon he walked off the practice field in evident disgust, with the squad, leaving the astounded Captain Harvey Brown to cope as best he could. Wednesday afternoon, while still voicing public displeasure at what he was seeing on the field, Rock blurted impulsively to me: "We'll knock them stiff." He knew that I understood this was not for publication; that I would continue, in print, to reflect the pessimistic face he wore for the squad.

He was uncanny in this ability to accurately assay the reactions of his men to a given situation. He was, as a coach, like a chemist or an alchemist. Give him the physical ingredients, and the time, and he would add the mystic drugs to insure victory.

XXX

Notre Dame players have always prayed before a football game; as any man prays in his own way, before any trial. This spiritual aspect was shielded from publicity until photographers, meeting the squad at Albany in 1921 for routine pictures, followed to Farrell Institute where they saw the boys receive Communion at the replica of the Grotto of Our Lady of Lourdes.

On the morning of the day when we were to leave for the Army game in 1923, I dropped into the Sacred Heart Church for a visit. The football squad was there with Rev. John F. O'Hara, then Prefect of Religion. He said there had been some publicity from the East that the Broadway musical-comedy star, Elsie Janis, "Sweetheart of the A.E.F." in World War I, would kick off for Army. He said: "Joan of Arc will kick off for Notre Dame." He gave each of us a Joan of Arc medal. It was only after I had lived intimately with the football squads for two years, that I learned that he had been giving the boys one of these medals before each game.

The 1923 Army game, from the Notre Dame angle, was a fantastically wonderful afternoon. Mounted police had to be called to handle the crowd outside Ebbets Field. Inside, the people were everywhere. There were bleachers on the side lines; and there also was the press box where I may have set some sort of record by servicing four Western Union wires. Elsie Janis did not kick off but she rode the Army mule about the field before the game. Valiant Joan of Arc made no tackles; but the Irish were all heroes in an almost flawless performance.

Layden had a field day—punting, passing, receiving passes, running. Young Dutch Bergman saved a touchdown with a tackling jewel. Crowley became the darling of the Brooklyn Irish by runs of

35 and 18 yards that led to the 13–0 victory. The ever-present Walter Eckersall, who officiated as head linesman, later wrote in the Chicago *Tribune:* "The heady work of Stuhldreher had much to do with the attack. The mighty Hewitt, who played fullback on the Pittsburgh eleven for three years, was unable to penetrate the Notre Dame forward wall for consistent gains."

Others on that Army team, which lost its first game in two seasons, were Ed Garbisch, Smythe, Mulligan, and Garrison Davidson, who was later the Cadets' head coach from 1933 through 1937, and subsequently as Lieutenant General Davidson to become Superintendent of the Academy at West Point.

"Notre Dame," Eckersall concluded, "was heralded as one of the greatest offensive machines ever to play in the East. It was especially lauded by Walter Camp and other well-known authorities who occupied seats on the side lines."

One of those who sat with Camp was Donold B. Lourie, Princeton All-American quarterback of 1920 who lived in the Midwest and had volunteered to scout the Irish for Bill Roper. He told me the story recently in his office: "I knew Rock slightly and when I appeared on the campus and told him I was to scout, he invited me in to his dressing room to hear him talk to the boys. I scouted the first two games at South Bend and then went to the Army game. Walter Camp invited me to sit with him on the side lines and I became so intrigued with Camp's conversation that I missed the forward pass play which Notre Dame used to score on the Army. After the game I saw Rock and explained my predicament. Without hesitation he gave me the scoring play, with each player's position, showed me how the play developed, exactly where the pass was intended and how it was completed. I reported that to Roper the next day, with a full explanation of how I had received the information. Much to our surprise Notre Dame used the pass twice against us the next week, exactly as Rockne had outlined, and completed the pass twice for substantial gains."

Lourie, now chairman of the board of the Quaker Oats Company, but still looking as if he could go at quarterback, smiled. "There's a sequel. I later told the story to Merrillat, the Army coach who also scouted Notre Dame at that time. He told me that he had once missed connections and missed the game he was to scout; so he had written Rock, who obligingly sent him *all* the plays Notre Dame had used in the game Merrillat had missed. Army figured it as a trick. They prepared for an entirely opposite type of attack. So, in the game, Rock used the plays he had sent to them, exactly as diagrammed, and beat them."

Giving the plays away was, for Rockne, not as foolhardy as it sounded. He gave them away at coaching schools; and to newspaper reporters. He always claimed it was the *execution* which counted. I could sit in the press box in later years and call the play from the direction of the shift—so it must have been easy enough work for scouts. But that still didn't stop the linemen from blocking and the backs from rambling.

I told Lourie how shocked I had been in 1921 when Rock hadn't even bothered to scout Army. At the blackboard he had told the squad: "They will hit inside here . . . Outside there . . . Occasionally they may do this . . . but you'll know it because . . ." And that's exactly what Army did. He seemed to understand the Army mind; so well that perhaps there might even have been some method in the '21 game when he had abandoned the shift for the second half. After all, was Army prepared for that? Rock was usually that far ahead of his opponents.

It is difficult for a Road Scholar to operate without a football team. I was about to break all the rules by paying for my own hotel room during the week between the Army and Princeton games; but Joe Byrne, ever thoughtful, put me up at the Newark Athletic Club, along with another graduated sophomore. Morris Starrett of Port Townsend, Washington, perhaps the original of Rock's "inefficient student managers" was then making the first of his many Farewell Tours with Notre Dame teams. I found the Manhattan sports editors quite eager for information about football's rising star, Mr. Rockne, and his flock of fleet meteors, but nothing I said matched their performance in the Princeton game. It was pretty much of a style show with the backs, behind a steadily improving offensive line, running like circus ponies in the center ring. Layden returned an intercepted pass 45 yards before retiring with an injury.

Hugh Fullerton, Sr., wrote this footnote for history: "Notre Dame swept to a 25–2 victory over Princeton today, put an end to the alleged supremacy of the East, and gave the Tigers, champions of 1922, one of the worst trouncings in the history of Nassau."

The Victory Parade continued: 35–7 over Georgia Tech and 34–7 over Purdue—with the backs taking turns front and center. Against Tech, Miller had touchdown runs of 59 and 23 yards—and had another of 89 yards called back. Stuhldreher secreted himself through the Rambling Wrecks for 46 yards on a punt return. Crowley earned the title of the Irish Eel with runs, passes, and points after touchdown.

The ensemble then proceeded toward Lincoln, Nebraska, to avenge their only defeat in 16 games; proceeded confidently since the Huskers, beefy as always, had been beaten by Red Grange and Illinois; and tied by Missouri and Kansas. Walter Eckersall wrote of this one: "The Cornhuskers outplayed Notre Dame in practically every department in the biggest surprise of the football season. Defensively they stopped most Notre Dame plays before they made much headway. It simply was a case of one team being alert and on its toes while the other did not show any of the dash or drive which featured its play in the Princeton and Army games."

XXXI

This was the second—and last—game the Four Horsemen lost. Both to Nebraska at Lincoln. In their sophomore season they had gone down gloriously after having been physically outmanned. But the '23 game was a drab performance, one of the few cases of operating failure in Rockne's career. He may have thought the revenge motif sufficient to get the boys "up." The boys probably thought so, too. They may also have begun to believe their sensational publicity. But regardless of the reason, this was a day when Rockne, the alchemist, had failed to find the potions which would bring his team up to par.

Actually Notre Dame did not get its touchdown in the 14–7 defeat until ten seconds before the game ended. It was one of those sad days, more frequent lately, but rare in the Rockne era when a defeat was always page-one news. But out of the gloom of the last period came two of the biggest laughs of the Notre Dame tradition—one of them a prize sparkle of the entire gridiron lore.

The Notre Dame song "When the Irish Backs Go Marching By," written about this time, was inspired by the parade of the Rockne soldiers. But there is frustration for runners who might have been stars in ordinary years but were pretty much unseen in the rush of air that follows pyrotechnics. It happens every year to some harassed gridders, just as it happens in business, politics, even, or perhaps especially, in love. It happened in '22 and '23 to Bergman and Maher, who could run with the Horsemen but were even lighter; to the fullbacks, Cerney, Enright, and Livergood; to Thomas; to others who never even made a letter.

It is the old, old story of the stand-ins behind super-healthy super-stars; and, among their other accomplishments, the Horsemen were incredibly healthy, in consideration of the assaults that must have been made, even in a legal way, upon their sturdy but unimpressive bodies. Stuhldreher weighed 154; Layden 168; Miller and Crowley each 165. But this was prime beef.

Notre Dame does not now (since 1951) play transfer students, and it is practically impossible for an athlete in real scholastic trouble to make up work in summer school (as Crowley did after the crap game suspension). But transfers were welcome in the days of which I write; and one of them became perhaps the most frustrated superior talent in gridiron history. Max Hauser may have been a throwback to the colorful period when footloose athletes switched from school to school for whatever reasons. They were called tramps in the old days, and usually they thought as the bricklayer who said of the textbooks handed to him at a football school: "If they had given me a trowel I'd have known what to do with it." But Max Hauser was no tramp. He had a good mind, his entrance credits were satisfactory.

Max had transferred from Lafayette, an Eastern leader in those days. He probably wanted to play under Rockne; and he had probably been inspired by the thought that, under Rockne, he could become another Gipp. It was not a grandiose thought because we all shared it at the time. Hauser was built like Gipp; had many of George's talents. He even looked like Gipp—except that he was a handsome Gipp. I walked along the street one day, wondered why the girls had all of a sudden begun to look at me—then realized they were gazing so invitingly at my companion, the handsome Hauser. He differed from Gipp in this field. I doubt if any pretty-girl-with-car had to be *sold* to Max.

He shared a room with Frank Doriot in the gym. It amused him to pretend to be afflicted by nightmares. Doriot, a hard-working, clean-minded young man who ordinarily slept well, found himself being awakened at night by moans, groans, and bloodthirsty yells. He would open his eyes to see his big roommate coming at him like Mr. Hyde. Doriot was a track man and there was a running track in the gym; and he ran many a race for his life out there in the chilling dark until he learned that Max was only funning.

Between Rockne and Hauser, my classmate Doriot had a hard life. Once, unpacking at Indiana, an important piece of equipment was "found lost." Rockne shouted: "If we lose this game it's your fault." (Rockne had packed the trunk.) Frankie recently told me that Rock once said to him: "You and Wallace have the same weakness—you like to travel with the football team."

Hauser was ineligible during his first year, but he worked out with the reserves often enough to support the impression that another Gipp was coming up. He was a triple-threat left halfback, which was going to complicate Rock's Layden-Crowley problem—a nice complication if you can get it. Max even seemed to have Gipp's lackadaisical attitude—which a Gipp could get away with.

When Max became eligible he was not quite a Gipp—not enough at least to crowd Crowley out of the picture. He didn't quite like the idea of being a substitute; but instead of going into high gear to prove that he was first-string, Max began to drag a little. Rock began to prod him, in his usual manner of stimulating laggards, but now Max exhibited another Gipp quality—a mordant wit. He talked back to the coach.

If Max *had* been another Gipp, he would have been at left halfback, or fullback; and Crowley and/or Layden would have had to fit in elsewhere, which they no doubt would have done. But Max was not a Gipp; and he dragged the body so much that he dropped back to third-string. He became just another guy around who got in after Crowley and Bergman had finished. But he made the traveling squad; and he was at Nebraska.

The trip had begun badly. Shortly after we arrived Rockne showed me a banner headline on the sports page of the Lincoln *Star: THE HORRIBLE HIBERNIANS ARRIVE TODAY.* It was, we knew, our friend Cy Sherman, the volatile sports editor, merely being alliterative; but Rock, no Hibernian himself, thought it in bad taste. Later, at what was supposed to be secret practice, numbers of Nebraska freshmen in green caps sat in the bleachers and jeered the great Rockne and his Horrible Hibernians. Other faces peered from windows of buildings which surrounded the field. Rock, burning at all this, said: "They want to see something—we'll show 'em something." So, on the spot, he put in a triple reverse, probably the one his Tricky Tiger team had used in grade-school days. And the boys worked it.

Midway in the fourth period of the game, it was apparent this was to be one of those bad days. The harder we tried the worse things went. The Cornhuskers, smelling Sunday morning's headlines, played like tigers, with some rustic vocal accompaniment also of questionable taste. The Husker fans in the stands were giving the first full throat to the elocutions of that night.

Rockne knelt on the side lines, fighting to live, searching for the way to redeem this lost cause as others had been redeemed. It was then that Max Hauser, the not-quite-second Gipp, with uniform still unsullied, got down off his high horse, put away his resentment, ate humble pie, knelt beside Rock and said:

"Put me in, Rock."

"It's all right, Max," Rock answered. "I'm saving you for the Junior Prom."

That's the true story of the Junior Prom gag that has been kicked over so many fields that it's become lopsided. But it also has a sequel. Rock relented; or perhaps it was merely another psychological inspiration. It would take another Gipp to win this one—so this was the time to find out if Max Hauser was another Gipp. So Max went in, with his clean uniform. Legend has it that this big, handsome, newest victim was greeted thus:

"Well—look who's here. Don't strut, Handsome—if you were any good you'd have been in here long ago."

"Well, you Irish Catholic so-and-so, the bench must be clean by now. When you gonna send for the Pope?"

Those are from the legend, true or false. The real kicker came later, and was given me by Bill Cerney: "The scene, 1923, Lincoln, Nebraska, Nebraska 14 ND 0. Three minutes to go. The Four Horsemen were out—except Stuhldreher. The other backs: Maher, Hauser, Cerney. We start from our own 20-yard line; slowly work to the 50 with about two minutes to go. We start to shift, left to right. A Nebraska man points to Hauser and hollers: 'Get that big Catholic so-and-so.'

"Hauser calls, 'Checks signals.' Everyone is on edge with him because we have only two minutes to score. Max says to Stuhldreher: 'Harry, would you mind informing the gentleman on the opposite side of the line that I am not a Catholic so-and-so—I am a Presbyterian so-and-so.' It got a laugh, we all relaxed—and went on from there and scored—on a pass from Stuhldreher to me, at fullback."

Max Hauser was a failure, perhaps his own; perhaps he was a problem that even Rockne could not solve. But he was basically a good guy who made the Notre Dame team that afternoon at Nebraska; and eventually an even bigger team. A few years later Max was coaching at Midland College at Fremont in that same state of Nebraska. A girl was drowning. Max came off the bench to save her— and lost his own life. So he did die like Gipp, heroically.

Superior football teams rejuvenate after an unexpected defeat, especially if the coach makes them feel that defeat is a hot iron that brands a scarlet letter. Poetically, perhaps, Butler was next on the schedule, and the memory of Castner's injury did not dim after Don Miller suffered a broken rib. When the game had been safely locked up, 34–7, in the final quarter, Rockne sent in the more rugged of his shock troops. This was the only time I ever knew a Rockne-coached group to play football that might have been described as "unpleasantly vigorous."

One of the lads who seemed to enjoy the informal exercise with the "married men" was Ward "Doc" Connell, who played third-string halfback opposite Max Hauser. Doc feared neither man nor ghost, as I learned when we shared a room in the supposedly haunted Washington Hall. At three in the morning he got bored waiting for the ghost to appear and yelled: "Come on you devils, come on." That roused the ghosts who, more recent research indicated, probably included Clarence "Pat" Manion, the political pundit.

Wilbur Eaton, a shock troop end, was the opposite type who some-times tied himself up with intensity. Rock had frequently warned him of closing his eyes as he was going for a big tackle. At a practice session after one of these failures, the coach did a little dance, hold-ing the edges of his pants and singing to the tune of the nursery rhyme:

> Wilbur closed his eyes
> Wilbur closed his eyes
> Heigh-ho the derrio,
> Wilbur closed his eyes.

After that Wilbur remembered not to close his eyes. A few years later I waited with several people to see Rock. When the door finally opened, Wilbur Eaton came out. He had been discussing some of his own coaching problems with Rock; he told me Rock never failed to answer his letters, in detail. The Master was still probably com-pensating for that embarrassment he had felt necessary. And it might just have won a big game.

XXXII

Rockne had created the post of Official News Correspondent to elim-inate what he called inaccurate reporting of athletic news by South Bend newspapermen to outside papers and press associations. The reporters did not entirely cease and desist. On my last day in South Bend the situation came to a boil—with Rockne doing most of the erupting.

The final game of the 1923 season at St. Louis did not seem im-portant; so I had decided to go with the squad to the Carnegie Tech game at Pittsburgh and from there to my home nearby. Quite by accident I was also pinch-hitting for the sports editor of the *Tribune*. A story came over the Associated Press wire from Indianapolis with a South Bend dateline. It said Notre Dame was going to drop Purdue in football and quoted the usual "responsible authority," which could

only mean Rockne. If true, I had been badly scooped. I called Rock
for verification and he established a new record for the leaping high
dudgeon. He was tired having his schedule-building threatened by
the "back room fiction writers" on the *News-Times.*

"Can I quote you on that?"

"Make it as strong as you can."

That afternoon the first edition of the *Tribune* carried this banner
across the top of the sports page: *ROCKNE RAPS BACK ROOM
FICTION WRITERS ON LOCAL MORNING NEWSPAPER.*

I had made the accompanying denial stronger by adding many
of the comments Rock had made on previous occasions.

The craft-conscious editors of the *Tribune* removed the banner
line in the later edition, but let the story ride. Since there was only
one local morning newspaper the *N-T* boys established a new local
record for the running high indignation. Three of them—the city
editor, sports editor, and Notre Dame correspondent—caught up
with me that evening at the Postal Telegraph office adjacent to the
lobby of the Oliver Hotel. They accused me of high crimes, including
character assassination; they were going to *murder me* in the morning paper. Since I was leaving South Bend permanently and hoped
to work in New York, this posed a serious problem. I denied the
allegations—forcefully; and when I was not set upon physically, we
got down to plain talk.

They said Rockne had denied my extensive quotes.

So we went looking for Rockne, who had recently been somewhere
around the lobby. He was not there. The train was leaving within
an hour; and the sports editor of the *News-Times* was making the
trip to Pittsburgh. We reached an agreement. He and I would talk
to Rockne on the train. If he continued to deny my quotes, they
would murder me the next day. If he admitted them, and bailed me
out, they would murder Rockne.

I was still traveling as a Road Scholar and had a trunk to check
to Pittsburgh. Mr. Hughes, the *News-Times* sports editor, turned out
to be much nicer to me than I had been to him and his editor. He
checked my trunk on his ticket. I also bought a berth from the conductor—thereby completing, on my valedictory, an educational masterpiece for all Road Scholars to shoot at. When these bits of business
had been taken care of, somewhere beyond Elkhart, Indiana, Mr.

Hughes and I began to hunt for Rockne. We found him in the smoker next to the baggage car, which was as far as he could go. The dialogue went like this:

"Rock, did you say I misquoted you?"

"No. I said I would deny anything you said that I hadn't said."

"Didn't you call them back room fiction writers?"

"I did."

"Didn't you say I could quote you as strong as I liked?"

"I did."

"Did I quote you as saying anything you hadn't said to me at one time or another?"

"No—you could have made it stronger."

I turned the witness over to Mr. Hughes who made the mistake of speaking harshly—after which the roof fell on him. He hadn't been around very long, but he had been caught in the middle of the old feud and had to answer for all the sins the *News-Times* had ever committed against K. K. Rockne; or at least those Rock thought they had committed. I never did see the *News-Times* of the next day.

The incident was typical of Rockne as I knew him. He could be wrong; he could be diplomatically cute; he could, on occasion, retreat from a ticklish issue. But when the showdown came he was always a stand-up guy. He never lied to me or failed to keep his word.

I shouldn't have done that to him; or to the fellows on the *News-Times*. I later learned to protect my friends who talked too fast.

We won the Carnegie game nicely, 26–0; but at home in Bellaire, Ohio, I sweated out the 13–0 finale against St. Louis. George Vergara recently wrote me about it: "We were playing at Sportsman's Park, the home of the Cardinals. It was a miserable, mean, muddy, rainy day. We were supposed to win handily. At half-time we went off the field with a 7–0 edge and Rockne was plainly worried. The mud had gotten into our eyes, ears, nose, and uniforms, so that we scarcely recognized one another.

"As we were crossing the field the effervescent, ebullient Crowley, who never took anything seriously, was joking and laughing with me. I turned around, and over my shoulder saw Rockne a few paces behind us. I told Jimmy to hush up. Jimmy laughingly replied:

'That's all right, he don't know who we are.' That was quite literally true. The only things visible were our eyes."

Crowley was the clown prince. Rock told of the time Jimmy came into the office with a recommendation for a player from his home town of Green Bay, Wisconsin.

"Good is he?" Rock asked.

"Awfully good."

"As good as you?"

"Well—perhaps not that—but awfully good."

The Horsemen were returning from Chicago in '24 after a lack-luster victory over Northwestern. On the train a drunk wandered into the Notre Dame car without a ticket. The conductor asked him where he thought he was going. "I guess nowhere," the drunk admitted.

"It's okay," Crowley said to the conductor. "He's one of the Four Horsemen. They've been going nowhere all day."

At the height of their fame they were much interviewed by newsmen. A sob sister, looking for a new angle, pursued them by mail, telegraph, telephone. Finally, on foot, she caught up with Crowley, who was tolerant and polite. "Who was she?" somebody asked.

"The second horsewoman," Crowley said. "Pestilence."

Vergara, recently mayor of New Rochelle, New York, was a regular end in '22 and '23, and a great one—tall, rangy, powerful, articulate, sensitive. He had played end at Fordham as a freshman, then transferred to Notre Dame. Technically that left him only two years of eligibility, but he wanted to finish the three years with the Horsemen group with whom he had started. But let George tell it:

"Rock once asked me where I had played before but I said nothing about Fordham. However, I discounted the fact that Rockne could read. When we came east to play West Point, there was a small squib in the evening *Sun* with the heading '*Ex-Fordham Sub Now Starring for ND.*' I am sure Rockne got to see this. At the end of my junior year, at the annual football banquet at the Oliver Hotel, Rockne, as was the custom, called on all the graduating members of the football team. I sat there in fear and trembling. He went right down the line and I thought I had fooled him when he failed to call on me. However, at the very end, he said we are now going to call on a young man who unfortunately played a little football in the

East before he came here—George Vergara. I stumbled to my feet with tears in my eyes.

"That same spring, I told Rockne that I was going to quit Notre Dame because I could not play the following year, 1924, which was the best year the Four Horsemen had. He told me that he would not let me quit and that I started at Notre Dame and I would finish there. I asked him about my scholarship and he told me not to worry about it, that I would coach the freshman football team the next year, which is just what happened. His determination not to let me quit was an inspiration to me in many a tough spot.

"The following fall, I coached and kept myself very busy, tried to make myself feel that I did not miss being a regular on the greatest football team ever produced at Notre Dame. Two or three years after I was graduated, I used to have recurring dreams in which I was sitting on the Notre Dame bench near Rockne during the 1924 Army game for which I had been declared ineligible as told above. In the dream it seems we were behind a little and as the first half was ending, Rock turned to me in this nightmare and said, 'Come into the dressing room at the half. I want you to put on a uniform.' I would protest and say, 'Coach, I am ineligible. Remember you told me this at the football banquet last year.' The rejoinder invariably was in his staccato, penetrating voice, 'Never mind—do as I tell you. Go in and get into your uniform.' The end of this nightmare found me sweating, trying to unravel the knots in my football shoes. Seems they had become all entangled to the point where I could not get into the shoes. When I recounted this nightmare, which must have taken place a half-dozen times, to a friend of mine, he christened me the fifth horseman—night-mare."

XXXIII

Rockne, a people-hungry man, walked an unobserved beat in what could have been leisure moments. Father Cavanaugh and Frank Hering are said to have given him elocution lessons—which would seem like teaching a fish how to swim; but Rock always went to headquarters to correct a deficiency. He often spoke of a small grocer named Zoss, whom he admired as a hustler and an exemplar of Americanism; two of the Zoss boys later became members of his football squads. One of his favorite sparring partners was John (Iron Hat) Sweeney, known to a generation of students as house officer at the Oliver. His circle of South Bend intimates increased through the years.

There were the Sunday visits to Doriot's room and the sessions with the records. On his New York trips he seemed to spend some time with Paul Whiteman, Isham Jones, and other top music men. He played the flute in the Monogram Club Orchestra. He visited the halls, especially those where his players lived. Ostensibly checking on their studies, he also practiced his individual psychology on these trips. He was always hungry for any information about his work, especially from newspapermen. After I began to travel with the top echelon sports writers I briefed him about personalities, felt free to make suggestions about publicity policy. He was always very receptive.

His chief escape from athletic tensions, apart from his reading and the considerable time he spent with his family, was undoubtedly his interest in chemistry. "Many an evening," Vincent Sweeney recalls, "Rock would drop in on Father Nieuwland. They would kick around problems and discuss formulae. Rock could talk intelligently and Father Nieuwland took him seriously. Since this was the time the Belgian was working on the final formula for the base for synthetic rubber, Rock might well have been in on those discussions. He was one of three people, the others being Father Nieuwland and myself, who had the combination for a secret lock to the office door Father Nieuwland had invented. Rock was the big man of the two to me. Father Nieuwland was just the guy I worked for." Sweeney smiled. "Father Nieuwland liked to hang around football, too."

(Father Nieuwland, like most Notre Dame priests, was a sports fan. I returned with the Yankees on an exhibition game around 1928. I sat next to Father Nieuwland at lunch. He quizzed me about Babe Ruth.)

Underneath all Rockne activity was the beat of football. In 1924 the artist was ready with his masterpiece and I was now looking at him as night sports editor of the Associated Press in New York. I had wandered in there with assists from Henry Farrell and Lady Luck at the very time they were looking for a bright young sports writer—and who brighter than one who had been a camera in the tail of the bright new Rockne comet? (My association with Rockne was later to help me break into magazines, books, and motion pictures.) They knew about Rockne in New York and every New Yorker who could find a ticket was in the Polo Grounds for the Army game. I was in the press box, still dispensing information but trying to act like an unbiased reporter. When the game ended, and after my bulletins had gone out, I sat, with the others, trying to think up a lead worthy of what I had seen. But down the line a bit, another chap was already writing:

"Outlined against a blue-gray October sky, the Four Horsemen rode again. In dramatic lore they are known as Famine, Pestilence, Destruction, and Death. These are only aliases. Their real names are Stuhldreher, Miller, Crowley, and Layden. They formed the crest of the South Bend cyclone before which another fighting Army football team was swept over the precipice of the Polo Grounds yesterday afternoon as 55,000 spectators peered down on the bewildering panorama spread on the green plain below.

"A cyclone can't be snared. It may be surrounded but somewhere it breaks through to keep on going. When the cyclone starts from South Bend, where the candlelights still gleam through the Indiana sycamores, those in the way must take to storm cellars at top speed. Yesterday the cyclone struck again, as Notre Dame beat the Army 13–7 with a set of backfield stars that ripped and crashed through a strong Army defense with more speed and power than the warring Cadets could meet.

"Notre Dame won its ninth game in twelve Army starts through the driving power of one of the greatest backfields that ever churned up the turf of any gridiron. Brilliant backfields may come and go but in Stuhldreher, Miller, Crowley, and Layden, covered by a fast and charging line, Notre Dame can take its place in front of the field . . . The Army had its share of stars in action, such stars as Garbisch, Farwick, Willson, Wood, Ellinger . . . but no such quartet who seemed to carry the mixed blood of the tiger and the antelope."

The story was a typical press box production. No time to study, or ponder, to edit or rewrite—with a telegraph operator waiting for each sheet, and sometimes copying as you wrote. The sports writer must be ready with his best, and that day, while immortalizing the Horsemen, Grantland Rice insured some measure of it for himself. The names of even the best sports writers tend to fade with their generations unless they leave behind a time-resistant medallion. As long as there is football, or a Notre Dame, the Four Horsemen will ride—and Rice in the carriage behind.

But as the Horsemen might have been just another backfield without the Rice story, both he and they might have inevitably found limbo had it not been for the young man who had succeeded me in a job that was no longer merely official news correspondent but, during my tenure, had evolved very definitely into publicity director. With sound instincts, George Strickler had spent some time between halves with Rice, Damon Runyon, and other influential writers. The talk had stressed the precision of the Notre Dame attack. Strickler later became publicity director of the National Football League and is now assistant sports editor of the Chicago *Tribune*. It is George's story, so let him tell it:

"I am very grateful to you for the opportunity to bring the Four Horsemen story back into proper perspective. Time and the retelling has distorted some of the facts.

"I had just seen Valentino and the Horseman film again, (for the fourth or fifth time) the night before we left the campus for New York. Brother Cyprian was showing it in Washington Hall. Those Horsemen got me. Especially Bull Montana.

"So I threw into the conversation: 'Just like the Four Horsemen.'

"Rice was the only one who picked it up. In later years my appreciation of Granny as a writer and a reporter grew as I recalled that others had the same opportunity to pick up a chance remark and build it into a classic, but missed it entirely.

"My pictures that year were taken by a commercial man named Christman, whose office was on the second floor across from the central fire station on Wayne Street. On Sunday after seeing Granny's story, I wired Christman to be at school the next day (Monday) and also wired my Dad, who worked for the university, to arrange for horses. Dad reserved them from a questionable riding stable run in conjunction with a coal and ice business on the race at La Salle Street, a few doors from Briese's Saloon.

"When I got back to South Bend on Monday afternoon, I dropped off and picked up the steeds. Practice was in session when I reached Cartier Field and the doors were locked. They were not going to let me in at first, but finally opened the gates and I rode thru, disrupting practice while Christman made the now well-known shot.

"Rock gave me hell in a polite way. He thought I had a swell idea. But he objected to the timing—or any timing for that matter, as you well know, that barged unannounced into his practice.

"Taking the horses out was a problem. I had never been astride anything but a bicycle up to that time. The trailers pulled me out of the saddle at least six times. Going back they started trotting and finally running as they headed for the 'barn' two miles away and I had all I could do to hang on and holler to everybody to stay out of our way.

"When I returned, I found a telegram from Bill Fox, one from old Joe Vila and one from the editor of the *Daily Oklahoman* in Oklahoma City, all suggesting what I had just done.

"If you will look closely at the picture, you will note that Crowley is sitting a little cock-eyed in the saddle. That's because he had the makings of a fine boil on one side of his bloomers."

As Edward "Moose" Krause, a former tackle who is now director of athletics at Notre Dame, frequently observes in his public statements, "In any election by a football team, the vote will always be seven to four." The linemen feel that they do the drudge work and that is why a lineman usually becomes, in his senior year, the captain, Cinderella-style. So when horses appeared on the Notre Dame practice field and the immortals posed for posterity, the linemen, standing around, had certain things to say; and one of their jibes was livid enough to live. "We are the Seven Mules who do all the work so these four fellows can gallop to fame." Captain Adam Walsh said it when the reporters heard it. "But I don't know who originated the phrase." Nobody else has ever claimed it so perhaps Adam, who had gone into the Army game with a bone broken in one hand, and come out of it with a small bone broken in the other hand, was just being modest.

At Princeton the next week Crowley scored two touchdowns and

Miller had another called back. The score was a modest 12–0. Charlie Caldwell, later Tiger coach, played in that game and later, in his book, gave the best description of Rockne football I've read: "Never in my life have I spent such a frustrating afternoon. The final score could have been 28–0 or possibly higher. The score didn't bother me —it was the way in which Rockne's men handled us, particularly me.

"The 1924 Princeton team was a better than average Princeton team . . . Yet I felt as if we were being toyed with. I was backing up the line and I don't believe I made a clean tackle all afternoon. I would get set to drop the ball-carrier in his tracks and someone would give me a nudge, just enough to throw me off balance, just enough pressure to make me miss. . . . There was no getting around it. I had been sold—hook, line, and sinker—by Rockne football. I wanted to coach, and more important, I wanted to learn everything I could about coaching a sport in which there were apparently a hundred and one opportunities to advance new thoughts, to develop partially explored theories and to blend the traditional with the unorthodox."

What Caldwell was sensing that day was the *new* thing Rockne had created, the blend of science with the artistic urge, the refinement of the game until all brutish elements seemed removed, leaving speed, imagination, grace—wrapped in such a flawless performance that, from the press box, the scene below looked like a well-rehearsed, finished motion picture in color. The Horsemen needed and utilized *space;* they swept wide, passed overhead; wasted little of their energy on interior body-to-body smashups. But when the defense spread to contain Crowley and Miller, Layden would find daylight for jet-darts down the middle; and that's all he ever needed —daylight. Ahead of the speed and guile of the Horsemen was the offensive blocking of the Mules. Any time you see a good running attack you are almost certain to see an experienced offensive line. Guiding it all was the artisan Rockne—and at the controls his little master mechanic, Stuhldreher.

Stuhldreher missed the 34–3 win over Georgia Tech but was back for the 38–3 romp over Wisconsin. He tells something of quarterback thinking, and of player dialogue during a game, in a letter to me. "In the Wisconsin game we noticed that Captain Jack Harris who had always played fullback was then playing the right tackle slot because injuries had riddled that position. It was only natural for us to play that point; and to do that we would shift to the left with Don Miller carrying and he was having a field day. After quite a spell of this, during a time out, Crowley came to me.

" 'Harry, do you know where my home is?'

" 'Sure, Green Bay.'

" 'Do you realize that six or seven thousand people are sitting in the stadium waiting to see their favorite son play and here I haven't even had my hands on the ball yet?'

"So Jim's wish was granted and he did himself proud."

Nebraska was coming up. The jinx team. And another good, big team, out to cement a place in history by being the only school to defeat the Four Horsemen—and never to be beaten by them—in three games. This one was played at Notre Dame, where the wooden stands had been increased to around 24,000 capacity; and you can be sure that Rock left no psychological weapons lying around unused this time; and that the students would keep the boys *up*.

Back in the East, watching some inconsequential (to me, on that day) Ivy League game, I got the depressing news that Nebraska had again scored first. I feared it was going to happen again—but this time there was too much class, too much desire, too much intelligence. During the early stages Nebraska had been repeating the '23 script—breaking through to stop the Notre Dame backs before they got under way. But after Stuhldreher had been flattened a few times, he made them pay. When men come storming into the backfield they leave other stations unguarded. So Stuhldreher passed into a defensive vacuum to Crowley who zigged and zagged and eeled for 80 yards and the tying touchdown.

That began a 34–6 parade. The Nebraska coach, Fred Dawson, waxed poetic in describing it: "The Four Horsemen used what was known as the Notre Dame shift: a four-man backfield movement to the left or right—in a dainty, graceful, dancing motion which was really beautiful to see! And a second or two after the Four Horsemen had landed squarely in their new positions, the ball was snapped and away they went—no longer like dancers but with a driving burst of speed . . . It was only with the supremest effort that my Nebraska teams had the great good fortune of winning from them in very close games in 1922 and 1923."

The difference in 1924 might be a good measure of the degree a senior team can improve over its junior year—if it can avoid that dread malady called "senioritis"—a compound of boredom and over-confidence. But the "Hosses and Mules" had too much pride for that; and Rockne too much fury. Still it was to take all the talent and class of all of them to prevent disaster in the final three games.

XXXIV

Notre Dame and Northwestern had been selected to open the new Chicago lake-front stadium known as Soldiers' Field; but the 100,000 crowd did not see the hyperbolic gyrations expected of the Horse-men. The batteries may have been down after Nebraska; bodies were beginning to show injuries after weekly jousts with bigger op-ponents; but mostly it was that old enemy mud. The running team is supposed to have an advantage on an "off-track"; and that may be true of a power offense. But the team that depends on speed, sharp change of pace, nifty ball-handling is always penalized in the "goo." It had rained all week and the field had not been covered.

(There is no suggestion that this was deliberate; though the Horse-men did sometimes encounter questionable terrain. A Big Ten coach, playing at another school the week after Notre Dame, went peering through the grass, claiming to be looking for "a couple of Rockne's fast halfbacks who disappeared in the veldt.")

Tim Lowry, a fine Northwestern center, said later: "We all looked forward to taking a crack at the famous Four Horsemen and their captain, Adam Walsh, who was a great leader and a great player . . . For the most part the Four Horsemen made a complete stop after the shift, as the rules demanded; but once in our territory the stops seemed to become shorter and shorter . . . Thanks to a couple of long drop kicks by 'Moon' Baker the score was only 7–6 in favor of Notre Dame going into the tail end of the last quarter . . . Then Elmer Layden intercepted a pass about midfield and scooted along the side line for a touchdown. Joe Lipske, the head linesman, marked a spot where we thought Layden had stepped out of bounds but then Joe changed his mind. And that was the ball game."

What the Wildcats had seen was a secret weapon which Layden, with Rockne's advice and consent, had been working on for three seasons. It is an orthodox weapon called pass interception—the always dangerous boomerang to the inflationary, easy-scoring pass attack, especially treacherous when directed at exceptionally fast defenders like the Horsemen. There had been almost identical plays in the two Nebraska defeats which, if reversed, could have transformed both into Irish victories—Nebraska passes to Dave Noble which Layden had almost intercepted, with a clear field ahead. In 1922 and 1923 Elmer had not quite acquired the savvy; but he was there in the Northwestern crisis with the defensive device which meant victory.

In the final game, against Carnegie Tech at Pittsburgh, the undefeated season was again in jeopardy. At half-time the score was 13–13. Layden was hurt and into this breach came one of the frustrated fullbacks, Bernie Livergood, a pile-driving plunger, who forced the ranging secondary defense back to their positions and opened up the Stuhldreher space program. In this, their final regular season game, the Horsemen celebrated by putting on the aerial display Rockne ordinarily permitted only when the running game was stopped. They completed 15 of 19 passes in the second half and 12 were consecutive passes. The ever-present Eckersall wrote: "Defeating Carnegie Tech today on Forbes Field 40–19, Notre Dame not only won the right to be rated the strongest football team in the country but gave an exhibition of forward passing never before equaled by any eleven."

Rockne had angled for a Rose Bowl invitation after the '20 and '21 seasons. Now he was invited to bring his Horsemen to meet the West Coast champion, coached by that older Master, Glenn "Pop" Warner, inventor of the Warner system which was then the only serious rival of the Notre Dame system of play.

Rockne could have protected his undefeated season by declining. But this was a competitive natural and Rockne the Sportsman never hesitated. During the month of December both squads prepared for the fray; rested their bruises, brightened their minds, charged their batteries. In those days the Rose Bowl had the field to itself. The country awaited what was truly a national championship game.

One of the last of the rugged individualists, Rockne was a great businessman for Notre Dame and all of football; but a mighty poor one for himself. He relied on handshakes, spoken agreements, sportsmanship. (After he died the job of schedule arranging was a complex one because of the unwritten agreements he had made.) Sometimes he was naïve, but, fortunately, he did have friends who protected him. Here are three telegrams to one of his agents on the Coast:

1924 DEC 2 HAVE ACCEPTED STANFORD INVITATION AND HAVE AGREED MANAGEMENT GAME IN HANDS STANFORD WE ARE TO RECEIVE TWO THOUSAND TICKETS ONE FIFTY EACH WILL YOU HANDLE SUGGEST YOU SEE MR HENRY ROSES COMMITTEE AS TO LOCATION SEATS WILL WRITE ON ITINERARY   ROCKNE.

He received an answering phone call informing him that "the $1.50 tickets are student tickets behind the goal post at the north end of the Rose Bowl; the regular tickets are $5.00 a copy; and we have informed the Tournament of Roses Committee, that we must get better seats and not the seats he had reserved at $1.50 each."

1924 DEC 9 . . . I HAVE SIGNED NO CONTRACT WE WILL GET SAME TICKET ARRANGEMENT AS STANFORD OR NO GAME SHOW THIS WIRE TO HENRY AND TELL HIM THAT I AM TIRED OF NO WORD ON ANYTHING WE ARE NO HICK COLLEGE AND INSIST ON EQUALITY WILL WRITE REGARDS KNUTE ROCKNE.

DEC 16 . . . I HAVE WIRED DAVIS ABOUT TEN TIMES I DON'T KNOW WHETHER TICKETS ARE COMING OR NOT ARRIVE WEDNESDAY SEVEN FIFTY AM LEAVE MORNING THIRD FORTY IN PARTY MARYLAND HOTEL PASADENA ALL SET REGARDS   ROCKNE.

His California friend informs me: "Mark Kelly was then sports editor of the Los Angeles *Examiner*. Bill Curley, Jr., was learning the newspaper trade at the sports desk of the old *Evening Herald*. We had Curley and Kelly write short paragraphs stating that Notre Dame was threatening to cancel the game because of no tickets. After that we got all the tickets we could use; in fact, as you remember, USC had been kicked out of the Pacific Coast Conference and were not getting any of the Pacific Coast allotment. We even got 1000 tickets for SC."

The ticket situation, along with a thousand other irritations, undoubtedly contributed to getting Rockne "up"—the prerequisite for getting his team "up"—for the great challenge of his life. On the way out—and this may have been part of the emotional conditioning of the squad—he talked to his captain. "When Rock cried out all his troubles to me on the Rose Bowl trip I swore that I would starve to death before I would ever coach a football team and endure all the things he had to endure. I haven't been doing anything but both ever since." There, of course, is the customary self-deprecatory touch. Adam Walsh has run for Congress, coached a world's championship pro team (the Rams), and earned other honors in football.

XXXV

In the early days of the Rose Bowl the Eastern team always faced two bugaboos: the hot weather and the change of climate. The Horsemen were to practice, as was customary, on Friday afternoon. Rip Miller recalls one of the Master's most scintillating ratiocinations: "Remember the 'delayed' auto tour which did not get us into the stadium until after sundown? I can still hear him selling the delightful *cool* weather in California. Of course, the next afternoon, it was hot as hell; but the Fox had accomplished his mission. We had slept well the night before and did not worry before the game about how hot it was going to be."

The game itself is often replayed in the "bull sessions" of gridiron reminiscence. Here are the highlights:

Rockne started his shock troops, as usual; but the pressure was heavy and the regulars came in much earlier than was customary. Stanford recovered a fumble on the Irish 15; and on fourth down Cuddleback scored a place kick from the 17-yard line to give Stanford a 3–0 lead. After the kickoff the Horsemen began to function. The first march carried to the Stanford 12 where the ball was lost. They were back on the Stanford 7-yard line when the period ended;

but tackle Joe Bach, one of the stoutest of the Seven Mules, had to leave the game with broken ribs. He was replaced by sophomore Joe Boland who played most of the game and lost 16 pounds. (Joe was to become a unique stone in the Notre Dame structure. He bore a remarkable facial resemblance to Rockne, became line coach under Elmer Layden, vice-president of the national Alumni Association, and, as a football telecaster on all major networks, a household name. When the Voice of the Irish was suddenly stilled by a heart attack early in 1960, I lost an oft-proved friend whose last service was an important contribution to this book. Joe Boland lived faithfully in the Rockne tradition of loyalty, simplicity, intelligence, charm, courage, and truth.)

Layden scored over right tackle. Crowley's point-after attempt was blocked and Notre Dame led 6–3.

Stanford came raging like a forest fire in a canyon, used its bull-dozer wing attack that ate ground in short gulps; but at the 20-yard line the quarterback called a surprise play which might have won the game for Stanford if it had worked—and probably did win it for Notre Dame. Nevers threw a flat pass toward his left end Ship-key; but now the secret weapon was well-oiled, cocked, and ready. Layden intercepted on his 15-yard line and ran 85 yards to the touch-down which, with Crowley's kick, gave Notre Dame a half-time edge 13–3.

This was only the beginning of what is known in Rose Bowl, Notre Dame, and Stanford tradition as Layden's Day. In the third quarter he punted from his 25-yard line to the Stanford 20. Solomon, otherwise a solid operator as the lead blocker for the Nevers plunges, fumbled; and end Ed Hunsinger, the one-time Interhall player who reached his peak this day, recovered and ran for a touchdown. Crowley kicked and the score was now a comfortable 20–3. But not safe.

Big Ernie Nevers, whom Pop Warner had placed ahead of Jim Thorpe on his all-time All-American (he had coached both) had been plagued all year with bad ankles; but they were plaguing Notre Dame this day. Stanford again pierced deep into Notre Dame territory. Now, with a 20–3 lead, and against a dangerous team, Stuhldreher violated ordinary Notre Dame strategy by passing. Nevers intercepted; and later passed to Shipkey for the touchdown which made it Notre Dame 20 Stanford 10; and put the Indians back in the ball game.

Rockne vindicated Stuhldreher with an inside explanation which should make every grandstand quarterback think a little before he criticizes the strategy of the men on the field: "The fact is that Stuhldreher had hurt his foot badly; we didn't know until the game was over that he had broken a bone and was suffering agony. Even this circumstance could not excuse passing on third down at that stage with his team leading. But Hunsinger, our right end, had told Stuhldreher that the Stanford halfback who should be covering him, did not follow him deeply into the scoring zone. So Stuhldreher called the indicated pass. Sure enough Hunsinger got into the clear, ready to race for the touchdown on receipt of the ball. A 45-yard pass would have done the trick and ordinarily that would have been a simple pass for Stuhldreher. But this time, as the plucky little quarterback squared himself to shoot, bringing down the foot with the broken bone to make his stance, excruciating pain shot through him, so that instead of his usual vigorous throw the ball sailed a feeble twenty yards.

"Yet Stuhldreher's tactics were sound—for so good a ball-thrower. Even if Hunsinger had failed to catch the ball and it had been intercepted, a 45-yard pass would have been useful as a punt. An incompleted pass would not have hurt because Layden was there to kick on the next down. And what a kicker Layden was that day! The entire team had wilted in the heat. They had to rely on Layden's punting, not their usual game."

Stanford, led by Nevers, was more accustomed to the heat. Down, down the field the Warner attack moved until there was first down on the two-yard line. A touchdown here and the rampaging Indians would be extremely dangerous.

That Rose Bowl goal-line stand is one of the peaks of Notre Dame football history. I think that every man in the lineup that day really believes that he had a piece of one of Nevers' legs during the next heroic four downs. But if this was the ball game, and all that rode with it, I have always thought it was won by perhaps the supreme demonstration of Rockne's ability to think under extreme pressure; to know his men and what to expect of each. In this situation he sent in a third-string tackle, John McMullen. In those days a substitute couldn't communicate until after the first play. McMullen got his bulk before Nevers. It was fourth down and one-foot. Stuhldreher chuckles: "We all rushed around John for the much needed help and information. 'What did Rock say?'

"'Rock said hold 'em.'"

Which is exactly what Big John did—thereby earning himself a place somewhere near Johnny One-Play O'Brien. This is my theory on the substitution: McMullen was one of those soft-spoken, mild-appearing powerful Irishmen who exploded in competition; but lacked that mental poise which Rockne always preached. Poise was not going to stop Nevers on the one-foot line. What was needed was a big guy who would explode. And Big John did.

Nevers is one of the most completely respected foes of Notre Dame through the years. Joe Boland, who was a prominent Horatius at this gridiron Thermopylae, raved: "I'll never forget that man. In my book he played football's greatest game that day, on two ankles that had been broken earlier in the year." Rockne said: "Nevers could do everything. He tore our line to shreds, ran the ends, forward-passed, and kicked. True, we held him on the one-yard line for four downs but by that time he was exhausted; and I sent in two fresh guards and a fresh tackle."

The game had not ended. Layden kicked out and Stanford came back. With time running out, and Nevers on the bench, the quarterback called for a pass—the flat pass again—this time thrown by Ed Walker (contrary to some accounts, Nevers did *not* throw the second pass) and again Layden, just beginning to learn how to use his secret weapon, intercepted and ran 60 yards for his third touchdown. Crowley made the point, which put a period to the most glamorous team that is ever likely to pound the turf in whatever years history may have left for college football.

Nevers was quoted: "I was very impressed with the perfect precision of the ballet-like shift of the Four Horsemen. Their speed and timing as a unit has never been equaled in the history of football . . . Sleepy Jim (a nuisance if there ever was one) Crowley had a wonderful change of pace evidenced by his ability to slice through a hole sideways. Elmer Layden, though on the light side and not a power runner, had speed and agility to cut most effectively through the

line. Miller was a very dangerous runner on reverses. Stuhldreher
was small and cocky but oh what a brainy quarterback."

After the game Stuhldreher revealed his broken foot. Crowley
went to a hospital suffering from exhaustion. (Like Rock, I don't
think Jimmy ever had any lost time due to football injury.) Rockne
called Crowley "the nerviest back I've ever known, the greatest in-
terferer for his weight I've ever seen, and a particularly effective
ball-carrier on the critical third down." There were the usual California postgame arguments: "Nevers was over on the fourth down;
Stanford outgained Notre Dame two-to-one from scrimmage and
made many more first downs." From his hospital bed Crowley uttered his valedictory as the official wit: "Next year in the major
leagues they aren't going to count the runs that come over—just the
bases on balls."

Seven of the 24 monogram men of the '24 squad are dead. They
included, in addition to Joe Boland, by coincidence, the two first-
string guards—Dr. John Weibel and Noble Kizer, coach and athletic
director at Purdue; and the two third-string halfbacks, Max Hauser
and "Doc" Connell. The others were Dr. Wilbur Eaton, and a
second-string guard, Vince Harrington, who, in 1942, resigned a Congressional seat (Iowa) to accept a commission in the Air Force.
Major Harrington died in England during the war.

The Four Horsemen, indestructible as ever, still ride as good
friends. They appear together about thirty times each year. Attorney
Miller is their "legal representative" but claims they give him as
much trouble as his incurable slice. "Nothing I do is ever right," he
laughed. Layden is an executive of the General American Transportation Company of Chicago. Crowley is in television, the coal
business and, for relaxation, boxing commissioner of Pennsylvania.
Stuhldreher is an assistant to the vice-president of U. S. Steel. They
still block for one another. "Crowley sometimes calls to sell us some
coal," Stuhlie chuckled. (When my young fellow, whom Crowley
had carried to St. Patrick's Cathedral in New York, turned up at
U. S. Steel looking for a job, Stuhldreher did some valuable quarterbacking.)

The night before a Notre Dame-Navy game in Cleveland, Miller
and Crowley were reminiscing. Don, father of five daughters, was
boasting that his first son, though only a few months old, was already

so tough he had thrown a block through a window that very day. "I am glad," Crowley said, "to finally hear of a Miller who can throw a block."

After a Notre Dame victory over Army, I went with Coach Layden and Joe Byrne on a few of those social calls the coach diplomatically makes on influential people who might be thinking of giving a building to the school. These over, we found ourselves in the neighborhood of Jimmy Crowley, then coaching at Fordham. George Vergara was there and they were happy because Fordham had also won. It so happened that out in Madison, Wisconsin, Coach Stuhldreher was celebrating a Wisconsin victory. So the three Old Horsemen had a fine time congratulating each other by phone. Later that evening Layden and Crowley sang the "Victory March," and cold sober too, at Jack White's rowdy-dowdy old Club 19.

Don Miller is one of those optimists who thinks just about anybody is "the best guy in two shoes." When he was U. S. District Attorney in Cleveland he was considered as a prosecutor for the Nuremberg Trials. But one of his small daughters objected: "Daddy—you can't. Before it was over you'd be saying Goering was the best guy in two shoes." I was once driving a new car from Cleveland to Notre Dame for a Minnesota game. Don Miller, my passenger, was reading the morning paper. On a good stretch of road I let the car out. "We just hit ninety," I said, which was high adventure to me. The speedy Horseman just continued to read the paper.

The five Millers of Notre Dame must be the most remarkable family in football history. Harry, recently retired from the legal department of the Du Pont Company, is the only All-American I know who has sired a son of equal stature—Creighton, who made it in 1943 under Frank Leahy. But with them, as everybody else, time gets in its charming little licks. At a recent Notre Dame class reunion I was in a car with Don, Gerry, and Walter. It was Gerry who said: "If anybody had told me that on the Friday night of my 30th Reunion I would be going downtown to South Bend looking for the best dish of ice cream—"

Gridiron goobers of the future, perhaps perusing such ancient lore as this, would have reason for thinking that Jack F. Rissman, though he cannot be found among the lists, must have stood very tall indeed among the immortals. Does his name not lead all the rest in the great trophies emblematic of national championships? It does, indeed. But I have news for posterity: To the best of my knowledge Jack F. Rissman was just a Chicago sportsman who was smart enough to get in on the ground floor of a very good thing.

Previous to 1924 the awarding of the national championship had been a matter of contentious debate. Rissman decided to put up a trophy to go to the team which would be scientifically picked by the Dickensen system of rating (later replaced by the Associated Press poll). It was to be retired by the school which first won it three times; and since it was Rissman's money, the trophy wound up with the name of the donor.

Presumably, it was also his idea; but there is a version which has the suggestion coming from the great Rockne, who won the first leg in '24, and retired it in 1930, just before his death. Notre Dame then provided the Knute K. Rockne Trophy which was retired by Minnesota in 1940. Minnesota put up the Dr. Henry L. Williams Trophy, in honor of its great coach who was the first prominent exponent of the shifting offense. Notre Dame retired the Williams Trophy in 1947 and offered the Reverend J. Hugh O'Donnell Trophy, honoring the 1914–15 center who became wartime president of the university. Oklahoma won possession in 1956; after which the Associated Press, whose annual poll still decides the winner, took over permanent sponsorship. Here is a quick glance at gridiron history:

RISSMAN TROPHY

1924	Notre Dame
1925	Dartmouth
1926	Stanford
1927	Illinois
1928	Southern California
1929	Notre Dame
1930	Notre Dame

ROCKNE TROPHY

1931	Southern California
1932	Michigan
1933	Michigan
1934	Minnesota

1935	Southern Methodist
1936	Minnesota
1937	Pittsburgh
1938	Notre Dame
1939	Southern California
1940	Minnesota

WILLIAMS TROPHY

1941	Minnesota
1942	Ohio State
1943	Notre Dame
1944	Army
1945	Army
1946	Notre Dame
1947	Notre Dame

O'DONNELL TROPHY

1948	Michigan
1949	Notre Dame
1950	Oklahoma
1951	Tennessee
1952	Michigan State
1953	Maryland
1954	Ohio State
1955	Oklahoma
1956	Oklahoma

ASSOCIATED PRESS TROPHY

1957	Auburn
1958	Louisiana State
1959	Syracuse

(Several other National Championship Trophies have been offered in recent years by responsible groups; but in most cases they all seem to agree on the winner. The AP Trophy has the same prestige of lineage that the Rose Bowl has over other Bowls; and that the *Collier's* All-American had until the magazine ceased publication in 1956. And, if I may, that the Francis Wallace Football Preview had over its field.)

XXXVI

After 1924 Father Sorin's "tight little boarding school" had become a national toast; and was on its way to becoming a great university. This would have happened in due time, regardless of football, because Notre Dame, of the French name and Irish background, is an almost fiercely American institution whose religious and geographical aspects have, from the earliest years, drawn vital students from all sections of the country. But it began with such a startling rush in the twenties because of the accidental presence of a homely, bald young Norwegian who had within him a tempestuous *jev* which so desperately wanted *ud*.

Rockne himself had no more idea of what was gestating within him than does any other bomb which ticks away in a suitcase. Those of us who were close to him at the time saw him as an intriguing, complex, attractive personality and a great football coach who had, in his seven years, won 60 games, lost four, and tied three. We knew that the compulsory disarmament by graduation had taken his entire 1924 starting eleven, seven men from his shock troops, five from his third team. Losing 23 of the first 33 would admittedly be a staggering blow to any coach. But Rockne wasn't *any* coach. We were inclined to share the sublime faith of the public in the ability of this gridiron Vulcan to hammer out, to order, another Gipp, another Four Horsemen, or some new fantastic compound of speed, brains, and courage from whatever human material was available.

When the Viking protested that he must lose several games in 1925, we smiled. And it seemed that he had been crying wolf, as usual, when the season began with a 41–0 win over Baylor and a 69–0 rout of Lombard. The 19–3 over Beloit should have been the tipoff, but it was thought that the team had merely idled that day, in preparation for Army the following week.

Rockne had obviously, and for the third time, hammered a group of sophomores into an invincible unit. With the victory string now at 16, and three more seasons to go with the new boys, where could it end? This was what New York was thinking when Notre Dame came to town. And because of the appetite for tickets, the game had been transferred to the Yankee Stadium—the fourth change of locale in as many years. South Bend had become aware of the bonanza on its doorstep, and this year the Studebaker Corporation had provided a fleet of convertibles to drive the squad from the old Belmont Hotel to the Stadium.

Army 27 Notre Dame 0.

It was the first Army victory since 1916 and the biggest score any school was ever to make against Rockne. The Cadets, with Light Horse Harry Wilson (Penn State), Tiny Hewitt (Pitt), and other imports from other colleges, were so good that a plebe named Christian Cagle, who had come from a small college in Louisiana, did little more than get his name in the lineup.

There were good men on that Irish squad—Flanagan, Edwards, Hearndon, O'Boyle, Parasien, Boland, Boeringer, Poliski, Smith, and Captain Clem Crowe, first of another famous family of Notre Dame athletes. They were met by the entire student body which had arisen at five o'clock and trudged three miles through heavy snow to the railroad station which has seen so much of dramatic Notre Dame history. The squad reacted, as Rockne squads had always done, 19-7 over Minnesota and 13-0 over Georgia Tech.

The next week, in the dressing room at Penn State, in the middle of his speech, Rockne burst out crying. It was miserable weather on a miserable field in the Pennsylvania mountains. The collapse of the strong-man coach left the squad emotionally numb, too. The score 0-0.

"What must you think of me?" Rock asked Joe Byrne and a few other friends.

"We think you're human, like the rest of us," Joe said. "And you'd better start to think so, too." That evening the party had to spend some time in Tyrone, Pennsylvania, awaiting a train. They wanted to shake Rock out of his deep depression. The handiest diversion was a shooting gallery. The shaken Rock took a shot, missed all the ducks, hit the supporting rod, knocked it loose—and all the ducks came tumbling down.

"What a shot," Rock laughed. It had been a miraculous tonic. He was out of it.

There was the usual strong reaction, 26–0 over Carnegie Tech; but at half-time the next week, the score was Northwestern 10 Notre Dame 0—and the Irish were facing the first defeat at home in twenty years; and under circumstances most disheartening. The events of that weekend have been among the most discussed, and most often distorted, of the legend. I will give you the facts from the people involved. And now we take you to the Notre Dame dressing room and regular tackle Joe Boland:

"We waited . . . and waited . . . *and* waited . . . in that silent, stuffy locker room . . . for Rockne to appear and to tell us what we had been doing wrong: to right it, as he usually did. But . . . no Rockne! He let us stew in our own mental juices until *after* the official had notified us we had just three minutes to kickoff.

"Not until then did he burst into the room. And, *burst* is the word! With his eyes almost popping . . . the cords in his thick neck standing out . . . and, his lower jaw projecting as he spoke, he addressed us like this: 'Hah! Fighting Irish, are you? . . . You look more like peaceful Swedes, to me! You . . . can have the honor of dandling your grandchildren on your knees . . . and . . . telling them . . . that *you* . . . played on the first team that ever *quit* . . . at Notre Dame! I'm through with you! I'm going to sit in the stands for the second half—'

"And . . . he strode out of the locker room!

"We almost broke down the door, scrambling for that field, for the start of the second half. Northwestern kicked-off . . . and, we moved 75 yards—on the ground!—without using an end run or forward pass!—to a touchdown. Then, the 'Cats—why, I'll never know! —kicked-off to us again . . . while we were still white-hot! Again, a steady march to another touchdown—again, no passes—all, slogged-out along-the-ground—and Northwestern was defeated 13 to 10! During that first march I took a quick peek at the side lines—there was Rock, hidden among the substitutes, twirling his cigar, taking it all in."

The star of the resurgence was fullback Rex Enright, one of the Layden shadows who had had the foresight to drop out of school for a year and return. Enright became a sort of Rockne at South Carolina. Shortly before his death in 1960, Rex wrote me a letter (with the customary modesty and self-deprecation) which is typical of the feeling the old boys have for their coach:

"A lot of water has gone over the dam since the days of Rock. My great love for him and the tremendous impression he made on my life have remained with me through the years. After many years of coaching I realize more and more the greatness of Rock.

"The terrible performance we were exhibiting on this particular occasion and our failing Rock at the time was heartbreaking. I am sure this had a great influence on our playing in the third quarter in which we scored two touchdowns. If you check the records you will find that Rockne had accepted the Catholic faith and taken his First Communion on the morning of this same Northwestern game in 1925." The conclusion seems obvious. The boys had undoubtedly decided among themselves to win that one for Rockne. As sometimes happens when emotion runs strong, they had probably been trying *too* hard in the first half. Rock's between-halves sarcasm had relieved all tightness, made them mad at themselves. The boy who got maddest of all, Enright, was not a Catholic.

Like all things close to him, religion was a subject Rockne rarely discussed. At the time of his death a football-coaching colleague, probably a non-Catholic, was quoted: "Rockne, while a great josher and humorist, had a serious side in which belief in right and loyalty to that belief were paramount. It never was generally known but Rockne was a Scottish Rite Mason until he left that order to become a member of the Catholic Church and after that step no more loyal Catholic ever lived. It involved a side of Rockne with which few were conversant and one day when a question of religion was mentioned, I said: 'Rock, it is so seldom a man takes such a step as you have, and one so seldom thinks of you in connection with such things, I wonder if you would mind telling me why you did that?'

"He hesitated just a moment and then answered quietly: 'Why should I mind telling you? You know, all this hurrying and battling we're going through is just an expression of our inner selves striving to find something better. The way I look at it, we're all here to try and find, each in his own way, the best road to our ultimate goal. I believe I've found my way and I shall travel it to the ultimate end.'"

Rock had taken Catholic instructions from Rev. Vincent Mooney, one of his former players and a close friend. Father Mooney, long associated with the Catholic Youth Movement, writes from Holy Rosary Rectory in Columbus, Ohio:

"I baptized him in the Old Log Chapel at Notre Dame, Friday, Nov. 20, 1925. His First Communion was in St. Edward's Hall, then the habitat of Father Sorin's Cadets. Bill and Knute, Jr., were kids in St. Ed's Grade School. Knute, Jr., made his first Communion Saturday morning, November 21, at the six o'clock Mass. To his surprise his dad marched down the aisle with him and knelt with him at the Communion rail. Tim Galvin, Chick Bader, and Al Ryan were on hand for the occasion."

Rev. John W. Cavanaugh, who knew Rock as a student, appointed him coach and edited his autobiography, wrote: "What the Catholic faith has meant to the Irish since the beginning of the fifth century, the Augsburg Confession has for four centuries meant to old-fashioned Lutherans generally, and most particularly, to the forebears of Rockne in the Scandinavian country. Two sets of influences had been working in his mind . . .

"Rockne's First Communion was an incident beautiful to the little group who witnessed it. Father Mooney arranged that Knute, Jr., should be at the end of the little procession moving to the altar in order that the stalwart father might walk beside his son. That Rockne had been baptized the day before was unknown generally on the campus; even the boys of his own family were not aware of it. When, therefore, Rockne stepped along at the side of his second son, the little fellow turned to his father and said: 'Daddy, don't you know you can't come with me; only Catholics receive Communion.' In such a public place and at such a solemn moment Rockne could not take 'time-out' for explanation; he affected not to hear. But a moment later Knute, Jr., said very earnestly: 'Daddy, you don't seem to understand; you can't receive Holy Communion. You're not a Catholic.'

"Out of the corner of his mouth Rockne whispered: 'It's all right. Father Mooney will tell you all about it.' When finally both arrived at the Communion rail Knute, Jr., looked questioningly at his father, then at Father Mooney. The padre was holding the Consecrated Host over the ciborium and he too found it an inappropriate time for explanations beyond whispering: 'Everything's all right, Junior; your Dad was baptized yesterday.' The moment was most touching."

The postscript to the autobiography gave this fragment of a speech

delivered by Rockne to a group of business and professional men at
the conclusion of the Laymen's Retreat at Notre Dame in the summer
of 1929: "One night before a big game in the East I was worried and
nervous about the outcome the next day and was unable to sleep. I
tossed and rolled and finally decided to get up and sit downstairs.
About five or six o'clock in the morning, while pacing the lobby, I
unexpectedly ran into two of my players hurrying out.

"I asked them where they were going at such an hour, though I
had an idea. Within the next few minutes my players continued
hurrying out and I decided to go along with them. They didn't realize
it but these youngsters were making a powerful impression on me
with their devotion, and when I saw all of them walking up to the
Communion rail to receive, and realized the hours of sleep they had
sacrificed, I understood for the first time what a powerful ally their
religion was to their work on the football field. Later on I had the
happiness of joining my boys at the Communion rail."

Rockne's reported membership in the Masonic fraternity is typical
of the confusions, usually caused by bad reporting, that grow in the
legends of the celebrated. I had accepted the report quoted above;
but in making routine inquiries could find no confirmation. Jesse
Harper never heard of it and writes: "And I think I would have
known." Father Mooney says: "I discussed that with him just once.
What the exact status was I do not know; but when I outlined the
Church's teaching he said: 'I'll buy that.'"

Just before his death Jay Wyatt told me: "I'm a Mason; but if Rock
was, I never knew about it. Once I came down to the campus to
sell him some athletic equipment. He noticed I was not wearing my
Masonic pin and asked where it was. I told him I had lost it. He
said: 'Now—you don't have to take it off just because you come to a
Catholic campus.'"

For the record I asked my old friend, Charles McElroy, Recorder
of Osiris Temple in Wheeling, West Virginia, for help. Later I received this note: "With reference to our conversation early in May,
I have authoritative information that Knute Rockne was never a
member of the Masonic Fraternity nor a Master Mason."

Religion must have been a continuing turmoil to this tempestuous
man. He had been exposed to Catholic philosophy; to that powerful
"soft-sell," the quiet example of devout Catholic men. He lived in

a Catholic home, was devoted to his family; and he was ever a man fiercely loyal to those closest to him. But there was the older loyalty to his first family and his earlier faith. It is my belief that he did not become a Catholic until he felt he had received clearance; and that the decision must have brought peace to this sector of his embattled mind. The essence of Catholic faith is that the soul, having come from God, is forever flying against the obstacles of life, in its desire to return to the happiness it can only find in the sight of God.

But there must have been little peace within Rockne the week after the tremendous comeback against Northwestern.

The team closed out its season—or was closed out—with a 17-0 defeat by the old nemesis Nebraska. The final record was seven victories, two defeats, one tie. It was a good record for a sophomore squad; and highly acceptable for any squad at most schools. But this was Rockne. He had lost two games in one season for the first time. There had also been an unexpected tie. Three times during the season Rockne had failed to do the thing which most set him apart from other coaches—pump enough of himself into a failing squad to bring it up to par.

Was Rockne human, after all? Had he passed his peak—and begun the slow descent to the coaching limbo which eventually engulfed the best of them, which, in the nature of humans, made every hero into a bore?

Yes—and no!

XXXVII

The 1925 season was the first indication that the third quarter of the wizard's career would bring the same troubles that come, logically and inevitably, to any successful man in any category. Little of the difficulty would come from his professional know-how or philosophy. It would come from his opponents, from his friends, from himself. The law of averages also operates against genius; and even more so, the laws of nature. These clouds had been looming and growing; '25 had merely dropped the first rain:

1. Opposing coaches had begun to regroup, to pack against this inordinate man. They had scouted him intensively, compared their notes, worked out joint defenses. Some operated through the Rules Committee to slow down his shift. He had compensated successfully enough against each such legislative move, but he was being forced to use heavier backs, and that meant giving up some speed. The full effect would be noted in the difference in average backfield weight between the Four Horsemen (164) and the 1929–30 group of Carideo, Savoldi, Schwartz, Brill (187).

2. High-school stars, eager to go to Notre Dame and become "a Four Horseman" were being met with this successfully persuasive argument from other coaches: "Why go to Notre Dame and sit on the bench—like all those good men who subbed for the Horsemen and Mules—and were never heard of? Come to our school, where we are not flooded with All-Americans, play regularly, and maybe make All-American." This argument seemed to have been especially effective with backfield men. It is a fact that in the 1925–28 period, Rockne produced no great backfield; and only two backfield "names" ranked high in the tradition: Christy Flanagan and John "Butch" Niemiec.

3. The pressures of success, which break so many men, were mounting within him. They were, in addition to the abnormally heavy demands of his many activities and lack of help at Notre Dame:

   a. Other schools were continually attempting to lure him away. He was continually being tempted. This developed an internal situation within the family at Notre Dame—already disturbed by the growing identification of Rockne as "Mr. Notre Dame." It also exposed prep-school talent to the argument: "Why go to Notre Dame to play for Rockne—if he's going to one of these other schools? He could move but you would be stuck."

   b. He was constantly taking on more outside activities: coaching schools, lecture dates, newspaper, magazine, radio work, motion picture shorts. As the stipends for these increased, he became increasingly incensed because he felt that a business manager with whom he had become involved was taking an unfair percentage for work that came to Rockne *because he was Rockne*—and not through the efforts of the manager.

4. Even such a tough body, vigorous mind, and vibrant nerves as Rockne's were, with advancing age, beginning to feel the strain of all the self-flagellation imposed by a man whose flaming temperament and passion for perfection magnified nuisances and irritations into world wars. Added to all this was poison from bad tonsils which he knew about but did nothing about—until later years.

5. As a result of all the foregoing, these things, which had been developing imperceptibly, were beginning to surface in 1925:

a. The supply of talent, especially backfield, had been tailing off; notably at the all-important position of quarterback—the "coach on the field." There was no "name" here between Stuhl-dreher ('24) and Carideo ('29).

b. Rockne, with so much on his mind, may not have given either the same amount of time or thought to his coaching. He may have (and how he would land on me for even suggesting this) unconsciously begun to slough off both the pursuit of talent, and its actual coaching.

c. Most important, as his health deteriorated, he no longer had the excess vitality and force necessary to keep a team at the victory level of the first half (1918–24) of his coaching career.

This is a hind-sight analysis. I could see an occasional moment when he seemed to show unaccustomed weakness, but the glances were brief. A perceptive junior on his squad did tell me in '25: "The Swede is not himself." But to the public in '25 he was still Superman, perhaps slowed down a little by sophomores. The public knew nothing about the locker-room collapse at Penn State in '25, and to my knowledge, it has never previously been in print.

But those in the locker room saw it for what it was. Immediately they insisted Rockne should take a rest when the season ended. His own state of fear is detected by the fact that he agreed. Florida was the first idea, but it was decided he should go to Europe, for a complete change of scene—and separation from his own propensity to get involved in the affairs of anybody who happened along, asking for help.

On January 26, 1926, Rockne sailed for Europe with Joe and Marie Byrne on the *DeGrasse*. When Byrne asked about his trunk, Rock jibed: "Who needs a trunk?" He had a suitcase which held a dinner coat, an extra business suit and enough other items to get by. On the boat he rested for a few days; but when he learned Helen Wills, the tennis champion, was aboard, he became her fan; and in her matches with Suzanne Lenglen he rooted for the American girl in American fashion; even did what he never did in football—criticized the officials.

In Paris he was surprised and delighted to discover that they knew about him. "He was a king among the Americans," Byrne said, "very big around Harry's Bar. As usual, he was available to all comers; and the word got around among the freeloaders. They would line up for him—and, as always, he was a soft touch."

The French made much out of the fact that he coached at *Notre Dame*. In return, with his flair for words, Rock spoke guidebook French, always ordered in French, made a big thing out of it. *Epinard* was easy because of the race horse of that name; but a clever scoundrel used Epinard as an entree, passed himself off as a very dear friend of Harry Sinclair, the owner of Zev, the American horse; and wound up by putting what the race-track people would call "a large bite" on Rockne. He became very friendly with the members of a band; but two of them were alumni of Nebraska. He spoke of the high grass on the football field and other distinguishing if undistinguished landmarks of Nebraska; they frequently played the Nebraska school song.

The triumphal tour continued in London. On the homeward boat were people he had met abroad. He enjoyed his vacation very much, including the press interview when he got to America—up to the point where somebody asked him about his religion. The immediate transformation came, the power in the eyes, the scythe in the voice, the blowtorch reaction: "And who the hell's business is that but mine?"

"There were tears in his eyes," Joe Byrne said, "when he took the train for home. He said: 'You don't know what this has done for me.' He was rested, ready to explode again. I think what really pleased him was the realization that he was an international celebrity. He needed that for his morale at that time."

Rock once told somebody he had a half-dozen friends and a million acquaintances. Jay Wyatt was one of the friends, Leo Ward another, Dr. Leo O'Donnell, and Joe Byrne certainly. Joe was the man Rock called in the early days when things needed to be done in the East; and Joe was much involved in the early Army games. The press gave him a title "Eastern representative of Notre Dame" which of course, was not true, though there was considerable truth in it. He was certainly Eastern representative of Rockne and he did many things for the university, which later made him a member of its Board of Lay Trustees.

As a former president of the Alumni Association I can truthfully say that the Notre Dame Alumni Club of New York has long been a strong and healthy group; but in the early days there were, perhaps, some unduly aggressive spirits who, Rock thought, had made an unequitable distribution of Army game tickets. When they also seemed to show a lack of appreciation of the services of his friend Joe Byrne, Rockne declared one of his world wars; but he was never scornful of a well-intended olive branch. So about 1926 I had a call from John Balfe, head of a new group of officers. Rockne was coming to town, they wanted to repair the breach, did I have any ideas about how to handle it? I did; but in settling one feud, I unwittingly set up another.

We set up a dinner at the Roosevelt Hotel. Rock, with his usual bewildering modesty, asked me what he should talk about. This corresponded, roughly, to Ingemar Johansson asking his secretary how to punch. I suggested that, since this was the off-season and sports news was scarce, it might be a good opportunity to give his side of the argument about shift legislation. He warmed to that. I invited all important sports writers; and to make sure the Press Associations gave it good coverage, had Rockne speak first. His speech blanketed the country the next day and delayed legislation for that year.

Westbrook Pegler was there, absorbing impressions for a column which appeared in 1930. It was one of Pegler's kinder efforts but it undoubtedly irritated Rockne more than any other single piece of writing—because it touched on certain things Rock thought nobody's business but his own. Here are excerpts of the column which, ironically, at the time, was called "Nobody's Business."

"New York, Dec. 13—At my first glimpse of him, close-up, Knute Rockne had the look of the old, punched-up preliminary fighter who becomes doortender in a speakeasy and sits in a shadowy table in a corner near the door at night, recalling the time he fought Billy

Papke in Peoria for $50. His nose is a bit mashed and his skull is more nude than otherwise. Maybe he was a preliminary fighter. I have heard so, but have never thought to ask him about it.

"On this night, several years ago, he was sitting at the head of a table in a small, compact and chummy gathering of New York alumni of the University of Notre Dame, nervously gulping draughts of smoke from a soggy cigar butt. Frank Wallace, then a recent alumnus of the university, who has lately written a football novel called *Huddle* about Rockne and the Notre Dame teams, was the master of such little ceremonies as there were. He would cast an eye about the room and light upon some cringing and apprehensive victim and say, 'And now we are going to hear from Brother So-and-So.'

"It was not until Brother Wallace—they were all brother to one another—called upon Brother Rockne for some remarks that Brother Rockne began to justify his reputation. He spoke in a jerky manner, as though he felt it was all nonsense for him to try to enlighten or entertain these fellow alumni of his, but there was a light of humor in his eyes and a plain, frank intelligence in his comments and, altogether, it was like an old, battered oil can giving champagne.

"I have mentioned the drinks at this meeting merely because drinks are customary at all alumni jollifications and at most reunions of the old athletes, including the coaches. But I am sure that anyone who really wants to know whether Knute Rockne likes a drink can find out by asking him. On the morality of liquor he is a liberal, unlike Mr. Stagg and Mr. Yost who take prohibition seriously and even testify to its fine effects.

"I see Mr. Rockne as a modest man who does not think much of himself, who is constantly amazed to find himself a great national celebrity, and who therefore wants to make all the money he can while he can, lest the public suddenly get next to him. He has a certain kind of confidence but not much assurance, as though always apprehensive that someone will put him to the necessity of proving that he is a great man. Sometimes, when he predicts that his team will lose a football game, he merely wants to tighten up his players, but I imagine that most times, when he says such things, that he is actually low-rating his own as he privately low-rates himself.

"If he were fully assured of his importance he would not burden himself with some of the obligations he constantly assumes. Last winter, in Florida, for instance, some promoter imposed on Rockne's reputation to declare a 'Knute Rockne Night' at a dog track . . . On another day, although it was dangerous for him to be on his feet, some high-school principal prevailed upon him to visit the school and address the students on sport. The compliment, he thought, deserved the sacrifice, and it was not long after this that he was on his way back home to see his doctor about a relapse.

"Gradually Mr. Rockne has changed into a showman and this has necessitated some little changes in his natural character for the platform appearances . . . If the public insists on regarding him as one of the greatest Americans of his time and paying him a fortune for chattering the same sort of conversation that he normally gives away by the hour to his friends, far be it from Mr. Rockne to dispute the customers or refuse their money."

Brother Pegler fancied it up here and there. Rock was already fluent in delivery; and the master of ceremonies also had a polished diction—none of them there Brothers—but the plug for *Huddle* was much appreciated. The column precipitated a violent feud. I was in the middle, tried to explain each to the other, once got them to shake hands—but it broke out worse than ever. Actually they were blood brothers, in the very area which made them clash—a gentle, sensitive, kind personality under the abrasive cover.

Rock's feud with Yost was imbedded in the ancient situation with Michigan when Rock was a freshman in 1910. Yost was still the demon to my student generation; so I was surprised, one day in 1939, to meet him in Layden's office. I accompanied them on a tour of the campus and we came to the foyer of the Rockne Memorial. There's a bust of Rockne there, a grim and fearsome bronze, a wide miss on his personality, but the face he had probably always turned to Yost. Yost just stood and looked for quite a while. Rock glared back. Layden, Jack Lavelle, and I said nothing. This was drama of a sort.

The following year (1940) I was a speaker at the Heisman Memorial Dinner when Tom Harmon of Michigan won the coveted trophy. Yost and Fritz Crisler were on the dais. I told the story of Yost's visit to Notre Dame and said I thought I had witnessed the end of the feud between two of football's toughest and greatest men. It was a bit on the delicate, daring side, since I had never cozied

187

up to Yost and did not know how he would react. After the dinner he sought me out—and thanked me for saying what I had. So, you see, there is quite a bit of Notre Dame-Michigan tradition, though mostly submerged, like icebergs.

XXXVIII

Being known as a friend of Rockne did a young fellow absolutely no harm around New York. I had moved to the New York *Post* where I covered football, boxing and baseball. A representative of the Polo Grounds asked me if I could do anything about getting the Army game moved back to their field from the Yankee Stadium. He said there would be a fur coat in it for my wife if I could swing it. He didn't say mink and he might have meant rabbit. I knew that Rock preferred the Polo Grounds. There seemed to be no moral issue involved, so I wrote Rock, and included the item of the coat. I had a very nice, almost apologetic letter. "As I told you, the playing field at the Polo Grounds is much better for our type of football; but the Army-Navy game will be played at the Polo Grounds next year and the Army people don't want to get into any political jam by having both games at the same grounds. Needless to say, of course, I regret this tough break very much."

I had broken into the magazine field with an article in *Scribner's Magazine*, titled "The Hypocrisy of Football Reform." It told of a case of realistic recruiting, involving alumni of two schools; and the idea was to reveal what was going on everywhere—and nothing really wrong with it—while the theoretical reformers were off dancing on their clouds. The fictional schools were Notre Dame and Princeton. The managing editor of *Scribner's* was Alfred S. Dashiell, recently out of Princeton. It was an honest effort to get at some truth; but I thought I'd better clear it with Rockne before publication. He wrote: "Glad to hear that you are getting over the hump and that everything is working well. I would like very much to look over your manuscript for *Scribner's* and I have some information for you that might be interesting."

Rather than howling about it, he actually helped me with the

piece. He had two basic ideas on this subject which the colleges have
been beating for forty years: (1) "Let the boys pay a little and work
a little; that will keep them well on the amateur side." (2) "Anytime
they all want to come out in the open on all this business, I'll take
my chances."

Scribner's didn't pay much money but it got around to the right
places. The article attracted some attention—and brought my first
invitation as a speaker, with an honorarium—from the Women's
Club of Providence, Rhode Island. Later, the ladies wanted to know
if I would be willing to debate the question with a well-known coach,
Knute Rockne of Notre Dame. That gave me pause. I didn't know
what Rock and I could debate since we agreed on most things, especially the meat of the *Scribner's* article. I checked with him. He
wrote: "Why not? We'll give them a show." They wrote me later
the debate had been canceled. Which was probably just as well. I
might have been the show. But we would have covered the subject
as they had never heard it before.

I was doing another job around New York of which Rockne knew
nothing but of which he would have approved. As I've told you, the
natural nickname of Notre Dame was the Fighting Irish. The press
associations, for some reason, had taken to using terms like Ramblers
and Nomads, which were offensive to Notre Dame people and had
lost whatever validity they might have had when the schedule began to assume the home-and-home basis at the time of the Four
Horsemen. At the Associated Press I learned that the ban had been
requested by Notre Dame, presumably at the request of some non-
Irish.

I began using the Irish nickname when I went to the *Post;* and
later it was well received by the millions, including many Irish, who
read the *Daily News.* Other papers picked it up, including the press
associations. So now we have Irish kilties in the band, shamrocks on
the top of the band caps, an Irish terrier mascot; Irish motifs at student demonstrations; and another of those fine moments in sport—at
Champaign, when the University of Illinois band stood before the
Notre Dame section and played the "Ave Maria." A nation that can
make a holiday of St. Paddy's Day can surely stand one "Irish" football team among all the animals of the jungle, the Battling Bishops
and other gridiron mascots.

Like most of his other close associates I tried to send Rockne a good football prospect when one appeared on my radar. It had cost me five dollars, which was almost a day's wages at the time, for a phone call to save one of them from the clutches of "bird dogs" from other schools. I presented the bill on Rock's next visit to New York. He paid it, with the usual injured air that attended any financial request. When he and Bonnie were leaving the hotel he gave me a letter to mail. It needed a two-cent stamp which I said I'd be glad to supply.

"Oh, no," he said, "I gave you the five—I'll give you the two." He also gave me a book he had been reading. It was Hemingway's volume of short stories *Men without Women,* and might possibly have been intended to remind me of my defections at the time of the Sheik contest. On impulse I asked him to autograph it, which he did; with no fancy comment for my grandchildren but the usual terse *K. K. Rockne.* If I can get Mr. Hemingway to autograph it sometime I will trade a genuine Rockne signature.

I was married in '25 and at the first opportunity took my bride to South Bend. The Rocknes had us to dinner, and later we went to the home of McCready Huston, editor of the *Tribune.* Both families had children in grade school and both were currently displeased at some educational wrinkle—correction—Huston was displeased, Rock was indignant. When he learned that my wife had been a teacher in Ohio he seemed to hold her personally responsible for all the sins of the South Bend school system. His eyes glared, his voice barked, his finger jabbed, exactly as if he were addressing some rhinoceros freshman tackle slow to get the right idea about blocking an end. My beautiful young bride quailed before this unexpected onslaught by the great Rockne.

"Don't let him bulldoze you, honey," I said. "He's talking about your racket now."

"All right, Mr. Rockne," and now the teacher was speaking firmly to a first-grader and pointing *her* finger, "let me tell you something. I'm tired trying to run my house according to your football strategy."

Rock loved it, as he always did when somebody gave him opposition. He was also no doubt pleased about the reference to his football system. (I do believe that adherence to sound gridiron strategy can become a valuable way, personal or professional, of life; I've since expanded the idea to my basic speech: "How To Quarterback Your Own Life.")

McCready Huston was one of several *Tribune* people who collaborated with Rockne on a famous column called "Bearskin" which appeared about this time. Always worried about the collection of fat in the head, Rockne invented the idea for an occasional column which would aim shafts at those players afflicted with "elephantiasis of the ego." The material obviously came from the inside and there was always suspicion that Rockne was involved. But occasionally "Bearskin" would take the hide off the coach; and would include references to sports writers and the downtown coaches.

It was a great success. Basically it was another form of goofing, and another use of humor and sarcasm in his coaching. It was revived occasionally after Rockne's death, but the Master's touch was missing (and in that phrase can be wrapped most of Notre Dame's recent gridiron woes). He had a definite flair for words and a wide range of knowledge. Once, in our early days, I sought to upstage him with my discovery of Chaucer. So he took Chaucer in stride and came back with John Wycliffe. That left me stranded. Our class hadn't yet come to Wycliffe.

He was as clever at adapting words or phrases into his vocabulary as in absorbing new formations into his system. He would borrow from H. L. Mencken or Freud or, in dire need, from Wallace. I was always searching for new expressions. One of them came out intestinal fortitude which Rockne popularized in his speeches and football lectures. Unless somebody can show its use before early 1921, I claim "intestinal fortitude"; along with "suicide schedule" and "watch-charm guard." And this seems a good place to nail down "lame-brain" and "monkey's uncle" which first appeared in my humorous short stories for *Redbook* in the late twenties.

Stories of Rock's kindness to his boys are as numerous as the boys themselves. He used to bring the small fry outside the gate into the Notre Dame home games—and one of these, about five years old at the time, was Joe Kuharich, his most recent successor. After his death Bonnie gave his watch to Father Vincent Brennan, stepson of Rock's veteran equipment superintendent, John "Mac" McAllister. Young Vince, as a neighborhood kid, had been one of Rock's protégés. Recently I met one of his old boys who said: "My mother died with cancer. It wasn't until we opened the safe deposit box that I found out Rock had been writing her pep talks for years."

He would go to anybody's home town to make a speech if he were asked. Joe Harmon, who was Adam Walsh's shadow at center, says, in a typical letter: "When he was Sales Promotion Manager for Studebaker he visited Louisville, and at my request came over to Xavier High School where I was coaching and gave a very fine talk. It really showed me the high type man that he was and it is something that I hold dear in my heart among his memories. I still have a picture of us taken on this occasion."

Paul McNulty, end on the '22 team and a great one, had a handicap unfamiliar to most Rockne players—no financial problems. Paul left school prematurely; and perhaps regretted it during the glamour days of the Horsemen. Later, as I get the story, Rock said to McNulty, in the presence of Bill Ingram, the Navy coach: "Paul was one of my finest ends—until he broke his slate." And Paul said to a friend: "That makes up for everything."

Rock would make a sparring partner out of you inside the lodge; but if he were in your home town, or with your friends, you were always the great guy. He had a habit of saying, to the home-town friends of one of his coaches: "If I should ever leave Notre Dame, I'd like Joe here, to succeed me." This led to confused nominations for his job after he died.

His coaching never stopped with graduation. He expected his graduates to come to him with their personal or business problems. I never made an important decision without asking his advice. Rock was the Grand Master of the Notre Dame lodge of coaches as long as he lived, and the actual leader of the football coaches, regardless of who held the formal title. He led the fight for job security in this most precarious of professions, constantly sought to elevate its standards, to increase its prestige. I once arranged for an article by him in *Liberty* magazine called "The Coaches' Rebellion" which led to coaches having a voice on the Rules Committee.

He was particularly kind to young coaches—and not necessarily his own. "It was my pleasure," Lou Little writes, "to have known him during my years of coaching at Georgetown. He was of great help to me and also gave me great inspiration. In fact, Coach Rockne came to Georgetown at my invitation to speak at our athletic dinner. He did it at his own expense. There was no particular reason for him to favor me, which goes to show his great interest in all young coaches . . . Perhaps the greatest compliment paid to me during the years when I was starting coaching was in 1930 when Coach Rockne insisted that I be the fourth official at the football game at the Polo Grounds when the former Notre Dame players played the New York Giants at the request of Mayor Walker. This game was for charity. During that game, even though the former Notre Dame players were being badly beaten, their main concern was, were they disappointing Coach Rockne? They spoke of him with great reverence."

Matty Bell, athletic director at Southern Methodist, writes: "In my opinion Rock's greatest asset was his personality for leadership with the boys he coached, and in the coaching profession. He provided a great opportunity for SMU in intersectional football by scheduling a game with the school in 1930. Although a tough competitor Rock was always real friendly with his opponents before and after the game."

Rock was particularly friendly with the Army group. Jay Wyatt, before his death, told me of the time he went with Rock, at the invitation of Coach Biff Jones and Graduate Manager (later Major General) Phil Fleming, on a fishing trip on the Harriman estate. The caretaker happened to be a Norwegian and the ever-suspicious Rock, who couldn't talk much Norwegian, smelled a trap set by two of his Army sparring partners. "He got me to fix it up with the caretaker so they could be alone," Wyatt chuckled. "Later, when Biff and Phil returned, they found Rock and the caretaker chattering Norwegian—as if Rock knew what he was talking about."

Through the years Rockne ran a quiet employment agency. There were always jobs for his graduates, and whenever people came seeking his services, he passed such opportunities on to coaches he had reason to know might be available. Here, from Bill Cerney, who was one of Rock's coaches at that time, is an intriguing story:

"It was 1925. Howard Jones, the man who had beaten Rock's great team of 1921, had left Iowa and taken over the reins at Duke University, which had just been founded by Wm. "Buck" Duke, the tobacco king of the world. Jones lost the first eight games of a nine-game schedule. He decided this was no place to stay. If he had another year like the past one, and the material was poor, he would be

dead and buried as a coach before his time. He called Rock from
Durham and explained the situation.

"About the same time a two-man committee from Southern California propositioned Rock to take over on his own terms. Finally
Rock said, 'Thanks, gentlemen, but I believe I will always be at Notre
Dame. It is my school and my coaching days will be spent here' . . .
One of the committee asked if he would or could recommend anyone. Now this is where Rock went to work as a tough bargainer for
his friend. 'Yes sir, I believe I have just the man you can use, a man
who beat one of my greatest teams, Howard Jones.' The committee
was surprised. 'Do you believe he would leave Duke?'

" 'He would if you would make him a decent offer.'

" 'Well, what would you consider fair, Mr. Rockne?'

" 'Ten thousand dollars and a ten-year contract.'

"That was the beginning of the Southern Cal series and a friendship that lasted until death . . . Fred Dawson, the man who beat
our 1922 and 1923 teams at Nebraska, was available in 1930. Rock
knew that Virginia was looking for a coach. So Dawson was hired
on Rock's recommendation . . . So Rock later got jobs for the only
two men who had defeated him in the six years between 1919 and
1924. This was the Rock that you and I knew, Frank, a man whose
heart was big, generous, and always considerate."

XXXIX

"The Swede is himself again," my observant friend on the squad,
now a savvy senior, said in 1926. And he also had the equipment he
needed—a seasoned varsity with a junior running star in Christy
Flanagan; and sound shock troops led by Johnny "Butch" Niemiec,
a fine sophomore all-round back. How these two got to Notre Dame
gives further proof of the casual nature of Rockne recruiting; and
why, perhaps, there was a tailing off of other superlative backfield
talent, especially at quarterback, during this period.

Flanagan had attended Culver Military Academy, not too far from
Notre Dame. There he had been much impressed by his tactical

officer, Paul Fogarty, a Notre Dame man who later wrote the lyrics
to "Betty Coed" (perhaps inspired by the lack of coeds at Notre
Dame). Flanagan, paying his own expenses, could have gone where
he chose. He chose Notre Dame because of Rockne's personality;
and remained there where freshman athletes must have seemed even
lower to him than McEvoy's student waiter who waited on student
waiters. Freshmen wore castoff varsity garments, worked out in a
far corner of the field, were brought over every so often to take their
lumps in scrimmage from varsity prima donnas.

"Sometimes," Christy chuckled recently, "it seemed as if he were
testing us, purposely trying to discourage us. I didn't even have shoes
that fit. It took me a long while to get up enough courage to face him
but one day I went into his office and told him I had a nine shoe
and an eight and would he please be so kind as to make them both
eights. Know what he yelled at me? 'What am I—a magician?' He
used to tell that story on me later on." Christy finally got two eights
by trading around with other frosh who had also been misshod.

Even after Flanagan had begun to scatter stardust Rock was slow
to let up on him. "If he really wanted to cut you down, he would
angle you over near the side lines where the students could listen.
Once he finished the list of my deficiencies by saying: 'You're just
a mollycoddle.' So that's all I heard around the campus for a while:
'Flanagan, you're just a mollycoddle.' That's what he wanted, of
course.

"One day I was in his office and he asked me to wait. He was
going to have a visitor and he wanted me to be present. The visitor
was a prep-school star from Iowa. He said he was being pursued by
everybody but that he wanted to come to Notre Dame and become
an All-American. You know what Rock said to that boy? He said:
'So you want to be an All-American? That's fine. So why don't you
go back to Iowa and be All-American there?' That's what he said to
that boy and that's exactly what that boy did. I could never figure
Rock. Do you know he fooled me more with his last pep talk than
he did with his first? And I thought I was a wise senior who knew
all his tricks."

Rock may have known the Iowa boy was shopping around, and
may have been rejecting, or testing a prima donna; and in doing so,
lost him. Or he may have been practicing some of the individual

psychology he used on Flanagan. "The week before a Minnesota game he just seemed to be running into me around the campus. He kept telling me I was going to have a big day against Minnesota, that they were made to order for me. So I had the biggest day I ever had." But Christy had his inning. "Junie became a fan of mine; and Rock had to come around with one of my pictures and ask me to please autograph it." Flanagan was thoroughly captivated by his coach and by Notre Dame. He was back at the spring game in '59, playing golf with his two student sons.

Niemiec, from my home town, was, like Rock and Gipp, about three years older than the average student. High-school football had saved him from our steel mills. He had also been much pursued, but he chose Notre Dame at a personal sacrifice. While there he worked as a "hasher" and at other jobs. Rock estimated Niemiec correctly as a thoroughly earnest chap whom criticism might hurt. Coming from opposite backgrounds, both Niemiec and Flanagan were at Notre Dame because they wanted to be. And Rock understood them so well that he could fit them into his pattern, at some sacrifice to each, without, as far as I could detect, the slightest resentment from either.

Had they played in the same backfield, with two comparable men, Rock could have had his fourth great quartet. He did try Niemiec at fullback, even though Butch weighed only 165; but he "had too many actions of the halfback." And he was the ideal "bell-cow" for the shock troops—a passer, runner, defensive man, and a great punter.

Rock had been frightened by what had happened in the Penn State dressing room; and by the results of the '25 season. He now had Hunk Anderson, Tom Lieb, and Tommy Mills as assistant coaches. Herbert Jones had begun to lay the foundations of an effective business office; the student management system had passed the "inefficient" stage; and Ruth Faulkner, who was to be his full-time secretary for the rest of his career, came along about that time. The Master could give more time to coaching, and the results were quite obvious as the squad swept the first eight games—and allowed only one touchdown to be scored against it.

Beloit was flattened by a horrendous 77–0 and the new juggernaut proceeded to Minneapolis accompanied by the Midwest segment of the circus which had already begun to form around Rockne. Ordinarily he was unapproachable before a game, but this day he paused on entering the stadium for a bit of a joke on Harry Kelly, a Notre Dame friend who was later to become Governor of Michigan. Rockne held the tickets for the insiders who would sit on the bench—the mark of distinction for a pigskin patron. Kelly, in the manner of the politician, had straggled. Rock ignored his frantic shouts, marched out of sight—and then, laughing, sent a student manager back with the ticket.

There was no more fun that day. Joe Boland, in trying to block a punt, had his leg broken by one of his own teammates. On the next play, fullback Freddy Collins hit the line, had his jaw broken in three places and took his place in the ambulance alongside Boland. At half-time Minnesota led 7-6.

Rockne said: "I didn't know whether to swoon or laugh idiotically at such savage breaks." What he did was read a telephone message from Boland and Collins to the squad between halves: "We're all through. All we can do is get the score when the game is over."

On the first play of the second half Flanagan ran 68 yards for a touchdown. Right halfback Bucky Dahman had previously run 70 yards. The final score was 20-7. The phone message was poetically, dramatically right. But neither desperation nor inspiration of themselves can produce touchdown runs. There has to be some mechanical blocking, learned the hard way through game experience and drudgery on the practice field. This 1926 squad had enough, now, of the savvy most of them had lacked as sophomores.

They continued to grow up with a 28-0 victory over Penn State, which had held them scoreless the year before. Against ever-troublesome Northwestern, the shock troops came through with the 6-0 victory on a "crisscross" pass from Art Parasien to Butch Niemiec which was to be repeated under more dramatic circumstances later in the season. It was 12-0 over Georgia Tech; and 26-0 over Indiana. (In the Hoosier game a Notre Dame man tackled Bennett, the Indiana star, at the side lines just before the Notre Dame bench. Rockne was caught in the melee. His leg was injured; which led to the still-recurrent theory that this injury caused his later phlebitis.)

Army was waiting at the Yankee Stadium, tough as usual, eager to retain the dominance it had established with the 27-0 triumph over this same Notre Dame squad the year before. And now we get into aspects of that "inside football" which becomes a form of chess, with human pawns, to the coaches.

The cardinal Notre Dame play, the bread-and-butter job, was what the boys called Old 51—the off-tackle slant they practiced so assiduously every day. It depended on the ability of the leading Notre Dame halfback to take the opposing end to the *outside*, and of the Notre Dame end to drive the opposing tackle *in*. This day Army coach "Biff" Jones came up with a jim-dandy defensive maneuver. He dropped his tackles back about a yard from the scrimmage line, and about a yard to the outside, so that, when the Notre Dame ends came looking for them, the Army tackles evaded the block. This may have been the first use of what has become known as the modern "stunting" or "jitterbug" defense—where the defensive players move around so much that the blockers cannot get to them.

But when men are deployed to bulwark another position, they leave unguarded the sector they had vacated. So, Rockne merely shifted to the now-vulnerable open space *inside* tackle. Harry O'Boyle, the fullback, now gained so consistently that the press box began to suspect he was a hidden weapon Rockne had held back to beat Army. O'Boyle, a rugged earnest competitor, was on his way to becoming an All-American in one afternoon; but on the first scrimmage play after the second-half kickoff, O'Boyle was stopped for no gain. On the next play Christy Flanagan ran 62 yards for a touchdown. The run is known in gridiron lore as the Perfect Play. I later saw a picture of it in the coaches room at West Point.

What had happened? After the play when O'Boyle had been stopped, right end John Wallace had reported to quarterback Gene Edwards that the Army left tackle, Sprague, was back on the line and Army had reverted to the orthodox defense. Rockne described the consequent operation:

"Edwards now called for Flanagan's favorite off-tackle play. Wallace blocked Sprague *in*. Hearndon, the leading halfback, took Harbold, the Army end, *out* of the play. Our right guard pulled out and deflected Murrell, the Army star fullback. Flanagan streaked through this opening, reversed his field through the secondary, tertiary, and quaternary defense men who had been picked off by our linemen from the other side, Ike Voedisch, Fred Miller, and Dick Smith."

That was it: 6–0; but enough.

Army had been the big one; and when Drake was taken 21–0, there remained only a routine struggle against Carnegie Tech—and then a relaxing train trip to Southern California for the finale against a new opponent, the Trojans. Rockne had other fish to fry that weekend so he sent the squad to Pittsburgh and the Tech game in charge of Hunk Anderson and Tommy Mills.

He got the score in the press box at the Army-Navy game in Chicago. Notre Dame 0 Carnegie Tech 19.

It was one of the great upsets in football history—scored over the man who had made his reputation by upsetting other giants.

Rockne the Superman had become Rockne the national laughingstock. The professor of psychology had exposed himself to his own favorite weapon by providing Coach Wally Steffen with a pep talk guaranteed to make any red-blooded football player explode: "Rockne thinks you're so poor he's gone to Chicago to see some real football players in the Army-Navy game."

Steffen, a Chicago judge who coached Tech as an avocation, poured brine into the wound by denying it had been an upset. It was, he insisted, a *setup*. Judge Steffen's little joke was to set up dramatic events two years later.

XL

Rockne, of course, had had reasons for being in Chicago. The Big Ten schedule-makers were meeting there. He was playing Navy the next year for the first time, and the Army-Navy game would give him a rare chance to scout both teams in person. He had thought that Carnegie Tech, on its record, would be taken in stride. He had taken what seemed a reasonable gamble; he had lost. He accepted the full responsibility, made no excuses or explanations.

What had happened at Pittsburgh? There were the usual extravagant rumors to fit an incredible event; actually it had been a classic deadfall set up by Rockne himself. He had made the mistake of telling his boys to concentrate on Southern California—while the second team would play most of the Carnegie game.

The day had turned up bitter cold, with snow, rain and a heavy field—conditions favorable to Tech. The Notre Dame players, with victory conceded by their cautious coach, were as cold, mentally and emotionally, as the weather. A miserable job of work had to be done—so let's get it over with.

The second team—shock troops—played the first quarter and half-way through the next, as planned. They could not score, but neither could the opponents.

The regulars came in. The script called for them to score at least once in the remaining time. But it was Tech which scored—and led by one touchdown at the half—chiefly due to the efforts of Howard Harpster, a slender but brainy sophomore quarterback who could pass and kick.

If Rock had been there between halves, the prescription would have called for him to pull something out of the bag, something to warm up these soggy champions whose spirits were as damp as their uniforms. Perhaps Rock couldn't have done it, either.

"In the second half," Niemiec said, "Tech got stronger as the game went on." That always happens in an upset. The supposed patsies begin to smell the Sunday morning headlines. They become invigorated, intoxicated. They become tigers, play like All-Americans. It's an old, old story. You see it repeated many times each season.

The hapless squad, "hating to face the student body," took an earlier train, arrived at the campus unobserved. The students later serenaded them at their halls, in the Irish manner of reserving the biggest welcome for the teams which need it most.

Because they were to leave Monday night for the Coast, there was an unaccustomed Sunday practice. Rockne told the players: "It was my fault. No blame is to be attached to Hunk or Tommy. Let's be glad we have a chance to redeem ourselves against Southern Cal."

On the train, when the players opened their bags, each found a program of the Carnegie Tech game.

Again, the law of averages and the laws of human nature. If it hadn't happened at Tech, it might have happened at Southern Cal, after a triumphant cross-country tour.

Notre Dame went into the last period at Los Angeles leading 7–6.

The heat was taking its toll. The Trojans poured through the exhausted linemen to take a 12–7 lead—with four minutes to go.

What now, Mr. Wizard? Any rabbits in the hat?

Facing another "bad season," and two straight defeats for the first time in his career, Rockne had little hope. Flanagan and most of the regulars were through for the day. There was no spark on the field. On the bench was a slightly built, left-handed quarterback, who hadn't played much because he had developed a heart murmur. Nothing actually serious but it hadn't been necessary to use him. He had a reckless confidence. It was in his eyes and manner now. "Art," Rock said, "those two left-handed passes 83 and 84."

"It's a cinch, Coach." The little man was charging the gates of Troy now defended by fire-snorting giants. On the first play he pulled a spinner which gained eight yards against a defense spread for passes. The Trojans yawned. No harm in such plays—

Number 84 was a pass to end "Chili" Walsh who gained 30 yards before he was nailed by the Trojan center and captain (and later coach) Jeff Cravath. A few more plays and Parasien had them on the 24-yard line—but with only thirty seconds to play.

The ball was passed, Parasien faded back, was lost behind the mob scene of blockers and rushers. Eighty thousand people were watching that group. None saw Niemiec, the chosen receiver, who had been knocked to the ground.

"It seemed like I was on the ground for an hour," Butch told me recently. "But I got up and took off for where I was supposed to be—and then I saw that hand come up over the crowd of players with the ball in it—that was all I saw—the hand with the ball in it. I caught the ball on the five-yard line and stumbled over the goal." Notre Dame 13 USC 12.

This was a Merriwell finish and a proper way to end a season, especially a Rockne season. It thrilled Rock—and that pro of the old pros, Hunk Anderson.

What lies back of such heroics? In this case, not much size, but plenty of desire, of confidence, of getting off the ground, of fighting to live, of a dynamic coach supplying thought and energy when the battery was down, and, very importantly, of boys on the field who wanted to play for this coach and this school—and because of that, would fight hardest when the going was roughest.

Niemiec was to throw passes later—and one would be immortalized.

Had I been doing my annual Football Preview in 1927 (it began just ten years later) I would probably have picked Notre Dame to go undefeated. A solid segment of upperclassmen, still led by Flanagan and Niemiec, was augmented by a fine group of sophomore linemen. After opening victories over an odd little stranger called Coe (which had the audacity to score) and Detroit, the squad took the first big one in style—a 19–6 win over Navy in the first game of the series which has become the longest continuous intersectional in football. Grantland Rice, the phrase-maker, coined a new one after this occasion: "Off-again Flanagan, On-again Niemiec." And with Niemiec on the shock troops now, was an All-American boy type—firm jaw, apple cheeks, eyes that were diamond-sharp and blue—who hit so hard he would sometimes have his mental moorings jarred—but would go on playing. This propensity of Jack Chevigny's was to set up perhaps the most famous single play in gridiron history.

It was 19–6 over Indiana and 26–7 over Georgia Tech. A little something was missing; there were no runaway scores, and everybody seemed able to score once against the Irish. There was considerable concern when Minnesota brought its rugged team led by Herb Joesting at fullback and Bronco Nagurski at tackle. But late in the fourth period the Irish held a 7–0 lead. The only break had come when Captain Johnny "Little Clipper" Smith had recovered a fumbled punt on the Gopher 20, and Niemiec had scored from there and kicked the extra point.

With about two minutes to go the shock troops were again in there to protect a slim lead, but it was their ball on their 30-yard line and the situation looked in hand. The next spring Niemiec took me to the spot on the field and replayed the sequence.

"It was our ball with third down and eight yards to go. Our quarterback played it safe and called a punt. Somebody argued with him, thought we should take advantage of the extra down to use up time and then punt on fourth down. So he changed the signal to a line play off a fake punt. It wasn't a bad idea. Such a surprise play might go; and if we made first down, we could easily run out the clock.

"So we lined up, with me back in punt formation. Our center Bud Boeringer [later All-American] passed the ball to our fullback, as the play called for. But the ball hit the fullback and Nagurski recovered it for a Minnesota first down on the Notre Dame 20-yard line."

What had happened? The fullback had not got the changed signal. And the incident proved another Rockne rule of action: the quarterback is the boss on the field. It was permissible to bring him information; but arguing invites just such a catastrophe as occurred. Now, as a result of the babel in the backfield, the complexion of the game had radically changed—and fifty-eight minutes of hard, winning effort were to be canceled. After recovering the fumble Minnesota had taken time out; and during the period, among other things, Coach Spears had sent in a tall end named Walsh.

The first three plays sent Joesting, a plunging specialist, into the line. The Notre Dame defense responded magnificently. It was fourth down and six yards to go—and time for the do-or-die play. Niemiec sensed what would happen—and covered the tall end, who would be his responsibility.

Niemiec was five-feet nine inches tall. Walsh, the opposing end, was six-feet four inches. The pass was perfectly thrown for this occasion—high. The tall man came down with it, as he must always come down with it if it is perfectly thrown. This time for a touchdown. A Gopher substitute named Pharmer came in, to kick the point which sent Minnesota home with a prized 7–7 tie.

Rockne undoubtedly had words for the quarterback and the backfield lawyer. He asked Niemiec only one question: "Did you misjudge it, Butch?"

"No—it was too high for me."

It was one of the penalties Rock sometimes had to pay for using the boxer-type player who invariably had to give away height and weight to opponents. But he was to remember this play—and capitalize on it brilliantly, in a more important game later on.

Rockne teams had always reacted violently after a defeat, and the Minnesota game had been a failure for Notre Dame regardless of what the scoreboard said. The boys would go roaring through Army —next week.

Army 18 Notre Dame 0.

After this game Army had another picture to place beside the Flanagan run on the walls of the coaching room. It was another perfect play, good for about 50 yards, executed by Chris Cagle, who that day began to earn himself a place among Notre Dame's beloved opponents.

For the first time a Rockne team had failed to come back after a failure.

The next week, against Drake, the weather was bitter cold at Des Moines. The field was frozen. With Southern California to follow at Soldiers' Field, Rockne wanted to protect his regulars. He had not intended to play Niemiec, or Flanagan, but he may have remembered what had happened the previous year at Carnegie Tech under similar conditions. "Go in and get a touchdown," he told Niemiec.

Niemiec went in, scored a touchdown. Somebody hit him from the side. He blacked out from pain. It was one of those cobralike stings of the gridiron—a knee.

Niemiec was out—and now Flanagan had to play on the treacherous Des Moines skating rink. The next week when Southern Cal came to mammoth Soldiers' Field to play before the largest crowd in the history of American football up to that time (and probably since) Niemiec was on the side lines and Flanagan had to carry the load at left half.

(Herbert Jones writes: "I have in my office a large oversized picture of the 1927 USC game. Imprinted thereon is 'Attendance 120,-000.' Some doubt this figure and it is an estimate; but I believe there were that many. Unfortunately, all of them did not pay to get in. It was our first game in the completed stadium [we had played Northwestern there in 1923 when only the sides were up] and I believe that the Chicago 'boys in the know' took us 'country boys' for a ride. Many friends of those working the gates were passed in. Also Rock had invited all of the Big Ten teams [they had finished their seasons the preceding Saturday] and these teams saw the game from the top of the colonnades on both sides. It was a mob. I am sure it was our biggest crowd and I have not heard of any bigger in the States—more paid, yes, but not more spectators.

"Our three biggest paid attendances have been: 1927, Southern Cal at Soldiers' Field, 99,198; 1928, Navy at Soldiers' Field, 103,081; 1930, Army at Soldiers' Field, 103,491 . . . We had a couple in Los Angeles where the attendance was announced as 104,000 plus, but this was a stile count and included everyone who went through the gates. The paid was less than the three above. . . . Another interesting fact about the games at Chicago: they all grossed over $400,000. No taxes then, and the prices were $7.00 for box seats and $3.00 for reserved. The 'take-home' was still considerable even after rental and other expenses.")

In the fourth period, Notre Dame, clinging to a 7–6 lead, halted the storming Trojans around the Irish 30-yard line and forced a punt. Safety man Charlie Riley tried for a running catch, juggled the ball and, while doing so, crossed into the end zone. He was hit hard, the ball bounded out of the field of play. The officials ruled a touchback and no score. The play precipitated a wild argument that can still be inflamed by any old match of memory. The Trojans claimed Riley had possession and control of the ball and that the play should have been ruled a safety which would have given them two points, an 8–7 lead, and perhaps an ultimate victory, instead of the 7–6 defeat. It was a judgment call, the most difficult an official is called to make.

(The controversy was typical of what was to follow in this famous series. In 1936 Notre Dame made 406 yards from scrimmage and 18 first downs—against 53 yards and one first down by the Trojans. In the waning moments a USC back roared 98 yards after intercepting one of those ill-advised flat passes. The Irish claimed an exuberant official, "pacing" the play, actually ran interference all the way. But the score, which resulted in a 13–13 tie, counted.)

The next week, while in Chicago for a knee treatment, Niemiec dropped in at Rockne's room at the old Auditorium Hotel (now Roosevelt University). The Master was in a merry mood as he tied his black tie before a mirror. "Five hundred dollars for opening the Auto Show. How about that?" He repeated it, at intervals, as if he could not believe such silly things went on in the world. "Five hundred dollars for a twenty-minute talk. Hmm!"

Rockne could show this immature side to his players because he knew, as they knew, he could change immediately and turn on the force. He was "Rock" to everybody except, in later years, his younger players. In that hotel room he was like a kid with an unexpected Christmas tree, laden with inexhaustible goodies.

He had three years to live. But what years!

205

XLI

As early as 1922, in my "Quad Wrangles" column, I had printed a blanket denial intended to cover the frequent rumors that Rockne was going to another school. This was my printed blanket report of his reaction to such irritating rumors: "Grr!!!$$###**!!" Nevertheless, on the evidence, he was a contract flirt who encouraged, even teased such offers, considered them, sometimes seemed to accept them, even to sign papers of various sorts which other schools chose to consider contracts.

Why did he reject them? Partly, no doubt, from loyalty. And perhaps his instinct gave him this clear picture: Go slow. At Notre Dame you have the type of boy and background and discipline most conducive to your type of football. At one of those other places little faculty men might throw intolerable halters on your activities. It is doubtful that, at any other school, Rockne would have been in position to make the immense sums he was just about to make in 1931. So his essential judgment, on this level, may have been as sound as on other levels.

There may have been another factor. Rock was born hungry in a hungry background. He had been an immigrant; the "lone Norse Protestant" among the Irish; a little man fighting bigger men on the field; a David battling the Western Conference giants. He may have welcomed (as Pegler had suggested) the little flatteries which came to him as a bolster to the astonishing lack of assurance (as an example) which would make him purple with fear before a speech which everybody else on the premises knew would be a smashing success.

His photographs reveal how he gradually grew out of that. There was less glare in the eyes, less intensity in the speech, more kindness in the face—all for the very good reason, I think, that there was less turbulence within; less, having proved much, for him to have to prove. I think his remarkable insight had told him all this would come; but that it would come sooner if he remained at Notre Dame. So that, as he flirted with other colleges, as he was taken to their mountaintops and sorely tempted, within himself, he knew he would accept none of their offers; that this was why he always gave himself that "verbal agreement" that "Notre Dame must be satisfied." I doubt if he ever asked Notre Dame to release him. I know that he did not in the most celebrated case—Columbia. With these background thoughts, let's look into the details of some of the contract negotiations—some of them bordering cloak-and-dagger, as he talked too much, then sought to elude entrapment.

Michigan State reports ownership of one of the souvenir Rockne "contracts." There were reported early romances with Iowa and Northwestern, Princeton and Wisconsin. The first rumors from Southern California began to come after the summer of 1924 when he held his first coaching school there. Here, in a frank letter, is background which probably reveals the general pattern: "During the summer, after the coaching school, at a party in his honor, Rock made a speech which, I suspect, later became his format. He began, as usual, by complimenting the fine country around Southern California; and all of the people around there. He built up the stature of his friends who lived there. He ventured the opinion that *if* he should ever consider leaving Notre Dame, *this* was the place to which he would like to bring his family and spend his declining years.

"During the '24 season the Coast Conference cut off USC in midseason. The stated reason was that the Trojan coach was exceeding the Conference speed limit in recruiting—the chronic complaint out here which finally wrecked the Conference 35 years later. It was plainly indicated that, if the Trojans were to return to the Old Homestead, they must produce a new coach. While this stew was simmering Rockne brought his Four Horsemen to the Rose Bowl and you know what happened. There was another banquet after the Bowl game at which Rock repeated his encomiums regarding our warm, benevolent countryside where it must be so nice to work and live. You can imagine the saliva this brought to the lips of the coachstarved Trojan folks.

"They contacted him, there were two or three quick, informal meetings and Rock, playing around this appetizing platter, must have talked too much. Rumors spread that he had signed a contract and was coming to USC. That caused him to go into his seclusion act. It had been publicized that the team was leaving for South Bend on the third of January. The friend who had been secluding the reluctant wizard drove him to the train. The USC dignitaries were there, contracts and fountain pens in hand.

"Rock had no intention of returning to South Bend with the team. He had been invited to Coronado on some other business; and Bonnie was going up to Seattle to visit with the Gus Dorais family. But to get rid of the importuning Trojans, Bonnie got on the train and Rock, with fast footwork, followed. They walked the length of the car, got off the other side, went out of the old Southern Pacific station, got into an old Model-T Ford which had been waiting there, and drove to San Diego; in second gear, incidentally, burning out the bearings.

"Regardless of what anybody says, Rockne at no time signed any contract to coach SC. He did some loose talking but had no intention of signing a coaching contract. Later there was talk that he had also agreed to come here and coach Loyola; but all he seemed to be doing then was to set up the job for Tom Lieb, who got it." In this context, it seems reasonable to guess that when the "two-man committee" came from USC to see Rock in 1925, he might have been setting up the Trojan job for Howard Jones. From these accounts it also seems reasonable to suspect that Rock had diplomatic talents the State Department could have used.

The Columbia incident in 1927 had the usual preliminary script, with Rockne being led to the mountaintop, tempted, seeming to agree; going back to Notre Dame to "get the consent of Notre Dame," writing, after a week, that he was sorry, Notre Dame would not release him, and the deal was off. Ordinarily, that would have ended the affair, as the others had ended, with a piece of paper rusting in somebody's archives.

But Jim Knapp, representing Columbia, and a man of some prominence around New York, told him Columbia was going to insist that the contract be honored. It is probable that he knew the background of the Rockne negotiations with other schools; or he may have thought that, faced with the threat of exposure as a contract jumper, Rock would come peacefully and Columbia would have its coach. There might even have been a bit of sport involved—if Knapp could land the big one who had wiggled away from so many others.

ROCKNE SIGNS WITH COLUMBIA

Rock, quite by accident, was in Philadelphia with John Neeson, another Notre Dame stalwart, when the newspapers carried the above headline. He came to New York, collected Joe Byrne, and they went to the office of Jimmy Carolyn, one of Rock's classmates who was assistant sports editor of the New York *Times*. They got in touch with Knapp. Rock admitted signing the penciled memorandum but stood pat on the verbal agreement release. Knapp was thus put in the position of the big city slicker trying to seduce the country boy from the old homestead. Columbia called off the pursuit.

Byrne told me Rock had tried to locate me the previous day. It seems I missed a great dramatic performance when Rockne finally forgave his good friend Jim Knapp for having put him in such an embarrassing position. But as the victor, assuming this magnanimous mantle, prepared to withdraw from the field, it broke out in another quarter. Rev. Matthew J. Walsh, president of Notre Dame, released this bomb: "Notre Dame will not stand in Mr. Rockne's way if he wishes to better himself."

It was on this second day that I made contact with Rockne. I was shocked at the change in the man. The force, the challenge, the power were gone. This was a weak, uncertain little fellow, looking for help, even from such a fledgling as me. He told me that, even before he had got back to Notre Dame after signing that penciled memorandum, with the verbal reservation, he had been so sure he did not want to leave Notre Dame that he hadn't even asked Father Walsh for permission, nor told him about the offer. I understood how this could be, for I understood Rockne, and I remembered the early morning he had stood crying on the baggage truck and said: "After this I will never leave Notre Dame as long as they want me."

A smaller man, attempting to prove that he was a big man, might have said, "Okay, Notre Dame, Columbia, here I come"—and accepted the $25,000 offer—which included $7500 for teaching chemistry. I was inclined to feel my school had been too rough on our great man. I also knew it had not been an easy thing for them to do, and that they must have had their reasons. Officially, the people involved at the time do not even now discuss l'affaire Columbia. But a man in position to know recently told me: "It was a calculated risk and the school would have been in a serious position if Rock had called their bluff and gone to Columbia. The situation had been building since all the hoorah following the 1924 season. Rockne would sometimes make commitments the university had not sanctioned. He was putting pressure on for the building of a stadium instead of the badly needed academic buildings.

"Actually, the rumors and reports of his leaving for other schools only got in the way of the stadium he wanted. Notre Dame knew that without Rockne to fill it, a big stadium might become the same debt-ridden white elephant as at other colleges. Nobody here questioned his greatness or his generosity. He was interested in sport, in boys, in a bigger and better college picture, in a finer America. He could have been selling the time, especially in later years, that he gave away to alumni groups, high schools, and other colleges. One time, for instance, Canisius College had a big meeting planned. They needed a major speaker. Somebody suggested Rockne but they decided they couldn't get him. One man said: 'He's a good guy—let's ask him.' So they asked him and he accepted—and paid his own expenses."

The true worth of what Rockne gave so freely to strangers was established in 1928 when he headed a tour of about 400 to the Amsterdam Olympic Games. The incident is so bizarre that I had passed it by as one of the fictions grown about the legend—until I received this voluntary eyewitness account from a Rockne classmate, John C. Burke, now of Stillwater, Minnesota. "The night before they left New York the tourists attended the musical *Good News*. Someone told me Rockne was to appear on the stage at that performance, so a number of us alumni attended. We expected that Rockne would probably take a bow from the stage.

"The professional actor who played the coach had delivered a pep talk to his actor players, an emotional speech, of course. The players had started to leave the dressing room to return for the 'second half'; but their coach said: 'Just a minute, boys. I want you to meet a friend of mine, Knute Rockne of Notre Dame.' At this point Rockne came on stage and got a big hand from the audience."

Perhaps that was all that had been intended, but this was Broadway, and the hero of a hundred such scenes in the little theaters of the gridiron responded to the stimulation. "Using Notre Dame tra-

dition and names," Burke writes, "he started slowly, using short staccato sentences; then he began to pace, to get madder and louder,
asking them 'what would Pete Vaughn think of the way you played
that first half—Pete Vaughn who broke the goal posts at Michigan in
1909 with his charge through the line for the winning score?' He went
on, bringing in other incidents and other players—Dimick, Philbrook and so on—then he went into his finish: 'Never mind the breaks
—make your own breaks—feet spread out, seats low—charge. Charge.
Charge.'"

It was, of course, a routine speech, such as the actor who played
the coach had given. But this was Rockne, the Barrymore of the Outdoor Stage, responding to the thrill of a challenge. It is very possible
that, as often happened in the dressing room, Rock forgot where he
was and began to believe himself. And the audience?

"You could see the embarrassment of the Broadway actor," Burke
continues, "at the power and dramatics that Rockne put into that
speech—so far superior to his poor imitation of a pep talk. You could
see the player-actors on stage thrill to the charge, and color up with
the excitement of that machine-gun blast. A man sitting next to
me said: 'I have officiated every Notre Dame-Georgia Tech game
played up to now. I have been in football all of my life—but that was
one of the most thrilling experiences of my career. I tingled from
the top of my head to my toes. It was positively electrifying.' And,"
Burke concluded, "it certainly was to me."

XLII

In 1928, with Flanagan gone, Niemiec moved up to the first string.
The day before the opening game, a "breather" with Loyola of New
Orleans, he reinjured the knee which had been ailing since the Drake
game of 1927. Troubles come to the troubled. Fullback Fred Collins
broke a wrist. With a few minutes to go and the score tied, 6–6,
Niemiec had to go in to pull out a 12–6 victory.

The next week, at Wisconsin, the grass was long on the playing
field. Tom Lieb, at that time on the Badger staff, did not show up to

greet the Notre Dame squad. Secret practice wasn't secret. Rock pulled his team from the practice field and worked them out in the ballroom of their hotel. In the game a shock troop punter's knee "locked" when he tried to punt. This 10,000-to-1 shot freak accident cost a touchdown. The final score: Wisconsin 22 Notre Dame 6.

Navy came to Soldiers' Field; so did 105,000 football fans, perhaps still a record college crowd, who did not believe anything could ever be seriously deficient with a Rockne team. The Irish won in the last period on a pass from Niemiec to Colrick, 7–0. No heroics, no magic. Just hard, routine work. That night at a mammoth alumni dinner Rockne received a tremendous ovation—and responded with the only bitterness I ever saw him display in public. He told them how, after the Wisconsin defeat, "eight trucks could have driven abreast down the street outside our dressing room—without hitting any alumni."

The shock troop system had been forgotten. Rockne was now being hard-put to find eleven reasonably healthy and capable people to start a game. He hadn't dared try any of his sophomores; but a tough Georgia Tech was coming and he tried to pull a rabbit out of the bag by making a fullback out of Joe Savoldi, a green, green, green sophomore with the potential of a Jim Thorpe. This magnificent gamble paid off—for Tech, which passed over Savoldi for an early touchdown. Georgia Tech 12 Notre Dame 0.

Drake was a comfortable 32–6 cushion, and Penn State was beaten 9–0 on another soggy field. After the game I gave Rockne one of the two technical suggestions I offered during all the time I had known him: I had seen Yale complete a lot of passes against Army by sending tall ends down against West Point's short safety man. Rock's scout also had this observation in his notes.

Army was waiting with another undefeated eleven led by Cagle, the Player-of-the-Year. I picked Notre Dame to win, in the face of 4–1 odds, for auld lang syne but with little hope. I knew that Niemiec was up every night treating his knee; that Collins would be in there with his wrist in a cast. This was Get-Even Year for Rockne's opponents.

Yet, in terms of the theater, Rockne was a star who could breathe brilliance into a pale play; who could inspire ordinary actors into extraordinary performance. The Swede obviously was not himself again, though it was hardly likely that even the young Rockne could have done anything about this situation. Still—this was New York, and Army, and this situation did have the elements—

Years later, Joe Williams would write in the New York *World-Telegram* of another Army game: "This is by no means the biggest game of the year or even of the day. And yet it has the Big Town in something approaching a mild hysteria. It's bigger than the World Series, the heavyweight championship fights . . . I have a feeling Knute Rockne contributed importantly to this unique situation. Rockne was the sort of fellow the Big Town goes for; an individualist, a leader, a showman. He was a legend even before he died. People around here talked in football terms of Rockne. The heritage lingers. There probably will be a number of people attending tomorrow's game who believe Rockne is still coaching. Unless you've been around here a number of years you can't appreciate the enduring imprint he left."

It was the 1928 Army game, which Rockne entered as leader of a band of martyrs into the colosseum, that left his deepest imprint on the Big Town. In his writing there was hardly a mention of it.

The pep talk before a game is as much a part of football tradition as the football. Nobody laughed forty years ago when Tad Jones said to a Yale squad, in sacerdotal tone: "Gentlemen, you are about to play football for Yale against Harvard. Never in your lives will you do anything so important." Later Herman Hickman, in a moment of heroic proportions, chose to deliver the oration of Spartacus to the Gladiators to his Elis. And so it has gone through the years, with the form and the mood changing as other styles to the times. It is all part of the spiritual preparation which makes jet-propelled missiles of human bodies, hurling at each other later on the field—and damned be him who first cries "Hold. Enough."

This day, in his direst need, Rockne delivered his masterpiece. In the little theater of the stone-and-concrete dressing room, he looked at his waiting boys. He knew the physical, mental, and moral qualities of every boy in the room. Individually, they would be outclassed by the Cadets they would have to face. Collectively they might have a chance—

Rockne said: "Before George Gipp died he said to me: 'Rock, someday when the going is real tough, ask the boys to go out and beat Army for me.'"

This was the day.

"It made our blood boil," Niemiec told me recently. "We had heard of Gipp as a nice fellow, a great player."

As the teams took the field the boys in the blue jerseys looked pathetic in comparison to the big, vibrant Cadets, but Notre Dame held the ball in midfield after having controlled it throughout most of the first period. I was surprised but grateful. The boys were making a good stand—but for how long?

Niemiec punted 52 yards out of bounds on the Army 2-yard line. Murrell punted out to the Army 37. Collins broke through and seemed headed for a touchdown until Cagle stopped him. Chevigny and Collins got a first down in two tries. Collins broke through to the two-yard line where he fumbled. ("Imagine my embarrassment," Freddy said later, "no ball.")

Notre Dame came back to the Army 37. Army held and that was the surprising first half.

Well, I thought, the boys have given them a show—regardless of what happens in the second half.

It seemed to be happening—and quickly. Army returned the second half kickoff to its 27-yard line, and in seven plays advanced 73 yards to a touchdown. Cagle threw a 41-yard pass to Messinger and later scored. The point was missed but it did not seem important at the time. Army looked good for plenty more, now that the dam had broken.

But the little lads in blue, like audacious bicycles through truck traffic, moved by short, steady dashes through the Army line 52 yards to the score. It was Chevigny who went over from the one-yard line— and then tossed the ball toward the sky with the exuberant shout: "One for the Gipper."

The point was missed. It was a 6–6 tie; and that's the way it looked as if it would end. It had slowly dawned on me that I could stop feeling sorry for my little boys, that while I had been willing to die gamely, they had been out there fighting to live. They had been bringing to life the couplet of the "Victory March":

> What though the odds be—great or small
> Old Notre Dame will win over all.

During the time-outs, Captain Fred Miller, a future millionaire, would lead the lads in short prayers. Center Tim Moynihan, the roistering son of a Chicago fire captain, would sit on the ground like an Indian, repeating: "It's in the bag. It's in the bag." After Miller's prayer, Tim would grin, like a John Wayne character: "Okay—let's play a little football, too." This was the Sorin principle: prayer *and* good works.

Late in the fourth period, it was Notre Dame which was again moving steadily toward the goal for what might be the winning score. The march had reached the Cadet 20. The stands were thundering approval. They were seeing, these people of faith, what they had come to see: Rockne and his lads performing a miracle; the hard way—*running through* that tremendous Army line. Then the gods who sit in the control rooms of the sky and direct these little things below, smiled and flicked a switch. The paean turned to the "Irish cry."

A signal had been missed. The ball was rolling toward the Notre Dame goal. The Army line, storming in, was after it. In those days they could have run this fumble 70 yards for the winning Army touchdown.

One Notre Dame man was back there. He pounced on the ball, hugged it—as the Army linemen hit him, fought him for it.

It was Notre Dame's ball, fourth down, with 16 yards to go, on its 32-yard line.

Notre Dame took time out. Now both groups of fans buzzed. It is in this high-powered delirium that young football players and older coaches must think. Players were around Chevigny asking him those questions. He had the smile but not the answers. How long he had been playing "out of his head" nobody would ever know. He had recovered that loose ball, saved the game through instinct. He was led off to a mighty cheer. And under that umbrella Rockne sent in, along with a new right halfback, a tall, slender sophomore end, who was a little light for defensive work, but he was a track man with speed, a sure pair of hands, a stout heart under pressure.

Sophomore Frank Carideo was in there at quarterback. As we have said, in these days the substitute could not talk until after the first play. But Carideo needed no message—once he saw O'Brien. There had been a dry run, of a sort, for this play—in the fading moments of the Loyola game O'Brien had caught two passes from Niemiec. Rockne had remembered the tall Minnesota end, jumping against Niemiec; and the scout report about the stumpy Army quarterback, Nave, who was still in there at safety.

It was a must-do play but the play itself was routine. Niemiec took the ball, rolled out, saw that his line was holding, knew he could throw the ball if O'Brien was there—O'Brien was there—and now the ball, high and true and leading, up there for Johnny to grab it—he had it—was juggling it, was falling—but over the goal line *with* the ball and into immortality.

Running outside the side lines from his place on the bench had been O'Brien's fellow sophomore from Southern California, Larry "Moon" Mullins. Years later, in a commissary on the Paramount lot in Hollywood they laughed over the play. "I told him," Mullins grinned, "if he hadn't caught that ball he might as well have kept on running all the way back to Los Angeles."

The try for extra point was missed. But nobody cared. The score was 12–6, it was getting dark and the game must be about over. There was no time clock in those days—which heightened the suspense.

The Irish script was simple: Stop Army on the kickoff. Take the ball away on downs.

But there was still a fellow in that Army backfield, an old Irish foe named Chris Cagle—one of the greatest open-field runners and most fiery competitors in gridiron history. This was his moment to arise—the moment of that fine, frustrated Army eleven—

The kickoff went to Cagle—a bad mistake right there. Down and across the field he swept—with Army blockers doing their jobs—past midfield—he might go all the way—

Freddy Collins nailed him at the side lines. But Cagle had returned 62 yards and now Army was crackling like lightning. Cagle continued to crackle, sparkle in the gloom. The play was furious, down in the shadows of the Notre Dame goal line, near home plate in the stadium. The crowd had lost all reason—and gone was the traditional poised neutrality of the press box.

I had my binoculars on the battle sector. There seemed to be time out—some discussion—

This was my lead in the game story for the *Daily News:*

"A huddled figure took off his headgear and threw it to the ground in disgust. The others began scurrying in various directions. Notre Dame had won 12–6. Army, needing six points to tie, had been on the Notre Dame three-yard line with fourth down and one-half yard to go. Well might the young man have thrown his headgear to the ground. He was an Army man, and Army, led by the scintillating star of the gridiron, Christian Keener Cagle, had just come 83 yards in a glorious effort to avert its first defeat of the year."

That night Rockne looked spent, tired, happy. He was smiling. He was quiet. It was one of only three times I remember him quiet.

XLIII

The next morning, in his suite at the Vanderbilt, he was vibrant again. He had read the newspapers. He told me that, along with the rest, I had missed the boat on who had the ball at the end of the game. It was, he said, Notre Dame's ball.

I checked my chart. He was right—as usual.

That afternoon the team left town, as always, on the New York Central. Also according to custom, I stood on the platform with three or four others while Joe Byrne led us in a "Big UND."

> UND. Rah! Rah!
> UND. Rah! Rah!
> Who rah? Who rah?
> UND. Rah! Rah!
> Team. Team. TEAM.

I felt a little conspicuous, as other adults watched us overripe sophomores on that Sunday afternoon. We returned to the Ritz-Carlton to talk it all over. It was here that Joe Byrne told me the story of the Gipp dressing-room speech.

The follow-up story usually gives more information on the game than the one done from the press box. I am quoting part of my Monday story which set in circulation the George Gipp speech that became part of football lore:

New York Daily News, Monday, Nov. 12, 1928

GIPP'S GHOST BEAT ARMY
Irish Hero's Deathbed
Request Inspired
Notre Dame

by Frank Wallace

George Gipp beat the Army in 1920 and died that fall, the outstanding football man of the year, mourned by the nation. Saturday, what was thought to be the weakest Notre Dame team in fifteen years, completely outplayed the Cadets, stopped the outstanding player of this season and provided the biggest upset of the campaign.

Notre Dame people regard the 12–6 victory over the Army as the most glorious in the history of the school; and the eleven men who played almost the entire game will forever be honored with Gipp, the Four Horsemen, Rockne, Dorais, Al Feeney and the rest.

Those boys overcame physical strength, pure form, theory and bad breaks. They played as few teams have ever played.

They were underdogs and that helped. They had Rockne and he helped. Football people knew that Rockne would fire up his boys in his speech before the game. This is what he told them—and perhaps you can understand the cold forgetfulness of self of those Irish kids.

"On his deathbed George Gipp told me that someday, when the time came, he wanted me to ask a Notre Dame team to beat the Army for him."

It was not a trick. George Gipp asked it. When Notre Dame's football need was greatest, it called on its beloved "Gipper" again.

The press went wrong on the situation at the end of the stirring battle. Actually Army had lost the ball on downs and the Notre Dame team was getting ready to line up for a kick or a safety when the officials called final time.

In the concluding paragraphs I gave the sequence of plays following Cagle's return of the kickoff, to prove the contention that Army had lost the ball. This argument remained live news for several days. But "One-Play" O'Brien and the George Gipp speech lived on. As previously related, Rockne questioned my use of the Gipp speech but accepted my reasoning—that it belonged to the tradition. He also used it in the *Collier's* articles, and there have been many distortions.

Do you think, perhaps, that I have overemphasized the importance of this game? Listen, then, to my sports editor, Paul Gallico, writing from the press box after the game:

"Long after the people had struggled off the playing field, the waves of play kept surging through the brain like heavy disturbing swells, uprooting all logical thought and still carrying the emotions on their curling crests. When football becomes a near-tragic race against time there is nothing like it for thrill, excitement or suspense. The game exerts its magic and you forget that it is just football and that one mustn't overemphasize . . . Hells bells and gongs of inferno! Let us overemphasize while we may. Tomorrow it will be too late. The enchantment which holds me still enthralled will be lifted. It will have been but a football game between two institutions which prepare for months for these hippodromes . . . As this is written the spell of Collins and Niemiec and Chevigny and Cagle is still on this mundane spot and one regrets that they have gone and that they are not still charging over the turf and flinging their bodies like living scythes through the air . . . I'm glad Notre Dame won the way they did. Do I mind being a boob on my prediction story? Gee no. It would have been heartbreaking to see them lose after so much gallant effort."

The heartbreak came the next week.

Two things can happen to a college football team the week after an emotional triumph: it can continue in the high gear of stimulation—*if* it is physically strong and technically sound. But if it is an inferior team which has drawn drastically from its emotional reserves, it is very apt to step on the starter and find the battery all but dead. The 1928 Notre Dame squad was inferior; and it was emotionally bankrupt, without spark, in the Carnegie game Rock wanted so badly to win. The cripples were hollow shells. Tech won 27–7; and the Irish score was made in the final period when Rock called in the sophomores whom he had not previously felt like risking in major competition.

It was much the same story in the climactic game at Los Angeles the following week. The Trojans avenged their two one-point defeats by a 27–14 triumph—and again the Irish heroes were such upcoming youngsters as Carideo, Mullins, Leahy, and O'Connor, with some help from junior Jack Elder, a track man who had come to football late and was still learning the trade. Niemiec had a wrenched neck to add to the swollen knee and other assorted bruises which caused Rock to describe him as Old Tape-and-Guts.

Rockne had now made records of a different sort. He had failed to win a game he badly wanted to win for personal reasons—Carnegie Tech. (Steffen had laughed and got away with it.) He had, for the first time in his career, lost two straight games. He had lost, in one season, as many games as in his first seven. He had seen Notre Dame defeated at home for the first time in a quarter-century.

I was flabbergasted recently, to hear, from a reliable source, that there had been some sort of a movement to have Rockne fired after the '28 season. There might have been a few such foolish faculty people. To Notre Dame generally the Army game had been worth any cost. I once asked Rock if the team that beat Army that day was not his favorite. He would never pick favorites, even among individuals; this time he just smiled, but his eyes talked. Personally, I don't think any football group ever gave more of itself.

In addition to Rockne, five others of the chief actors in that game died tragically. Johnny O'Brien joined the staff of Elmer Layden at his alma mater in 1936. On March 12, 1937, while returning from a tour-of-duty speech, he was killed in an automobile accident. (The Spring Game of that year was played for the benefit of his family. Acting captain of the Varsity which beat the Old-Timers 7–0, was Joe Kuharich.)

Freddy Miller became the millionaire president of the Miller Brewing Company, an important patron of sport on radio and television. He retained his interest in Notre Dame, was serving as a "volunteer coach" under Frank Leahy when his private plane crashed, killing him and his Notre Dame student son. Fred had never lost the faith which made him lead the prayers in the '28 Army game. He was a daily Communicant. He and his son had received Communion the morning of the day they died. Tim Moynihan died just a few years ago, after an auto accident.

Chris Cagle, who was to figure in another emblazoned play in the '29 Army game, never failed to show up, usually along with Elmer Oliphant, at the Notre Dame alumni parties in New York. The game doesn't end on the field and Chris knew he had a place in the Irish tradition. He died in a subway accident in Manhattan.

Then there was Jack Chevigny. In 1929 he joined Rockne as a coach, later went to Texas as a very young head man, came back with a team that ruined Elmer Layden's opening game as Notre Dame head coach in '34. In 1944 he visited me at Beverly Hills. He was in charge of troop entertainment for Marines at Camp Pendleton. Always bristling with ideas, he had a project by which he hoped to have motion picture companies sponsor Marine divisions. I took him to M-G-M to see James Kevin McGuinness, an executive producer who had been a top-flight New York sports columnist. Chevigny, then an overage Marine lieutenant, clenched his fist, and with all the old football fire, said: "Marines are expendable."

The next year he died leading a suicide wave in the landing at Iwo Jima. You can guess *how* he died.

Niemiec became a high-school coach and is now a first-aid specialist with construction companies. He is still calm, poised, rugged, and true—as fine a representative of Notre Dame as I know. But he sometimes gets irritated with strangers who tell him all about the pass to Johnny "One-Play" O'Brien.

"By the way," Butch asked one of them, "who threw that pass?"

"Who cares who threw the pass?" the expert answered.

Rock cared. He called Niemiec the Old Bell Cow. After the 1928 season the citizens of Bellaire, Ohio, "The All-American Town," decided to have a testimonial dinner honoring Niemiec and Oliver "Mike" Miles, another of our citizens who had made All-American that year as Princeton fullback. The committee wanted their coaches. I contacted Rockne, who agreed immediately. The dinner plans fell through, so Rockne never got to Bellaire. He knew about us, since we had sent him, in addition to Niemiec and Poliski, Joe Sheeketski and Jim Harris. He had a routine he would give in hick dialogue, about how the constable met the train in Bellaire. He would, on occasion, refer to Niemiec and Poliski as "the Bellaire bankers."

Along with other possessions, I had acquired, in my early Manhattan days, a Homburg hat, spats, and a walking stick. These were reserved for proper occasions; one of which was definitely not the Notre Dame team headquarters at the Westchester Country Club. But I wore them for one reason—to get Rock's reaction. Something had happened to upset him. I smiled, with graduate sophistication. "Wallace—what are you laughing at—with that dude paraphernalia?

It's only recently you shook that Bellaire clay off your heels." The trip was a success.

XLIV

At a time when Ohio State was looking for a football coach, the veteran Buckeye Athletic Director, Lynn St. John, reminisced on a previous experience. "There was only one time when I felt justified in hiring a man without talking to anybody else. That was after the 1928 season when we were looking for a successor to Dr. Jack Wilce . . . I was sitting in my office when a call came from Major John Griffith, Athletic Commissioner of the Conference. He said he had a young fellow in his office who was interested in our coaching position. He was Knute Rockne. So he put Rockne on the phone and sure enough he was interested in leaving Notre Dame and in getting into the Big Ten. We talked awhile and finally made an engagement to meet at the coaches meeting which was being held shortly after at New Orleans."

Hub Atkinson, then chairman of the Board of Trustees at Ohio State, later told me of the details of the talks at New Orleans. He said that Rock gave these reasons for wanting to come to State: (a) Notre Dame had promised to build him a football stadium out of football profits but was building other buildings instead. (b) He wanted to get into the Conference to get cracks at Zuppke of Illinois and Yost of Michigan, neither of whom would play him while he was at Notre Dame.

Rockne wanted $10,000 salary, with a full professorship. He wanted the right to hold a coaching school, to write for a newspaper syndicate. Out of these activities he expected to net about $35,000. He wanted the right to name his own assistants. Ohio State was willing; but, and now came the familiar: "Rock said to keep it tentative until he had a chance to talk to Notre Dame"; and a somewhat new proviso, probably born of the Columbia episode: "There must absolutely be no premature publicity."

(Rockne had been considerably chastened by the Columbia experience. In Philadelphia, John Neeson had sternly demanded: "What about all these things?" After it was all over Rock and Joe Byrne were walking in the rain. A few bits of paper were floating down the gutter. "Don't sign any of those," Byrne laughed.)

But the publicity broke almost immediately at New Orleans. Rockne was annoyed, the deal was called off, without prejudice, on the part of Ohio State. Their version was that the Studebaker people intervened to keep Rockne in South Bend. "It was shortly after this," Atkinson told me, "that Rock made a deal with Studebaker to lecture to their salesmen; and from that he moved into the executive end and was to have a car named after him."

I can only speculate, but the Ohio State incident could have been a near-miss. Rock would have heard any talk by a fringe element about getting him fired, and he would have reacted seriously to that. Studebaker did want to keep him in South Bend, as we will see a little later. After this flurry subsided, his major motivation seems to have been a sharp comeback in '29. When Hunk Anderson left to go to St. Louis University as head coach in '29, Rock may have begun to think about building a permanent coaching staff, headed by a top assistant who could take over details.

The man he had in mind was Adam Walsh, captain of the Four Horsemen and certainly one of Rockne's personal favorites among the boys he had coached. Adam writes: "I was invited by Rock to be his assistant in 1929. I had agreed to a three-year contract from him by telegram. Two days later he called me from Philadelphia, asking me if I wouldn't take the line coaching job at Yale, because I would be the first 'outsider' on their varsity staff. He felt that would help the name of Notre Dame. Naturally, as always, I did what Rock wanted me to do, to the best of my ability."

The following, from Joe Boland, may help to explain this bond between Rock and his boys:

"Scene: Springfield, Ohio . . . August 1929 . . . Coaching school conducted by Rockne . . . with Jack Chevigny and myself demonstrating for him . . . and rooming, side by side, with connecting doors open. Last night or so of the school, a thief cleaned all of us of money—leaving everything else, but going through each room with the thoroughness of a vacuum cleaner! I was a pretty blue guy— no dough: no pay check from my first job as head coach until the first of October: transportation to St. Paul and living expenses needed. Sitting in my room next morning, contemplating the evils of life, when Rock came in . . . said: 'You lost all the money you had last night, didn't you?' 'Yes,' I replied. Whereupon . . . he dropped a thick roll of bills into my lap (he had cashed a sizable check, to take care of his own and these needs) and said: 'That should hold you until you get paid, kid!'

"Never a mention of a loan—or a gift: obviously, he felt Chev (for whom he did the same thing) and I were *his* responsibilities! And he was going to take care of his boys!

"He got his money . . . needless to say: but the manner in which he *gave* it . . . that defies description, as it typified Rock!"

Having placed Walsh at Yale, "to help the name of Notre Dame," Rock brought Tom Lieb back from Wisconsin as line coach and first assistant and, though neither could suspect it at the time, to do a uniquely valuable (and generally overlooked) coaching job during the season. Lieb handled most of the spring practice as Rock flew over the country on Studebaker assignments. "It was a good thing I did have that responsibility," Tom wrote me, "because after the first game with Indiana, Rock had to go to bed. The next week I was at his home every morning, and ran the noon lectures and afternoon practices. On Thursday morning Rock had a copy of *Gray's Anatomy* on his bed. He called Dr. Sensenich and said: 'Doc, I think I have a phlebitis.'"

Unfortunately, Rockne was right again, and the stage was set for the most bizarre of all his exploits. The already famed Irish squad now became a traveling stock company (the stadium was being built and all games were played on the road) each week presenting some fantastic new drama of the Outdoor Theater, conceived, written, and directed by the Master who, on occasions, would scorn medical advice and rise from his couch to personally star. He had several things going for him.

(1) Lieb, his stage manager, had been his assistant for several years, knew his methods and had a general grasp of the Rockne psychology. A bluff, genial extrovert who was more apt to enjoy responsibility than panic before it, Tom was just about perfectly cast and proved to be one of the great pinchhitters in the history of sport. Mornings and evenings he spent in the sickroom. When Rock came

to practice, or went to the two road games, Lieb helped him dress, carried him in his arms from one resting place to another. Rock was the overseer, but Lieb personally directed six winning games.

(2) The Rules Committee, which had finally legislated the shift to a definite one-second stop, had already forced Rockne to gradually turn to a heavier type of football player, averaging about ten pounds more than the Four Horsemen group.

(3) Graduation losses had been light; his new squad would be composed of seasoned seniors and some very promising juniors who had acquired experience in the disaster period of the two final games in '28. Marty Brill, a rough transfer from Penn was at right half. The sophomores were promising; and one, Marchmont Schwartz, was good enough to give Jack Elder backing at the important left-halfback spot.

(4) Through the combination of these events Rockne would again, as the season progressed, have in smooth working order the system of starting shock troops, following with varsity, returning to shock troops and winding up with sophomores.

(5) Most important, perhaps, he again had a "coach on the field," a top-flight quarterback in the person of Frank Carideo, who could also take over first-string punting and when necessary, passing.

(6) The Master, supposed to abstain from even thinking football, had nothing to do but lie there and dream—and scheme.

The first big test came at Baltimore in the Navy game. I had left the *Daily News* to free-lance, and had joined the circus brigade which felt life was not complete without a View from the Bench— the very worst place in any stadium from which to see a football game. But a bench ticket also included dressing-room privileges; and this was a phase of the Rockne coaching which had previously been mostly hearsay for me, as I had always been in the press box.

So I was on hand for the first of the Master's personal performances, a "remote" as the TV people might now style it. Before the game the regulars began to be called from the room to a nearby alcove where a telephone had been installed. Rockne was calling from South Bend. He talked, calmly, technically, personally, to each of his regulars—and finally to Tom Lieb. (The technique has since frequently been utilized by other hospitalized coaches. Niemiec used it to win a high-school game.)

The atmosphere on the bench that day was cool, poised. Rockne had supplied the proper touch—and Lieb did nothing to disturb it. Frank Carideo, knocked to his knees, threw a forward pass that was a key play in the winning touchdown of the 14–7 victory.

A 19–0 win over Wisconsin, almost reversing the 6–22 debacle of the preceding campaign, was a measure of how this squad had improved in one year.

Carnegie Tech, the self-proclaimed "jinx team," was next.

This was the one Rockne had planned for; it was the one he was going to have, even if it killed him—as the doctors warned him it might. The danger was that emotion, or excitement, or mere activity, might dislodge the clot from his leg, send it racing through the blood stream, where it would pass through his heart or the big artery at the base of the brain—causing a heart attack or a brain stroke.

XLV

Rockne got out of bed to coach from a platform erected on the practice field. His period of thinking had convinced him that one man might be the key to victory over a bruising Tech team that knew Notre Dame would be coming for a fight to the kill. The man Rock wanted in there was Joe Savoldi, the potential Jim Thorpe, who had come to this country from near Milan, Italy, at the age of thirteen— not too many years before. At Notre Dame, as a sophomore, as previously related, he had been pushed in over his head; and after that disastrous Georgia Tech experiment, there had been neither time nor opportunity to salvage him. Savoldi had been Rock's special project in the spring training and pre-season practice of '29; but after Rock had been taken from the scene, somebody had made the bad mistake of questioning Joe's courage. Bewildered, he had, for a week or two, quit the team.

Now Rock brought him back, had him running at fullback again, sometimes on the first eleven. I can still remember Rock's metallic voice booming out from the loud-speaker on the platform where he sat, legs stretched out, well-bundled against the cold: "Nice going, Savoldi. Big Joe is going to *go* in there Saturday. Attababy Savoldi. Big Joe will go. Big Joe will go." It rang out for all to hear, for the squad, the campus, the countryside, for Big Joe to hear. The Gridiron Vulcan was at his anvil, hammering out a psychological repair job for an emergency.

When the team left for Pittsburgh, Rockne was on the train. The next morning he lay on a divan in his room at the Pittsburgh Athletic Club, bandied wisecracks, dispensed tickets to his friends of the press, especially those from the Big Town. I was one of them, representing the biggest circulation of all; but I was a member of the family and didn't count. When I offered to trade him two tickets for three, to take care of an added starter from my family, he reacted, as always, as if I were seeking the gold fillings from his teeth. But he gave me the tickets. He was, as they say at the race track, going in his best form, happy to be back in the swing of things, where there was challenge, action, competition.

That afternoon he was wheeled to the gymnasium floor where the squad walked through signals.

But that night the door was closed. There was no party. There were alarming reports.

Fifteen minutes before game time the next afternoon the Pitt Stadium was already filled, waiting for this grudge game, between players and coaches, which had been advertised from coast to coast. But there was a prologue which none of the seventy thousand in the stands could have imagined.

An automobile drove through the stadium gates and to the entrance of the dressing rooms.

Inside the boys were waiting, wondering. The boys had heard the rumors.

The door opened. Tom Lieb came in, carrying Rockne in his arms, as if he were a baby. Lieb placed Rockne on a table. He sat there, legs stretched out, staring ahead. He wore tan, high-top shoes and black overshoes—and overshoes on Rockne seemed the symbol of his weakness. His face was very sober, very set. His eyes were static. This was like watching a calm over mercury.

For five minutes he sat there, immobile. The seconds were long in a football locker room where boys were dressed, waiting to run and explode. Time was running out. Two o'clock would be soon. But Rock looked at nobody, seemed hardly conscious of anybody or anything about him.

The boys were sitting before him, on benches, like they do in a grade-school picture. They were like grade-school kids as they looked at him, away from him, bit their lips, glanced at the floor, did other things to get through that silence—the boys who were to make football history by winning nineteen straight tough games and two successive national championships—Twomey, Carideo, Moynihan, Savoldi, Law, Brill, Conley, Elder, O'Brien, O'Connor, Colrick, Culver, Kassis, Metzger, Donoghue, Nash, Yarr, Vezie, Schwartz, Leahy, Mullins . . .

It would have been ludicrous if it had not been serious—the great, strong, fierce, indomitable, dynamic Rockne being carried into a locker room like a baby and left sitting there with black overshoes on tan high-tops—

There were about five of us back of the lockers where we could see but not be seen. There were some wet eyes. You may think this a very silly business to get so emotional about, but this was in 1929, just a few days before the stock market crashed and a new era dawned. This was Rockne and Notre Dame; and across the way were Steffen and Carnegie Tech, the tormentors.

Behind the lockers Dr. Maurice Keady was whispering: "If he lets go, and that clot dislodges, hits his heart or his brain—he's got an even chance of never leaving this dressing room alive."

It began. When his voice came it was strong. This is close to an actual record of the words he used:

"A lot of water has gone under the bridge since I first came to Notre Dame—but I don't know when I've ever wanted to win a game as badly as this one.

"I don't care what happens after today.

"Why do you think I'm taking a chance like this? To see you lose?" (He was beginning to shout.)

"They'll be primed. They'll be tough. They think they have your number. *Are you going to let it happen again?*"

Quiet again. I don't know what the boys were doing. I could not see. All of us behind the lockers had heads down.

Now he shot the works. He let go. I watched his face through a space between the lockers. As he talked his mobile features distorted with almost insane determination. This was the supreme effort of a great fighter. His voice was vibrant, strong:

"Go out there and crack 'em. Crack 'em. *Crack 'em.* Fight to live. Fight to win. Fight to live. *Fight to win—win—win—*WIN—"

He was shouting, screaming, pouring his sick self into them—

They were leaving, running, leaving a savage roar among the reverberating tiles. As the last of them left, Rock collapsed.

His eyes were shut. His face was in pain. He was sweating. The doctor, at his side throughout, felt the pulse, gently mopped the sweat from his face.

Rock wanted to win more than he wanted to live.

It was not easy that day in the Pitt Stadium. He and his squad knew what they were up against, what they had asked for. This would be as near a fight to the death as any one of them would ever face without weapons.

There was no talk on the field this day. It was grim, hard, savage, no quarter asked or given. But remarkably clean, as if this were an affair of honor, not to be cheapened. I was on the bench, close to the side lines. I could see it—and hear it. That's football—when you can *hear* the bodies hit.

Rock was calm, efficient, in his wheel chair. There was no sign of weakness. He was the general, the dynamo, the source of wisdom, of strength, of guidance.

No score in the first half. Nobody came close. Notre Dame was a bit better on offense, but fumbles had stopped their moves.

Rockne knew what had caused that. They were wound too tight. Between halves, he relaxed them a little. He was now calm as an executive in a conference room. "They'll pass this half."

In the second half they passed. Notre Dame was alert.

Tech gathered for the frontal assault. Their strong man, Karcis, a human cement barrel, hit our strong man, Marty Brill. Marty was driven back, just a trifle, but back.

Notre Dame stopped the charge. Tech was forced to punt.

Jack Elder is famous in football tradition for a run he would make later that year. But the one Rockne wanted most came now. The track man had learned the things a football man had to know to be effective in the big time. Elder returned a punt 35 yards to the Tech seven-yard line.

This was it. The showdown. The meeting in the street of football's Dodge City. And now Rockne called on Big Joe. This was the moment he had foreseen. Now was the time for Big Joe to go.

Everybody in the stadium, perhaps on radio, knew what was coming. Big Joe was the ball-carrier, but ten men were ahead of him, and eleven men were opposing. There was no deception. This was man-style.

Four times Big Joe Savoldi gathered his weight and speed into a projectile, hurled it at the tiny stretch his mates had made in the Tartan armor. Three yards—two yards—one yard.

Fourth and one.

Big Joe scored.

There was more than a quarter left to play. But Notre Dame had the seven points, and put the stamp of finality on the victory by protecting it with such savagery that Tech never came close.

The big danger the next week, with Rockne back in bed, was the letdown after the emotional surge. But this was a hungry squad, a strong squad, a prosperous squad which was repaying the debts of 1928. With the Wisconsin and Carnegie Tech accounts settled, they repaid Georgia Tech 26–6. And after Drake had been safely passed, 19–6, there remained the last of the '28 conquerors, Southern California.

The game was played at Soldiers' Field on a brilliant November day before another 100,000 crowd. Rockne had put this one on the pre-game chemist scales and decided it would also need his presence. He let go again in the dressing room; but, having survived the first threat at Carnegie Tech, we were not seriously disturbed about this one.

Southern Cal, a team notable for its grind-'em-out tactics with tailbacks carrying the brunt of the offense, threw a surprise punch with an immediate long pass that went for 50 yards and a quick touchdown. As the Trojan rooters (they always bring special trains to these Irish games) tumulted, a Notre Dame shock troop back was led from the field with an egg already formed over an eye. Presumably something had happened to his vision, permitting the Trojan receiver to get clear. He was undoubtedly more chagrined than pained at that embarrassing moment. His name was O'Connor—Paul "Bucky" O'Connor. Remember the name. The Trojans will never forget it.

Rockne had also prepared a deadfall into which the obliging Trojans kindly fell. Later he wrote: "In our 1929 season many Notre Dame enthusiasts wondered why our forward-passing game was not very much in evidence. Although ill in bed, I knew the Trojans had been scouting all our games, and must have been impressed by the fact that we had won all of them without the pass. That was kept undercover so that, as probably happened, their scouts would report our passing game was of no consequence. But we completed five long passes that won the game."

The surprise passer turned out to be Elder, the track man, thought to be only a runner. And the receiver was junior end Tom Conley. The Irish led 7–6. Then "Racehorse" Russell Saunders justified his title by doing what no other player had ever done against a Rockne team—ran a kickoff back for a touchdown. Again the Trojans indulged their odd weakness by missing the try for the extra point. The Irish finally won 13–12, for their third one-point victory in the first four years of the Trojan series.

That night Rockne was back in bed, happy and bright when I brought a visitor I knew he would want to see, Alan Gould, sports editor of the Associated Press. Little Jackie was asleep, his arms about his father's neck. Later that night the clot dislodged, passed through the heart, bypassed the brain and lodged in the other leg. Rockne was permitted no more recklessness, but the team was now ready for whatever came.

Northwestern, usually good for a close game, was beaten 26–6. Tim Moynihan's leg was broken, ending his career; but the roistering rascal came East with the team for the Army game, joined up with the victorious alumni, sat on a bed with a glass in his hand, and established the custom of autographing the surgical cast.

Two big hurdles were overcome in the 7–0 finale against Army. One was the familiar Chris Cagle, perhaps the most dangerous optional pass-or-run backfield man in college football history. The other hazard was the weather—eight degrees above zero. But the stands were packed, as always, and, as always, their patron Rockne, even in absentia, provided a new thrill.

Cagle's optional play was exciting because he would dart and dash and artfully dodge around the field, sometimes twenty yards back of the line of scrimmage. Chasing this fox kept the Irish players warm on this frigid afternoon. Finally, on one of these scatter plays, Chris let go toward Messinger, his right end, who had crossed over to the left. It was a touchdown play—for Notre Dame. Elder, who had followed his man across, took that do-or-die chance of getting in front of his man to intercept. The football senior had the savvy to time it perfectly—and the track star took off straight down the right side lines. One Army defender took a flying shot at him near midfield—and after he missed, Jack was homing for the longest run of the Army-Notre Dame series. I had always scored it as 96 yards, but later, when we served on the Alumni Board together, he convinced me it was 98 yards.

Like most of Rockne's great moments, this one had been carefully prepared. The Friday practice was held on the golf course at Westchester Country Club, in Rye, New York, where the squad was quartered before the game. The big "gallery" watching the practice did not know that there was deep design behind the long passes Lieb himself was throwing to the "Army right end" who was crossing over to his left—with Jack Elder defending. Once, when the ball went into some trees, Elder shouted: "I can't cover him in these trees."

Rockne's personal relationship with the Army people, extending from his day there as a player, was unique. He was a particular favorite of Colonel Herman J. Koehler, Master of the Sword and Army's Grand Old Man of that era. When the two service schools broke off relations and Notre Dame became the big game for each, Rockne's considerable talents as a diplomat were severely taxed. I was called to West Point, not as a writer but as a friend of Rockne and a Notre Dame insider. Army felt that Rock had sided with Navy. Colonel Koehler felt particularly let down. They had a publicity release prepared which would, in effect, have forced Rockne, and Notre Dame, to choose between Army or Navy. I told them that, from what I knew about Rock's feeling for Army, there must surely be some mistake. I asked them to hold the release until I had a chance to talk with him. He immediately called Army to clear the situation.

Later Army did release a statement, probably as a tactical maneuver in the conflict with Navy: but the sting was out and the ultimatum extracted. It caused practically no embarrassment because it had been scheduled for release the day after what Wall Street still calls Black Tuesday. And sports wound up among the ads that afternoon.

There was a fraternal feeling among Army and Notre Dame aficionados around New York in those days. Each year Alan Gould and I would arrange for a table at the Baseball Writers Dinner. Alan would invite the Army football brass. I would bring Joe Byrne and Dr. Maurice Keady, among others. In 1931 the Army people started it off with an afternoon cocktail party. I came home next morning, wearing the top hat and stick of a sedate officer who had, sensibly, retired early. Later an extremely beautiful young lady brought in a hat to the Knox store in the Roosevelt Hotel building and asked the astonished manager to please send it to Major Philip B. Fleming, U. S. Military Academy, West Point, New York. The lady was my wife. It was the easiest way we could think of to return the top hat.

XLVI

Rockne was back on top. He was going to stay on top, go out at the top, but I never saw him so low as on a late afternoon of the next February on the sands of Miami Beach. The phlebitis had dramatized his coaching during the '29 season, but it had now sentenced him to just sit in a bathing suit and hope the sun would bring him back to normal activity without the danger of any moment being his final one.

This day he had been to the doctor, as invalids often go, hopefully. The news had been, if not bad, discouraging. He would have to sit some more.

So he was sitting, staring out to sea, seeing nothing. And hearing nothing. I was trying to be bright, hopeful. I just didn't get through to him. This was not Rockne. There was no force inside storming from his eyes, agitating his voice. There was no twirling cigar. This face was flat, totally uninteresting; the body was just a series of lumps on the sand. No stranger, passing by, would see in this mediocrity one of the glamorous figures of his times, who before the year had ended, would again give high voltage to the football season, and a short while later, stun the country to its individual marrows as no private citizen had ever done.

That was Rockne in February, on the beach with his family around him.

When I next saw him, in the early fall, the Swede was himself again, in the basement offices of the Main Building. Tom Lieb had gone to Los Angeles to take the Loyola job Rockne had arranged for him. Hunk Anderson was back as top sergeant. Jack Chevigny, Tim Moynihan, and Ike Voedisch were also coaching. There were now student managers, business managers, squad doctors, trainers, equipment managers, and all sorts of other people to do all sorts of jobs Rockne had previously done for himself. This left him free for the two things about football he liked best—coaching his boys, and entertaining his old friends of the press, who, in their ways, also loved the guy. When they kidded him about all his help he said: "I don't know what goes on around here any more."

He would take time out occasionally to tighten the bandages which were to guard against a recurrence of the phlebitis. He called them his spare tires. He said, in the presence of Arch Ward and myself, that Joe Petritz was the best publicity helper he ever had; it got the proper laugh from our colleagues and the gentleman was pleased.

Somebody told of the time "Pop" Warner had drawn on a tablecloth the diagram of his famous reverse play. While Pop was explaining its operation, Rock had joshed: "It only works on paper." And of the panel radio show when Rock had been at the microphone and Babe Ruth, who did not know a football from an ostrich egg but was interested in lingerie, asked: "Rock, why do your football players wear silk pants?" And Rock had replied: "To keep their opponents' minds off the game. Next?"

At the beginning of his last and finest season, Rockne seemed happier and more contented than I had ever known him to be. He had learned to live with the phlebitis which was no longer a serious deterrent regardless of rumors following his death that "he hadn't long to live anyhow." The tonsils had been removed, ridding him of that poisonous stream. His nervous system had been toned. The doctors at the Mayo Clinic had gone over him from head to foot. His mind was rested after the long enforced idleness. He had a good squad coming up. He was again leaping at life—and over the horizon all sorts of people were waving that money he wanted so badly for the security of his two families.

He had his new stadium. In characteristic fashion he had supervised every detail, even to the extent of going to Ann Arbor to look at the stadium Yost had built. (He found many mistakes of course but copied the best features.) It is not unlikely that, after the Ohio State episode, there had been a firm understanding, with Studebaker as an interested party, that, if a stadium were built, Rockne would be around to fill it. The structure itself was mostly financed out of commitments for future ticket sales instead of the interest-hungry bonds which had become concrete chaplets around the necks of other schools, notably Pitt. Once the decision was made, Notre Dame had given its Ziegfeld a theater worthy of his talents, but there must have been anxious moments when, almost immediately after the job had begun, the country began to descend into a long depression, and Rockne's coaching future was threatened by his illness. If Notre Dame had known it was to have Rockne for only one more year, there would have been no new stadium at that time.

Rock had now completely achieved his "suicide schedule." It was to open with Southern Methodist which, using Coach Ray Morrison's "flying circus," was pointing for Notre Dame and a place in the national firmament. On the last play of the final practice, Rockne had permanently lost his regular left tackle, Frank Leahy. Early in the game his other tackle, Dick Donoghue, suffered a puzzling bone injury which was to count him out. This was no good omen for a bright new season, nor was the informal opener exactly what Rockne's doctor might have ordered, but it was a faithful preview of future productions in the House that Rock Built.

"I think we learned more in this game about defending against passes than fifty lectures could have told us," Frank Carideo said. Sparked by a 48-yard pass from Mason to Kattman, the Methodists made the first touchdown in the new Irish stadium in four plays. One minute later Joe Savoldi had avenged this effrontery with a 98-yard kickoff return. A Carideo punt runback set up the next score which put Notre Dame ahead. The Mustangs passed the length of the field to tie it, 14–14, just before the end of the half. A great catch of a pass by Ed Kosky finally got the Irish in front 20–14, but it took three late interceptions by Tommy Yarr, the half-Indian center, to definitely rope and tie the wild young hosses from Dallas. In between there had been open-field heroics and touchdown saves by both squads—and a 60-yard touchdown dash by Larry Mullins that was called back.

Navy came for the formal opening which was given all the pomp and gala enthusiasm due the glamorous past and present stature of Notre Dame, and to the eminence of Rockne. As Father Sorin had built the university and raised aloft the statue of Our Lady high on a golden dome, so the one-time "lone Norse Protestant" had raised the battlements of the stadium for all men to see. To those of us who, seeing a Great Stone Face among the bricks, thought it should be called Rockne Stadium, the man himself, with characteristic modesty, said quickly: No!

As usual, Notre Dame rose to a significant occasion. Torches, flaming red, marked the three-block long procession of stout fellows who chanted the hike song and the "Victory March." South Bend turned out. An Indiana moon shone down on 20,000 people. Air bombs went off. Set pieces blazed out a welcome to the Navy, spelled out the Notre Dame monogram, unfurled the American colors.

Rockne spoke briefly. Admiral Samuel S. Robison told of Navy's friendly relations with Notre Dame. Reverend Charles L. O'Donnell, the poet-president, told the story of Gipp at West Point—"reflecting all who had gone before and come after Gipp, which was why this stadium could be built." There were cheers for everybody, including Gilbert K. Chesterton, who was then lecturing at Notre Dame:

> He's a man.
> Who's a man?
> He's a Notre Dame man.
> Chesterton! Chesterton! *Chesterton.*

"My, they're angry," said the Englishman. He was standing with Rockne—and I'd liked to have heard their conversation. I'd particularly have liked to have caught Rock affecting an English accent, which he might well have done, since he hospitably adapted to environment.

(After the '30 season, Carideo's friends from White Plains, New

York, gave him a big dinner at the Hotel Astor. When home-town speakers pronounced it Car*iday*o, instead of the Car*ide*o by which he had become famous, Rock, in his speech also referred to Car*iday*o. Notre *Dame* is rhymed with *game;* but if a learned person chose to call it *dam* or *dom*, Rockne would obligingly go along, sometimes changing the pronunciation midway in a speech.)

The next afternoon, before the game began, Frank Hering, accepted in tradition as Notre Dame's first coach of any permanence, said: "Tradition is a compound of reverence and pride and unselfish service. Notre Dame traditions live. Notre Dame teams have thrilled millions of spectators and inspired the youth of the nation to play the game of football—and the game of life—in the spirit of the rules."

The whistle blew and the 1930 Notre Dame team, with Joe Savoldi (at fullback for the injured Mullins) leading the way, proceeded to its task with a 26–2 victory. When it was over, Bill Ingram, the Navy coach, became a prophet of record. "Not only was a fine stadium dedicated but there was ushered in the greatest Notre Dame team in the history of football."

XLVII

Frank Hering had said: "Tradition lives at Notre Dame." In 1928 Carnegie had violated the tradition that Notre Dame never lost at home. That indignity had to be redeemed the following week. It was grim for a while as neither line gave. Then, as if by arrangement, the strong men met again. A hole opened in the line and Karcis, the "human cement barrel" came rolling through—and was met by a headlong, head-on tackle by our Mr. Brill. This time it was Karcis who got up slowly. (Brill later told me he had brooded since Karcis had jarred him the preceding year.) With a 21–6 lead, two minutes to go, and nearing another score over the "jinx" team and its kidding coach, Rock put in his reserves.

Pitt was an old Irish sparmate, but the next game would be the first between Rockne and the rising Jock Sutherland, whose Panthers, also undefeated in 1929, ranked just behind Notre Dame. The game had a national championship flavor and drew a record crowd of 70,000 to the Pitt hilltop stadium (thereby delighting the banks which held the stadium bonds that hadn't been earning interest).

On the first play from scrimmage Marchy Schwartz slid through an aperture arranged by the Philadelphia firm of Conley and Brill— the old off-tackle play with the end blocking *in* and the halfback *out*. Once into the corridor Marchy broke from two tacklers to drop behind forming interference and complete a 60-yard touchdown run. It was a knockout punch, and thereafter the pattern was much the same. Notre Dame would kick off, take the ball away from the panting Panthers, and stage another unstoppable march. Four touchdowns in less than one half was against all Rockne's principles; so he sent in the shock troops. Bucky O'Connor—remember the name— ran for 41 and 20 yards and added the fifth score. At half-time it was 35–0. In the second half Rock used reserves and Pitt scored 19 points. In later years Jock Sutherland told me: "Rock could have beaten me 100–0 that day."

The next week it was Notre Dame 27 Indiana 0. But the Hoosiers were not taken in hand or even in comfortable fashion. At half-time the score was 0–0. Jack Elder, covering for the Chicago *Herald-Examiner*, wrote: "A lot of words must have been said during the intermission" meaning that Rockne had reached into himself to pump vitality into a squad due for a letdown after four straight weeks of high excitement.

Next came Penn, a good Ivy League squad which had, the preceding week, won over a previously undefeated Kansas eleven. A record crowd of 80,000, including Mayor Jimmy Walker of New York, filled Franklin Field for the only Eastern appearance of Notre Dame. Ed Pollock wrote in the Philadelphia *Public Ledger:* "The largest crowd saw the greatest team of the season and perhaps the best of all time, run up the highest score, 60–20, against Pennsylvania made within recollection of even the grayest-haired alumnus . . . If Penn tacklers were clever enough to diagnose the mystery plays of the master coach as executed by the talented first team, they were swept aside by interference which for effectiveness and *poetry of motion* has had no parallel on Franklin Field within the memory of this writer."

Grantland Rice wrote: "Notre Dame's first team actually beat Penn 43–0 in less than 30 minutes of play. Rockne and Notre Dame passed on far beyond the Four Horsemen. With Carideo, Brill, Savoldi, and Schwartz they put on a combination of four antelopes, four charging buffaloes, four digdigs and four eels." Your humble servant, in the New York *Daily News*, was more conservative: "Notre Dame, the wonder football team of modern times, played a game of superlatives here today . . . Marty Brill, who wasn't good enough for Penn as a sophomore, was the sentimental and actual star in the parade of Irish backs. He made three of the nine Notre Dame touchdowns, following runs of 66, 36, and 25 yards."

Marty Brill was the story. He had been enrolled at the University of Pennsylvania, felt unwelcome, came unsolicited to Notre Dame, lost a year of eligibility in the transfer, became so very popular with the students that the team had looked forward to the Penn game as "Marty's Day." There was nothing Rockne could have done, unless he risked mutiny, about that first-half score. The Brill story has been distorted by the report that Marty's father had offered $1000 for each touchdown he made against Penn. Both assured me it was not true.

The squad dinner following the Penn game was quiet. Not even Rockne would sit at the head table. I believe they all sensed, as I did, that something unusual was happening, that they were a part of it— and just a little afraid of it. I asked Rockne that night: "What's happening? Anything I don't know about?"

He shrugged, did not smile. "They're just taking the stuff, doing things right."

This was perfection, right off the blackboard, with every man doing his job. People fear perfection, or anything approaching it. But this being earth, perfection is rare.

Joe Savoldi had learned to run like an eel, defend against passes, back up the line. He might have really become the modern Jim Thorpe. But Joe hadn't learned not to sue for divorce in the middle of the football season, especially at Notre Dame where, apart from the religious obligation, students were not even supposed to be married.

That was all for Joe, but he did well as a wrestler, where they did not have silly rules; and he later did very well, for a fellow whose courage had once been questioned by a southpaw psychologist, in

World War II behind the lines in Italy with the Cloak and Dagger squad.

Larry Mullins was a better all-round player than Savoldi, a fine team and morale man, which was why he was first-string when his knee was not ailing. But it was uncertain, and the departure of Jumping Joe in mid-season set in motion a series of events which were to thoroughly test the best college squad in football history—and send the last season of the greatest coach down to a thundering climax. In other words—you ain't heard nothin' yet.

Rockne's final margin over other coaches came from his superior ability to foresee *how much* of *what kind* of stimulation his squad needed *when;* and to provide it. He could do this because of his insight into human beings; and his ability to transfer from himself to his players the energy needed to keep their emotional batteries at top level of efficiency. (If I repeat this every so often it is because this is the explanation for the success or failure of almost any football coach, or, probably, of any leader in any field.)

Having lost, in Savoldi, a valuable cog in his whirring machine, and with Mullins an ever-doubtful factor because of recurrent injuries, Rockne the Engineer reached into his reserves and brought out sophomore Dan Hanley, a big broth of 190 pounds, six feet, one and one-half inches, who could also punt. Though no Savoldi as a runner, he looked good enough in the 28–7 victory over Drake to back up Mullins. And Rockne now had his machine tuned up for the last lap, the Big Three who, this year, all were really *big.* They were: Northwestern, the undefeated Big Ten champion; Army, once-tied but undefeated; Southern California—beaten early, but so sensational thereafter that the Irish, undefeated for 19 games, and hailed with superlatives, were actually to enter their game as 5–3 underdogs.

XLVIII

Bert McGrane of the Des Moines *Register-Tribune* received permission to report Rockne's pep talk before the Northwestern game.

Very few coaches would have done this, and Rock would have done it for very few writers. Bert reported: "Twenty minutes of death-like stillness—then the atmosphere is electrified. Rockne bites off every burning word. He speaks in sharp ringing tones. He tells them what the game means. He wants it clean as a whistle. He wants them to fight, *fight*, FIGHT. Rockne's talk requires perhaps forty seconds. His men dash out. Fifty fighting hearts are pumping. Fighting blood is coursing. There must have been silence of the Rockne variety in the Argonne or at Château Thierry."

At first Notre Dame gained almost at will. Then the illusion gave way to reality. Coach Dick Hanley had also played a scene in the Northwestern dressing room. The Wildcats rallied with savagery. The half ended without a score. Now, in the dressing room, Rock gave them his homely prescription: "Work more as a team, less as individuals."

In the second half Northwestern never got beyond the Irish 40-yard line. But with five minutes to go, it looked like a scoreless tie. Then, again, the perfect play, Old 51 with Schwartz approaching the goal where only the safety man stood between him and victory—

A long, lean mate, coming down and across (also off the blackboard), eliminated the safety man. Who was that? Johnny "One-Play" O'Brien, now a senior, had clicked again in the moment of high emergency. The final score: 14–0.

Now there were two—Army and USC. And Army this year was coming to Chicago, presumably as a Midwest rallying point for propaganda-morale purposes; and to Soldiers' Field, because its 110,000 capacity could accommodate almost twice as many spectators as the 58,000 of the new Notre Dame Stadium.

Undefeated, once-tied Army coming to Chicago would seem to have engrossed even Rockne's complete attention, but these were the early days of the great depression, Rockne's name was a crowd-getter, and promoters in three great cities, Chicago, New York, and Los Angeles, had asked him to coach charity games. This amazing man who couldn't say no, had agreed to all three—with none promising anything more to him personally than the headaches, and in one case, a financial loss, they finally delivered.

The Chicago charity game, between old stars from Notre Dame and Northwestern, was to be played at Soldiers' Field on Thanksgiving Day morning, two days before the Army game. But down at Notre Dame, where Rockne was coaching the varsity and the Old Pros (as they called themselves), a heavy snow drove both groups indoors to the dirt floor of the old gym—where the basketball and indoor track squads were already at work.

Everybody was working for sweet charity but the sour weatherman. On the morning of Thanksgiving Day it was two above zero in Chicago. The Pro game was observed by 2000 crazy people, not including me. I don't even know who won—but Rex Enright had a rib broken, and Rockne got clipped for $3000. I have seen correspondence from both sides of this venture by well-meaning but ill-advised people who probably were satisfied to charge it to experience. For a little while it even seemed that Rockne had learned to say no—but only for a little while.

The night before the Army game the Chicago alumni staged a big victory powwow. As the recent author of *Huddle*, a book in which Notre Dame and Rockne were thinly disguised, I made the end of the dais, among the coaches of other schools who had been defeated that fall. The oratorical competition was terrific but I got a smart-alecky freshman idea: I complained that Notre Dame alumni had been cheated of one of the great pleasures of the alumni of other schools—because we never got a chance to fire our coach.

Everybody seemed to think it a cute idea, especially those defeated coaches who might even then have been just a few strides ahead of the alumni wolf pack. Everybody, that is, but Rockne. Busy as always with many other things, he was late for the dinner, and he had had to stand at the door and listen to his former literary bus boy trying to be funny about Rockne. Attended by the usual retinue, he marched by me, giving me the best glare I had received since the days of the Sheik contest. A few months later, of course, I didn't think it was so funny, either, after we had got rid of our coach.

The next day it rained. The crowd went out anyhow, as football crowds do (and this is something Khrushchev should have seen) defying the pneumonia germ. The rain became sleet, the field was a slithering mess. Here was the day for the upset.

XLIX

Just before the kickoff came a rare winter thunderstorm—a noonday darkness eerie with gongs of doom; easy, in hindsight, to interpret as a fitting farewell to Chicago, where Rockne had begun his athletic career.

Robert F. Kelley of the New York *Times*, wrote: "Two teams never played under worse conditions. The threatened snow did not come but in its place was a steady, drizzling rain that half-froze as it fell. It turned the field into a slimy mess that made it a feat for a man to stand up, much less run or change direction. Passes were tried but only two were completed."

Larry Mullins, bad knee and all, was the best mudder, kept the Irish on the attack; but the Army line was strong enough, with the help of General Mud. Again it looked like a scoreless tie—and that would have gone on the books as the Upset.

Again, without warning, and from midfield, it was Schwartz on Old 51, the bread-and-butter play practiced so patiently day in and day out. Five yards from the scrimmage line one Army man slithered off Marchy's pads. Thereafter he was on his own. Carideo kicked the point, which nobody thought important.

At a lecture before this game I had heard Rockne say something which surely belongs in Army lore: "Army will not quit." And so Army quickly proved. After the next kickoff Carideo dropped back to punt, to protect the lead, and avoid a fumble deep in Irish territory. But a gate was left open and Dick King, a substitute left end, got through to block the punt, follow it into the end zone and fall on it for a touchdown. The score was now Notre Dame 7 Army 6.

Kelley wrote: "With the crowd pouring down on the field and standing along the side lines, Army's drop-kick specialist, Broshus, came off the bench, peeled off his sweater to wipe the soggy ball. He took his place—"

Time, of course, stood still.

"The ball was passed but Notre Dame used the same weapon that had served Army. A cloud of blue-shirted players came through and smothered the kick and Army was beaten."

And now the stage was set for the finale, the climax of the saga, a small-sized saga in itself.

We were to leave at one o'clock on Sunday afternoon for the Coast. I dropped in Rockne's suite as he was dictating last-minute notes to his secretary Ruth Faulkner. One of the things he told her was to wire the Mayor's Committee in New York that the "game with the Giants was off." I asked if I could use that and he snorted for me to go ahead. So I hurriedly prepared the little bomb which was to shock the Big Town.

Mayor Jimmy Walker had organized a committee of sports writers to help raise a relief fund for the needy. Their prize project had been a charity game between the New York Giants' professional team and a group of Rockne's ex-stars. Rock had agreed, as usual, to do a favor for his friend Jimmy Walker, his friends the sports writers, and his friends the needy of New York. The Giants, and all professional football people, were no doubt delighted. In these early days the argument had been building up as to whether the pros were superior to the college teams. Rockne had obligingly agreed to put it to a test under conditions most favorable to the professionals. He was staking his own prestige, that of the Four Horsemen, of Notre Dame and of college football; planning to send college seniors and old fellows like the Hosses and Mules—who hadn't had a uniform on for six years or more—against a co-ordinated, conditioned, and well-rehearsed pro team. (When the call came to Crowley, asking if he were in shape, Jimmy wired back: FORGET ABOUT ME. GET THOSE LINEMEN IN SHAPE.)

It was a bad match for Notre Dame, for college football, but most of all for Rockne, who was, under all the strains, going downhill again, obviously approaching another collapse. None of his friends, in position to observe him closely during this period, wanted him to go through with this game. Perhaps we had convinced him, or perhaps he had had enough of sweet charity after that $3000 clip on the Chicago game, and the close call against Army. So I wrote the story, filed it, got on the train in that spot every reporter dreams about—with my big "beat" all tucked away where nobody could get to it.

The next afternoon I was writing my story. Rockne came along and sat down. Warren Brown and J. P. McEvoy joined us. The wits crackled. There were some comments about the town of Pratt, Kansas, we were approaching. Rock told an anecdote which ended: "Can you imagine me comparing myself with H. L. Mencken?"

"Yes," McEvoy said. Rock laughed. Everybody laughed. It was the last laugh on the trip. At Pratt the outside world caught up with us. There were messages from Mayor Walker's Committee, and others, asking about the Wallace story. The claim was that there had been no cancellation from Rockne himself. This could have been a trick, to permit Rock to save face, if he had had a change of heart; in which case my great scoop would have turned into a great sour lemon. (I later learned that Paul Gallico, in the face of denials, had decided I was close enough to Rockne for the *Daily News* to stand on the story against the town.)

"Take a wire," Rock barked to me. I took many wires.

The cancellation was official.

The next day Rock called Warren Brown and me, the two reporters on the train, and told us he had real troubles.

Mullins had hurt his knee again in the Army game. We could announce that Hanley would play fullback, and it would be all right with Rockne if we pointed out that Hanley was a green sophomore with hardly any experience and that he lacked the speed to fit into the backfield.

Confidentially, however, and he asked that we guard this secret, he was going to try to make a fullback out of Bucky O'Connor, who had been Brill's substitute at right halfback.

"They always expect me to pull a rabbit out of the hat out here," Rock said with a wry grin. "I'm going to try to give them one."

L

The decision to send me to California had been sudden. It was two above zero when we left Chicago. And ninety above when we reached Tucson, Arizona. If any of the natives are still wondering,

I was the guy in the black derby hat, carrying the velvet-collared overcoat.

On Wednesday the squad practiced at the University of Arizona stadium before 5000 people, including a few Los Angeles reporters. None but the official party knew that the fellow wearing Hanley's number was O'Connor. The workout was mostly for exercise, most welcome to boys who had been playing in cold, snow, and mud.

There was no publicity man on this trip and I found myself returning to the job as things began to pile up in Tucson. Messages were coming from New York about the Giant game, and from the Coast about the Trojan game—tickets, speeches, appearances, tickets. There were calls about the Los Angeles charity game. At his top form, Rock would have made an entertaining show of all this, but he was beginning to get a bit ragged.

Bonnie was worried. I asked if she wanted me to try to do something. She said she'd be glad if somebody could. So we double-teamed him. He agreed to let me handle the phone; he agreed to take a nap. When Rock began to agree to things like that, instead of blowing you down, he really needed help.

So I got on the phone, had a lovely time saying "no" from coast to coast. I canceled a service club speech he was to make in the hotel—for free, of course. In the lobby I was approached by Bill Henry, then sports editor for the Los Angeles *Times;* and such a good one that he knew Dan Hanley was the story. "Introduce me to Hanley, will you?" And he pointed to Bucky O'Connor.

I was a newspaperman and Bill Henry was also a good friend. But I was a Notre Dame man, back on the old beat as publicity man—and the O'Connor story was in confidence. There was no way out of this unless Bucky was very sharp.

"Dan Hanley," I said to Bucky, very slowly, "this is Bill Henry, sports editor of the Los Angeles *Times*. He wants to ask you how it feels to be an unknown sophomore about to take the place of Larry Mullins in the big game."

"Okay," Bucky grinned. "Let's go some place and sit down, Mr. Henry, away from this crowd." Bucky was fast, indeed. And the deception was probably helped because he was a map-of-Ireland, black Irishman.

I had arranged for an old friend, Jack Murphy of Harold Lloyd

Productions, to make the trip west with the squad. Breakfast service was slow in the squad dining room. Rock fumed about it, went to the main dining room. Later Murphy and I were waiting for a cab. One pulled up. Rockne got out. Very obviously something had gone wrong. Out at the stadium there was very secret practice.

"Wrong?" He snorted at my query. "Everything's wrong. Practice? Nobody else is interested in practice. Why should I be? I'm going back to South Bend." He started into the hotel. "Hunk and Chev are as bad as the rest."

Murphy, a Notre Dame rooter, was a candidate for apoplexy. All those people in Hollywood going nuts over this game, with sky-high ticket prices—and Rockne going back to South Bend!

We went to the field where secret practice was being held.

When the gate opened every head turned our way. They were hoping it would be Rockne.

Hunk had the first team, Chevigny the second. It was true that the two coaches had been across the border into Mexico the night before, but they had not gone until the boys had been bedded down; they were bright and eager this morning. They had been late for practice for the same reason everybody else was late—because of the slow service in the dining room.

Rockne had been at the field ahead of all of them because he had gone to the main dining room. It had pleased him this time, to include his two coaches in the blanket interdiction. I don't know if he had taken them into his confidence, but it wouldn't have been necessary. They had been around long enough to recognize one of his productions.

Finally Rock returned. He walked slowly down the side line, passed the first team without even giving them a glance, went to the second team, looked them over for a while. The message was plain: "If I do change my mind and stay, this will be my team."

"Everybody up." They came from all corners of the field as if drawn by a great magnet. He talked and, as usual with his scripts, it was basically true. He was wearing down again. The doctors had wanted him to go to the Mayo Clinic. He was the magnanimous parent trying hard to understand. Were they really interested in the Southern Cal game? If they *were* and if they *wanted* him to stay—

The giant roar! Then, as if nothing unusual had happened, the wheels began to whir. It was a spirited practice. The voices of the coaches rang out like sirens. The winter poisons were being sweated out. Spring had come to the squad again.

In the showers, after the workout, for the first time in my experience, I heard a Notre Dame squad singing its own "Victory March" —and really pouring it out as they slapped and smacked at one another.

I knew then it was going to be a horse on Troy.

Rock made use of another of his old wheel horses that day. Tom Lieb, coaching at Loyola, had been quoted as saying that the Trojans were much too strong; the Irish were over the hill; Hanley would be no adequate sub for Savoldi or Mullins.

The clipping from the Los Angeles newspaper had been duly pasted on the bulletin board in the locker room. It got noised about, somehow, that Lieb was a traitor who was selling out to the enemy because his bread-and-butter was now in Los Angeles. At the time (and until recently) I had thought it was part of another act, either arranged by Rockne or instituted by Lieb, who would have known how well it would fit into the pre-game psychology; later the story would come out and the boys would understand. Now here's a recent note from Lieb:

"A thing that has never been cleared up, and left me a black sheep with some Notre Dame alumni and friends, is that I picked USC to win and wired Rockne what I was doing to help him in his plans. Rock handed my wire to Hunk who read it to the squad, with a few adjectives about their coach of the year before. When the team arrived, I met the train and the boys would not speak to me. We played the act well and it was one of Rock's greatest team preparations. When Metzger got hurt, I left the game and went down to the dressing room—but had to hold Bert down on the table and tell him the truth. Those boys were really poisoned against Lieb."

Another version is that Rockne, with his fetish about loyalty, was displeased about Tom's "getting into the act." I heard nothing from him about it at the time, and Rock seemed to have thought the situation repaired two months later, with a typical gesture. A friend wrote me: "Rockne was here on February 16, 1931, on a Studebaker tour. Lieb met him and that apparent misunderstanding seemed to have been smoothed out. As evidence of this, Rock went to Loyola with Tom to show that everything was friendly." And I've never met a Notre Dame man who hasn't been friendly to Lieb, or had the slightest doubt about his loyalty or intentions in that famous speech of thirty years ago.

It was a routine that probably helped win; but, as often happens, somebody got burned by the backfire. So what about such flimflam? Is it necessary? Or desirable? The answer depends on how badly you want to win. Rock had wanted to win badly enough in '29 to risk his life. He knew how badly his boys wanted to beat the Trojans. He also knew they had been idling toward the "down day." It was not too hard to see, for anybody who had been around for a while. The trick was in knowing what to do about it in advance. Rockne knew what to do; and had done it. On reflection, few of those boys would really think he would leave them and go back to South Bend. But he had, for that little while during the play, made them believe it; as, indeed, he had probably made himself believe it.

The practice that afternoon was dead-serious. The gates were tightly shut against everybody. This was when the real construction work on the O'Connor rabbit was done. The boys had had their shock. Now it was time for the perfection of detail.

The train trip to Los Angeles was a relaxed daylight ride. On the way I got acquainted with guard Tom Kassis. He was depressed. Here was a boy of twenty-two explaining to me how he had become disillusioned about certain things since he had entered Notre Dame as a freshman. That is not unusual talk for a senior.

Kassis had one of those "trick knees." The University of Arizona had a trainer so supposedly expert on bandaging such knees to keep them in place that Rockne carted him from Tucson to Los Angeles. His primary job was to bandage Kassis. Jim Harris, now assisting Dr. Eddie Anderson at Holy Cross, remembered: "So he bandaged Tom expertly, but as soon as Tom got off the table the knee popped out. You should have heard Rock. I never saw him so mad." But somebody, perhaps Rock himself, did a better job with the knee.

After the game I sought out Kassis to return his topcoat which I had borrowed. They told me that Tom was in the hospital.

"I didn't see him get hurt."

"He didn't. He played himself to exhaustion."

At Notre Dame, and perhaps Southern California, there is a picture of another perfect play. It is a frontal shot, done by some expert cameraman, of Bucky O'Connor seeming to stroll through a wide, wide hole inside his right tackle. Once into the open Bucky became a halfback again, ran as he had run on long jaunts against Pitt and Penn, slithering his hips, stepping aside from defensive bulls with the grace of a matador. Seeming to be cut off at the side lines (exactly as at Pitt and Penn), he pirouetted, let the tackler go out of bounds. Bucky then cut back into the open, attended by those Irish interferers who seem to spring from the ground on such occasions.

O'Connor's run was a poem of gridiron power and poise set to speed and deception. It has, without the shadow of any doubt, been viewed by more people than any single play in gridiron history. How do I know this? Because, the next summer, at Paramount, while writing the screenplay for the picture *Touchdown* (from my novel *Stadium*), we had built our studio football scenes around that newsreel run of O'Connor's. Later I saw Bucky running for a half-dozen other picture epics. You may possibly yet see him on television on the old, old shows. If the hero is wearing what looks like big white shoulder pads, that's Dr. Paul O'Connor. The jerseys were special costuming for Rock's production that day. I've never seen them used since.

Anything that happened after O'Connor's run had to be anticlimax, though there was plenty of it, and almost exclusively Notre Dame. The powerful Trojans seemed to have fallen into the very pit of complacent adulation Rockne had detoured around. Bucky O'Connor made them pay big for that big eye they had given him the preceding year. He gained almost as much yardage as the entire Trojan team. Notre Dame rolled up 433 yards to 140.

"What you didn't expect," wrote George Shaffer of the Chicago *Tribune* service, "and the circumstance that has left the Coast in a football stupor, is the fact that Bucky O'Connor, secretly converted from a second-string halfback to a first-string fullback, was the star of the game in his swan song. What a swan song for Bucky!"

And for Rockne. That evening he was where he most liked to be, with his boys at dinner after a great victory. This was that third time I had seen him quiet. He was completely fulfilled. His voice was oddly gentle but the eyes twinkled. "They always expect me to show them a rabbit out here."

As usual, the magician had a little something going for him. O'Connor had played a few weeks at fullback as a freshman. But it is still the most spectacular trick in the history of the outdoor stage.

That night, on the kitchen floor at the Mullins home in Pasadena, a quiet young fellow who hadn't been able to play all year because of a gimpy knee, reinjured it—playing tiddlywinks. His name? Frank Leahy.

Rockne? Oh, he had flown back to coach the Notre Dame Old Pros against the New York Giants for his friend Mayor Jimmy Walker, his friends the New York sports writers, and his friends the needy of New York.

He got whupped, good, as he figured to be; but he made $100,000 for the relief fund. Technically it was the last "game" he ever coached; sentimentally it was a sort of reunion of representatives from the boys of the various groups he had coached. They were pushed around by the conditioned professionals, but, as always, they had a few laughs. After Layden was hit on the first play he asked the official: "How much time is left?" Crowley was manhandled; and while they were asking him those questions he asked two of his own: "How many people are here today? And what are they all doing down on the field, in Giant uniforms?" The only enjoyment Rock got out of it, you can be sure, was the doing of a good deed.

He then took off to return to the coast to coach another group of Notre Dame Old Pros against some Trojan Old Pros in Los Angeles, for what he thought was charity. But the doctors mercifully flagged him down and put him in the Mayo Clinic.

The promoters of the Coast game threatened to sue him. It was after this experience that Rock wrote a friend: "I possibly trust people too much and seem surprised when I find I am getting the worst of it, but maybe that's just as well."

After a rest, checkup, and warning, Rock came out in time to attend the victory dinner of his two-time National Champions. In this proud setting he publicly apologized to a player whose injury he had once questioned. Early the next winter, in what may have been his last appearance as a speaker at a sports event, he told his listeners the story of what he called "my greatest coaching mistake."

It involved the nuisance abhorred by all coaches—the aggressive father, usually a former athlete himself, who cannot understand why his boy isn't on the first team and has concluded, usually before witnesses, that it's because "the coach won't give him a chance." One of these got so objectionable that Rock invited him to a practice session where his boy was given every chance. He not only failed but revealed the reason for his failure: he was very probably in football only to please his father. Everybody had known that—including, undoubtedly, the mother—but the father. Well, the father knew it now.

Rock said: "He stood there with tears on his cheeks. That was my greatest mistake in coaching. I should have found some other way."

LI

Rockne's discovery of the Wonderful World of Easy Money seems to have been made late in 1927 when the Chicago Automobile Show paid him $500 for a twenty-minute talk. Probably as a result of this appearance he spoke to Graham-Paige dealers in New York, Detroit, and Chicago. His association with Studebaker followed naturally.

Rock worked under four contracts with Studebaker. Under the first, from May 1, 1928, to April 30, 1929, he addressed twenty-one sales meetings in all parts of the country in January, February, and March 1929. The timing, ideal for both the company and the coach, fitted nicely into the automobile selling campaign and came between the end of the football season and spring training.

The second contract ran from May 1, 1929, to April 30, 1930; but this was the period of his thrombosis. A new contract was signed for May 1, 1930. He had filled fourteen engagements under this, all in the first months of 1931, when the company gave him the title of Sales Promotion Manager and a new contract which was to run until April 30, 1932. He held this title for exactly twelve days.

Excerpts from a Rockne letter of January 13, 1931, give glimpses of his affairs at that time:

(In relation to the Los Angeles All-Star Game): "As to the matter of my being in any way liable for not having been there, that seems to be rather absurd in view of the fact that at the time I was laying in the hospital at the Mayo Clinic; and in view of what the doctors wired."

(In relation to his general health): "The doctors at Mayo claim that writing an article a day is impossible and they thought that it would be better for my peace of mind not to write at all, at least for a year or two, until I get back to normal. Next fall they may allow me to write an article once a week."

Other correspondence indicated that Rockne might have been marking time until 1932, when he would put all of his business affairs on a new basis.

Would he have then given up coaching and gone with Studebaker as an executive? Certainly Studebaker was very serious about Rockne. Paul Hoffman was quoted: "My extreme admiration for him is best shown by the fact that at the time of his death he occupied an important sales post with us and was destined to go far had he lived." In attempting to follow through on a selling program Rock had laid out, Hoffman listed his qualifications, developed in football but already transposed to business as: (1) *Selection*—ability to select superior human material. (2) *Training*—ability to teach his men. (3) *Supervision*—salesmen would respond to Rockne's "perfect" type of discipline. (4) *Inspiration*—his understanding contact with individuals as well as the group.

Leo Ward, who was very close to Rockne in his last months, told me: "He was then [February 1931] satisfied in his own mind that coaching was a thing of the past and he was looking for some means to capitalize on his reputation." The means were certainly available. Rockne at forty-three must have known, and his doctors had surely warned him, that his way of coaching football was taking a toll his body could not continue to pay. (At forty-four, his pupil, Frank Leahy, who went at it the same hard way, *had* to quit coaching.) But I think Rock would have proceeded slowly. Football, and all of its aspects, fulfilled him, challenged his *jev*. He loved to work with boys. Despite his occasional outcries about faculty interference, he was a dictator at Notre Dame; the actual leader of the football coaches; the head of the "Notre Dame Lodge." He had the Studebaker connection so close by. He could dabble profitably in writing, radio, motion pictures, and other activities, pick up the side money.

Rockne was intensely shrewd about people, even if his generosity and his response to any sort of challenge sometimes made him appear naïve. Although he had grown in poise and assurance, he was still hungry and cautious. It may well have occurred to him that other coaches who had been campus demigods, and national figures as long as they remained in college football headlines, faded rather quickly when the spotlight moved away from them. At Notre Dame he was *Rockne;* and for a reasonable number of years, probably would continue to be.

What kind of a businessman would he have become? Or actor? Or writer? Or any of the other occupations which were beckoning? I'd say *as good as he wanted to be.* How good would he have wanted to be? Would he have thrown all of his tremendous talents into these other things as in football?

I doubt it, especially in business, unless they allowed him to be what he was in football—a brilliant individualist, keeping his own hidden books, ad-libbing his own scripts, jumping out on the uncharted course, taking the desperate leap his intellectual intuition told him was in the right direction.

That was Rockne. That was how he had to operate. It doesn't sound like the description of the Corporation Man. Rock would have gone nuts, governed by committees.

My guess is that he would have drifted along as he had been doing; marking time; keeping the home base of coaching but training more men to take over more of the detailed work.

After signing the final Studebaker contract March 19, 1931, Rockne flew to Coral Gables where his wife, Mary Jean, and Jackie were spending the winter at a modest rented house. I saw him at the Hialeah Race Track on Saturday, March 21. As always now, he received the VIP treatment, and was being escorted by the official greeter of the city. Bonnie was with him. Mary was with me. They invited us to go along with them to the exclusive executive quarters of the track, far above the teeming masses below.

He was contentedly relaxed; he did not seem to have to prove anything. I did not feel like a sparring partner this last day but more like a kid brother. We had been together through a lot of the stirring action in the last eleven years; the top deck at Hialeah was a very far piece from the sheeted dormitories of rugged old Nostra Domina a Lacu. It was nice just to sit and enjoy it. We saw him for the final time in the parking lot. He waved good-by.

After a week at Coral Gables, he returned to South Bend to prepare for a trip to Los Angeles. But his mother would have a birthday while he was gone, so he went to Chicago a day ahead to visit with her and his sisters. He took a night train from Chicago to Kansas City where he was met in the morning by another old friend from student days at Notre Dame, Dr. D. M. Nigro. The two older boys, Bill and Knute, Jr. (Junie), were in the Pembroke Country Day School there. Rock had intended to visit with them but the train had been late. Before he left he sent a wire to Bonnie. "His last words to me," Dr. Nigro writes, "were that he would be sure to stop off on his way back to see the boys. The weather was fair at take-off."

There were two pilots and five other passengers. One was C. A. Robrecht of Wheeling, West Virginia, father of a Notre Dame graduate whom I had escorted to the school as a freshman. Mr. Robrecht would probably have recognized Rockne. They may have talked. Rock was easy to talk to.

Rock would have been thinking of the business which had brought him into the plane. Because he was so secretive about personal affairs, there are varying explanations. Jay Wyatt said he was to be honor guest at a Chamber of Commerce breakfast in Los Angeles. Father Cavanaugh wrote that it was in connection with a motion picture *The Spirit of Notre Dame*. (This picture was made by Universal shortly after his death.) He might have been going to see RKO which was "talking $50,000"—assumedly about *Good News*. I was later told it was in connection with my novel *Huddle*. I knew nothing of that but do know that David O. Selznick had tried to interest Rockne in playing the part of the coach patterned after him. He would probably have been preparing some choice words for the "fraternal racketeers and unemployed promoters" of the All-Star game. There would have been some legal talk about the agent's contract he was planning to terminate. Very probably there would have been Studebaker business. The deal Hearst was offering—$100,000 for newspaper writing—had been discussed on a previous trip to Los Angeles and was still, presumably, awaiting Rockne's decision.

He would have had many things to think about—probably more than suggested here—and you can be sure he would be preparing his offense, from his knowledge of people in the mass, the nature of the business involved and, above all, his instinctive judgments of the individuals involved. He would have been considering tactics, possible psychological gimmicks, the mood, the performance; or, if necessary, man-to-man, on-the-line talk. He would be ready. He would enjoy it. He would thrill to the challenge. At forty-three, though slightly damaged physically, he was at the absolute top of his mental, emotional, instinctive powers; and of his world. He was what an immigrant can become in this fabulous soil of freedom.

LII

BY UNITED PRESS

Bazaar, Kansas, March 31—Knute Rockne, noted Notre Dame football coach, and seven other men were killed in an airplane crash near here today.

Edward Baker, a farmer, was feeding stock on the Stewart Baker farm, and was watching the plane when it flew over.

Suddenly, he said, there was an explosion and the ship fell to earth.

The plane was flying at a low altitude because of the cloudy weather.

Members of the Baker household heard the explosion and rushed to the scene, half a mile away.

The first flash to Emporia that Rockne was among the dead shocked the entire world and business and industry halted while all sources of communication were placed into service to determine the truth of the report.

(Houston, Texas, *Post-Dispatch*) A copy desk man emerged from the Associated Press printer room with a long string of copy.

He spread his paper on the desk before him, quickly scanning the dispatches from Paris, New York, Washington, Detroit, Kansas City.

A few brief paragraphs told of an earthquake in Managua, Nicaragua. He paused for a moment, visualized a streamer headline.

His eye ran down the string of copy—stock market, murder, romance, divorce. His expression was unchanged.

Suddenly the copyreader jumped from his chair. His face was white, his mouth open. In a moment he shouted:

"My God, Rockne's dead."

Like a flash the cry "Rockne's dead" reverberated through the *Post-Dispatch* plant.

It echoed through the editorial offices, ran down the stairs to the business office. Reporters, printers, and executives stared speechlessly at the bit of paper upon which a mechanical telegraph had impressed the words ROCKNE'S DEAD.

It was a big story, the biggest of the year, someone suggested. But it was not of the story these newspapermen were thinking. Hardboiled newspapermen! There were moist eyes in the group around the copy desk.

Not much like the movie version of a big story breaking in a newspaper office. But a true picture.

It was Tuesday, March 31, 1931, around noon. I was in the office of the Railway Express in Miami, shipping the manuscript of my second novel *Stadium* to my agent. I was going back to the *Daily News* on a regular basis. Our car was packed for driving north the next morning.

My wife came into the office. She was crying. The newsboys were selling extras. Rockne was dead.

We drove to the house in Coral Gables (2202 North Greenway) where we had visited. Mrs. Rockne was not yet there. She had been spending the day with the Tom O'Neills on the beach. George Hussey, the official greeter of the city, was there with about four other people. The telegrams were already arriving. On top was the one Rock had sent from Kansas City: LEAVING RIGHT NOW STOP WILL BE AT BILTMORE STOP LOVE AND KISSES.

The next wire was from Dorais—roommate, teammate, best man, best friend.

When Bonnie returned with the O'Neills, she was calm. Like the rest of us, she was waiting for that second message, with the typical wisecrack. This was a peculiar period in which people tried to make time stand still. She repeated, every so often: "I just don't believe it."

But finally she said to Jackie: "Your Daddy has gone away. He loved you so."

Jackie, playing around the house, asked: "Did my Daddy get killed in an airplane?" It was just another marvelous thing his wonderful Daddy had done.

The packing began. There was an old trunk which Rock must have had since student days—if he had a trunk then—for there were initials, painted on the inside in the familiar scrawl K. K. R.

A football wouldn't fit in the trunk. I suggested we deflate it.

"Oh no—" Bonnie cried. "Knute blew that up himself." Somewhere Rockne's breath may still be in an old football—as it is in the game.

Calls came from Notre Dame. The first tentative plans for the funeral (a horrible word coming from nowhere, and one Rockne would have fought for the personal indignities it meant to his person).

It was Holy Week. There could be no Mass. The funeral would have to be postponed until the following Monday (April 6).

Bonnie and the children and an official delegation would go on a special car. We decided to drive to South Bend.

The curtain had risen for the final act. It was in motion.

"It is not too much to say," Father Cavanaugh wrote, "that the world went pale, trembled, almost wept. On the campus at Notre Dame, men with frozen faces looked hard into one another's eyes and passed by unspeaking when the news was confirmed.

"Although Easter examinations were nearly concluded, school was at once declared in vacation because neither faculty nor students were fit to work. All day long it was impossible to reach Notre Dame by telephone, so clogged were the wires.

"Every student on the campus hurried to the University church. Impressive young stalwarts bowed before the altar with a characteristic Notre Dame absence of shame for honest devotion."

William L. White, son of the distinguished Emporia *Gazette* editor William Allen White, described the scene:

"On a wind-swept promontory of the Flint Hills, out of sight of any vestige of human habitation, lies the twisted wreckage of a giant Fokker, its three motors buried deep in the stony soil, which carried to death Knute Rockne, the Viking of football, two pilots and five other passengers. . . .

"Among the first to reach the wreckage was R. Z. Blackburn, who was feeding his cattle in a pasture. He heard the roar of the morning mail plane. It is just at this point in the Flint Hills that the old stage road, marked by furrows in the prairie sod, intersects with the transcontinental air mail line marked by flashing beacon lights, running between Kansas City and Wichita.

"The hum of airplane motors was a familiar sound to Blackburn. Today the plane was invisible above the gray clouds which hung a scant one thousand feet above the Flint Hills. After dying away in the fog, the hum returned and attracted his attention. Something apparently was wrong with the regular morning mail plane. He looked up from his work in time to see the silver Fokker drop like a plummet from the low-hanging clouds. Behind it fluttered a severed silver wing.

"Its motors still roaring, the Fokker disappeared behind a hill, there was a splintering thud and the motors ceased."

I have often wondered about the final moments of this man who fought to live. His rosaries were found nearby. Now the unimpressive body was still, and much, much less impressive than before.

White's story continued: "Early in the afternoon as the news spread that a mail plane was down and Knute Rockne was dead, airplanes from Wichita zoomed overhead, swooped like great birds curiously inspecting a wounded fellow and settled unsteadily on neighboring hills.

"Khaki-clad pilots were driving away a crowd of excited, overgrown boys who were tearing bits of fabric for souvenirs. Cowboys were viewing the tangled aluminum from their saddles, their ponies stamping nervously at the unfamiliar odor of gasoline . . . an endless stream of curiosity seekers trudging from their motor cars parked along the road. Miraculously, there had been no fire.

"So died the great Viking of football, on a high hill overlooking a prairie, at the crossroads of the old forgotten stage road and the new highway of the air, and at his bier keeping vigil on the hilltop stood, not the Four Horsemen of Notre Dame, but four sun-tanned horsemen of the plains, forcing back from the tangled wreckage a gaping, curious crowd.

"Swiftly and painlessly he passed from a land of far horizons into a horizon without bounds."

LIII

Any person who was old enough in 1931 to remember, can probably tell you just where and how he received the shock of Rockne's death. (I have heard it from a hundred people who never knew him, but the most astonishing was this comment from Eugene "Bud" P. McIndoe of Pittsburgh, Pennsylvania, whom I met on a plane recently: "According to the family tradition, I was born at about the time Rockne died, March 31, 1931.") Bill Alexander, then coach at Georgia Tech, told of an Atlanta newsboy who, after arranging his papers for sale, read the headline—then rubbed his eyes and wandered away from his stand. The Southern California band interrupted a concert on the steps of the Oakland City Hall to play taps. FBI Agent Harvey Foster, then a youth in South Bend, saw people cry on the streets. Bonnie later wrote:

"I had left our police dog, Noxie, in care of my sister in South Bend. My sister, an unusually safe reporter, tells me that at the moment Knute was falling to earth, the dog uttered a sound that was not the sound of a dog but curiously like a human cry. At the same time his eyes shed tears. Commanded to rise, he laid his forepaws on my sister's shoulders, laid his jowl against her cheek, all the while lamenting bitterly."

Messages were received from President Herbert Hoover, King Haakon of Norway and his Minister in Washington; from Secretary of War Patrick J. Hurley, and U. S. Army Chief of Staff General Douglas MacArthur; from Ring Lardner, Babe Ruth, Jack Dempsey, Gene Tunney; from senators, representatives, heads of industries and unions. College presidents and others of the learned professions helped to complete a "eulogy of the illustrious." The mayors of most big cities and governors of many states sent messages. The legislatures of a dozen states paused to memorialize him. The outpouring from college football was a roll call.

Judge Wally Steffen: "Rockne's dead! What a terrible import those two words have. It was an honor to have known the man. He was a commanding figure, a gracious winner, and a good sport in defeat. I am deeply grieved at his death."

Elmer Layden: "He was a daddy to us all. We even went to him if we fell in love with a new girl."

Frank Carideo: "I hope God takes care of him like he took care of us."

Major John L. Griffith, Commissioner of the Big Ten: "Knute Rockne's death is a greater loss to society than to football. This country, that appreciates the things Knute stood for, paid him, during his lifetime, some of the tribute he deserved. His true worth to society will be recognized more and more as time goes on."

Pop Warner: "The greatest figure in football—and one man with no enemies."

Bill Bingham (Harvard): "One of the greatest geniuses of his time."

Fielding Yost: "Football has lost its most colorful figure and outstanding coach."

Alonzo Stagg: "I was impressed with his human qualities, his warm, friendly, generous, unselfish personality. He was always ready for the give-and-take of life—and willing to give more than he took."

His mother and sisters heard the news by radio. One of the sisters collapsed. The pioneer mother said: "It is God's will and we must not question it."

LIV

Tuesday: Dr. Nigro and the two elder boys accompanied the body from Cottonwood Falls to Emporia, and by night train, to Kansas City, where the party was met by the official delegation from Notre Dame: Rev. Michael Mulcaire, vice-president of the university; Hunk Anderson and Jack Chevigny of the coaching staff; and Howard "Cap" Edwards of South Bend, one of Rock's closest associates.

Wednesday: On the campus, 2000 students attended a low Mass celebrated by Rev. Charles L. O'Donnell, Notre Dame president.

And in the town of South Bend: "In the homes, offices, cafes and hotels there is but one topic of conversation. Everybody is talking of Rockne, sketching back over his life, his deeds, his sayings. It is still unbelievable."

Some 10,000 people were crowded into Dearborn Station when the train bearing the body arrived in Chicago. Other thousands lined the streets between the Dearborn and La Salle Street stations while the body was transferred; the latter station was "so packed the crowds became unmanageable."

At South Bend the crowd began to gather shortly after ten o'clock, an hour before the train was due. Bared heads were bowed as Rockne's casket was lifted from the train . . . Down the ramps it was borne on an express cart—the same, perhaps, upon which he had stood, crying, after the Iowa game in '21, and promised: "After this, I will never leave Notre Dame as long as they want me to stay."

Homage to Rockne was a tragic contrast to the homage of years past. In the throng were leaders of the city's business, professional, and social life; and early arrivals from among the ranks of his players.

Holy Thursday: Rockne's body rested in the McGann Funeral Home. The bronze casket was closed and would remain closed. (He would have resented having to lie there while the curious stared at him.) Except for the coroner's jury and other officials at Cottonwood Falls, nobody except Dr. Nigro had seen or would see the body.

A guard of honor stood watch. All were members of the Monogram Club. Frank Carideo and Marchy Schwartz took the first two hours. The watch would continue until the body was lowered into the grave.

Mrs. Rockne and her two younger children left their train at Englewood (Chicago). The widow was joined by Rock's mother and four sisters: Miss Florence Rockne, Miss Louise Rockne, Mrs. Henry Stiles, and Mrs. Walter Leggett. Father O'Hara met them. They came to South Bend by car. There Mrs. Rockne was joined by her mother, Mrs. Hulda Jones.

The aeronautics branch of the Department of Commerce announced that the propeller of one of the motors had broken, due to a "structural defect," causing vibration which shook one wing off.

Other details were announced: The plane had left Kansas City at 9:15 A.M. Pilot Robert Frye radioed "bad weather" at 10:31. The time of the crash was estimated between 10:45 and 11:00. This *opinion* was ventured by other pilots: "The pilot might have decided to go back to Kansas City. To get bearings from the ground, the plane would have to lose considerable altitude. In doing so, the plane might have gone into a dive that caused the wing to pull out."

Had the pilot gone a few miles farther, he would have found fair weather ahead. Level pasture land would have permitted landing. Had Rockne, who constantly warred against imperfections, been sacrificed to an imperfection over which he could have no control?

It was decided to hold the funeral on Saturday, April 4, instead of Monday.

Good Friday: In chill, drizzling rain Rockne's body was taken to the modest home on East Wayne Street, to lie in state in the living room.

The great and the humble stood in silent tribute; sent more messages (one, from a railroad switchman, was in pencil). Editorials were published, poems were being composed. Flowers came in an endless stream. There was no doubt about Rockne's place in the hearts of people. And none would have been more surprised, or embarrassed, than the man himself.

Long furls of black-and-white bunting hung from the Church of the Sacred Heart, and from the football stadium.

The funeral would be held from the church. Admission would be by card. Bonnie thought Knute would want it kept simple. Because of Holy Week, there could be no Mass of Requiem. That would be sung the next Thursday after the students had returned from the Easter vacation.

Holy Saturday: "There seemed to be a note of irony in the brightness of the afternoon. Life in the trees and the soil was beginning to bloom. The air was softened and the harshness of winter was gone. Life was vivid everywhere and the desire to live welled up anew."

But they were burying Rockne, the symbol of spring, of resiliency.

The funeral was going to the nation by CBS radio. All business had halted in South Bend and neighboring Mishawaka. Shops, industries, and offices were closed. The South Shore train and bus service would halt for one full minute, all along its system. Police and firemen guarded the funeral route. At the cemetery, the Boy Scouts, long his special favorites, would gather.

More than one hundred cars rolled in the procession which was headed by city and state police. Crowds waited on the campus grass. At the door to the church the body was lifted by Tom Conley and Tommy Yarr, captain and captain-elect of the football team; Carideo and Schwartz, Mullins and Brill. The clergy waited at the door. The Rt. Rev. John Francis Noll, Bishop of Fort Wayne, conducted the solemn and majestic ritual. The Moreau Choir sang the Gregorian chant.

Rockne's class of 1914 served as honor guard, and some had come a thousand miles. They included Gus Dorais, Al Feeney, Ray Eichenlaub, Joe Byrne, Freeman Fitzgerald, Mal Elward, Ralph Lathrop, Walter Clements, Fred Gushurst, Emmett Keefe, Arthur Larkin—and Johnny Plant, one of the two men who had started it all by selling Rockne on Notre Dame.

In the long rows of church pews: Harper, Phelan, Madigan, the Four Horsemen (Stuhldreher, Layden, Crowley, and Miller), Walsh, Barry, Kiley, Eddie Anderson, Wynne—the roll call through the years.

And the Norwegian Consul, delegated by King Haakon; and Steffen, Warner, Tad Jones, Howard Jones—the long, long roll of coaches, officials, athletic directors, writers, the Studebaker and other business people; the "downtown coaches"; newspaper people, faculty people.

Father O'Donnell, the poet-president, who had been a war chaplain and had known tragedy, said, in his sermon: "In this Holy Week of Christ's passion and death there has occurred a tragic event which accounts for our presence here today. Knute Rockne is dead. And who was he? Ask the President of the United States, who dispatched a personal message of tribute. Ask the King of Norway, who sends a special delegation . . . Ask the thousands of newspapermen, whose labor of love in his memory has stirred a reading public of 125,000,000 Americans; ask the men and women from every walk of life; ask the children, the boys of America, ask any and all of these, who was this

man whose death has struck the nation with dismay and has everywhere bowed heads in grief.

"What was the secret of his irresistible appeal to all sorts and
conditions of men? Who shall pluck out the heart of his mystery and
lay bare the inner source of the power he had?

"I do not know the answer. But I find myself in this hour of piteous
loss and pained bewilderment recalling the words of Christ: 'Thou
shalt love the Lord thy God with thy whole heart. This is the first
and greatest commandment. And the second is like unto this: thou
shalt love thy neighbor as thyself.'

"I think, supremely, he loved his neighbor, his fellow man, with
genuine, deep love. In an age that has stamped itself as the era of
the 'go-getter'—a horrible word for what is all too often a ruthless
thing—he was a 'go-giver'—a not much better word but it means a
divine thing.

"He made use of all the proper and the legitimate methods of
modern activity to be essentially not modern at all; to be quite ele-
mentarily human and Christian, giving himself, spending himself
like water, not for himself, but for others. And once again, in his
case most illustriously is verified the Christian paradox—he has cast
away to keep, he has lost his life to find it. This is not death but
immortality."

In Highland Cemetery, away from the campus, is a tree called
Council Oak where Allouez, and possibly Marquette, had held talks
with the Indians. Nearby is where they laid him. And as his widow,
his mother, his children, his "boys," his friends crowded round, an airplane roared above. The body was down but the *jev* was *ud*.

When the funeral time was moved up from Monday to Saturday
my wife and I were caught in ice and fog in the West Virginia mountains. No planes were up. I did not see the closed casket or watch
them throw dirt on Rockne.

LV

The respect philosophers hold for what they call the Common Estimation was fully justified by the poll on Rockne, as expressed in the

telegrams, letters, editorials, poems, religious and other memorials. They would form a volume in themselves. Here are representative samples from the beat walked by this ubiquitous officer of the court of humanity:

President Hoover (telegram): "Mr. Rockne so contributed to a cleanness and high purpose and sportsmanship in athletics that his passing is a national loss."

Ex-President Calvin Coolidge: "A great man, an inspiring leader and a profound teacher. He put intellectual and moral value into games. Right living and right thinking went into his victories. His activities had the benefit of publicity but that does not account for his hold on young men."

New York *Times:* "Millions of citizens who knew nothing about Knute Rockne the man, regard his death, in the words of President Hoover, as 'a national loss.' His death produced a sensation in this country which reveals college football as a national institution."

Cleveland *Press:* "In the past generation it was Buffalo Bill. For this generation it was Knute Rockne. The boy had a profound respect for Knute Rockne. Knute Rockne had a profound respect for the boy. By some sort of process, each read the other's mind and heart. They were heroes to each other. Millions of boys and men and girls and women bow in grief at the news that Knute Rockne is dead. For millions he was greater than the President of the United States."

The Youngstown *Vindicator:* "Anyone who can fire the manhood of others as he did is in every way admirable . . . We all have latent powers that need to be stirred and awakened; Rockne did this, not merely for the men of the Notre Dame squad but for all the healthy young men of the country. Just as we learn history best through the biographies of great men, so in the chronicle of our own time, the life of Knute Rockne, exerting an extraordinary influence for good, will be remembered long after the Nicaraguan earthquake is forgotten."

Will Rogers: "We thought it would take a President or a great public man's death to make a whole nation, regardless of age, race or creed, shake their heads in real, sincere sorrow . . . Well, that's what this country did today, Knute, for you. You died one of our national heroes. Notre Dame was your address but every gridiron in America was your home."

Frank Hering (in the *Eagle Magazine*): "Our generation will not see such another phenomenon as this: A man without political honors, without wealth, without the support of powerful organizations, rising to such heights of popular approval as Rockne has attained . . . Rockne's life and the honor paid him testify to the recognition of character and worth in our republic . . . Hundreds of thousands are deprived of a hero whose achievements added zest to workaday lives . . . He is the greatest exemplar of clean athletics, the finest inspiration to the schoolboys of America that history offers."

"Deaf students of Illinois School for Deaf, Jacksonville, grieve over passing of Knute Rockne whom they admire greatly. He was at our banquet and gave inspiring talk. Always good to me despite my deafness." S. Robey Burns.

"We mourn the loss of our beloved friend Rock." B'Nai B'Rith of South Bend.

"We all mourn the loss of a truly great man." Mr. and Mrs. Howard Chandler Christy.

"Knute Rockne was a strong moral force and an inspiration to the youth of our land. Fourteen hundred orphan children of Moosehart, Illinois, will always remember his timely and inspiring talks to them." James J. Davis.

"A man like Rockne did more spiritual good than a thousand professional evangelists. His career was a sermon on right living. It is not distorting values to say that he was a more important figure than any state governor, senator, college president or professor. Indeed, one cannot think of any American whose death would have intimately affected so many of his fellow countrymen as Rockne's did." (From an unidentified New York journalist.)

Bellaire, Ohio, *Leader:* "The Soul of Knute Rockne will be the subject of the sermon at the Sons of Israel Temple Friday evening. The sermon was delivered previously at Columbus by Rabbi Jacob Tarish, one of the outstanding rabbis of the country and was broadcast."

"I read that youth has no idols nowadays. But they had one at Notre Dame." (Westbrook Pegler)

Edgar Guest, in a radio tribute: "Boys down through the future will remember Rockne and be brave; they will remember him and be clean; they will think of him and give their best of life."

James L. Knox (Harvard): "One man like Rockne means more to our country than a million reformers; and if football produces one Rockne in each generation, the nation can ill afford to curtail football."

Very Reverend Rudolph J. Eichorn, president of Canisius College: "A Guiding Providence had directed him to the field of sport and in that field he was the apostle of clean living and fair play. A gallant gentleman, a chivalrous fighter, an inspiring master who, with a football and the white rectangles of a gridiron, knew how to help youth plot the best moves of life."

News-Times, South Bend: "But from Rockne the national character one must separate that strange and strangely sweet person who was Rockne the man. Rockne the man was in some ways Rockne the perennial boy . . . The essence of his personality was the attitude of a boy still advancing through a glorious and inviting world; the morning dawning with adventures just ahead; no day like yesterday . . . Rockne a sad and broken old man was an impossible thought. He was a man to burst bonds."

"Your husband was ever ready to cooperate in promoting true Americanism among boys who entered into the American Legion program." Lawrence J. Fenlon, Commander Cook County Council.

North Carolina Christian Advocate (Methodist): "He was a king among men. We have not at any time met a man with greater personal magnetism—not even William Jennings Bryan. We were surprised to find out how much he knew about North Carolina."

"Have played against your husband's team at Georgia Tech. The whitest man that ever lived. We loved him down here at Tech." Raymond C. Eubanks, Rome, Georgia.

"KPO radio station, San Francisco, read at its regular noonday scripture broadcast from the gospel of St. John, chapter fourteen, verses one to seven."

Rt. Rev. Francis Clement Kelley, Bishop of Oklahoma: "When I heard of Rockne's death, something unusual happened, for tears came into eyes that I thought had long ago shed all they could hold. That was a light triumph for a dead man whose face I never saw. Now I know that I was only one of a multitude who had never spoken a word to Rockne but who loved the kind of man he was. . . . Rockne was Sorin without a cassock and breviary . . ."

The Denver *News:* "No other death could have brought more universal sorrow than this. Knute Rockne's name was a household word. He had long since o'erleaped the sports page. Boys who could not yet read could tell you about Rockne . . . There have been big figures in the sports world but none who attained the size of Rockne. In all his career there was never the slightest taint of unfairness, of unethical practice, of lack of sportsmanship . . . This little Norwegian immigrant attained a place in the college life of America which no other man has ever held . . . The game is ended. And in every department of play Knute Rockne won."

H. V. Millard, Decatur, Illinois, *Review:* "He would give as much time to the sports editor of the small town daily as to the boys on the metropolitan sheets. He was not a politician who would pick out the men who would do him the most good. Rockne needed no one to favor him in any way for he was in a class by himself."

Bob Nesbit, Terre Haute *Star:* "The fighting spirit with which his teams were steeped brought him through safely. But he didn't have a fighting chance out there on those Kansas prairies yesterday."

Longview (Washington) *News:* "His earthly remains will lie beneath the sod somewhere, but his spirit—ah, there's the thing that tells the man!"

"It was Rockne, with his marvellous Notre Dame teams and through his own powerful personality, who made football the national institution it is today." Damon Runyon.

"A great hero and Christian gentleman has left to his family a good name better than all price. God rest his sterling soul." Joseph Scott, Los Angeles attorney.

Detroit *News:* "The essence of Rockne's character was its complete masculinity, a circumstance calculated to set him apart in an age which has somehow lost the edge of an earlier virility. He was a man's man, and particularly a boy's man, with a remarkable insight into the aspirations and tendencies of youth, and an almost unique capacity for inducing the adolescent character to realize its full stature and strength."

This was the public image of Rockne, the man who, unknown to himself, became the Great Stone Face of the Gridiron; whose life gave America a new conception of the importance of sport in American life, and the indoctrination of youth in basic American virtues.

An anonymous editorial writer summed it up: "It has been a splendid thing for the youth of this world to have had a President of the United States, as well as great leaders of thought and opinion in all walks of life, render admiring tributes to this man, who lived so simply and who strove so honestly to prepare men for the larger battles and games of life."

And not just America and Norway. Bob Fox of Denver, who was in Peking, China, the day of the accident, reported that a Peking newspaper carried a full column on the death of Rockne.

Rockne often said: "Give our boys footballs for their hands instead of guns." In that sentence, and its implications, may lie the greatest loss to his country and, who knows, the world.

LVI

As long as men have souls, Knute Rockne cannot die
His legend shall grow mighty, pure, in time.
And you, who now receive in death the son you loved in life—who
    knew him best—go on!
Be true to his tradition—he'll know, from where he treads a mightier
    sod.

Oh envied Notre Dame!

(concluding lines of a poem by Carroll B. Chouinard, Graduate Student at the University of Wisconsin, 1931)

What thought Notre Dame?

Jim Armstrong, editor of Notre Dame's *The Alumnus:* "In many places, to many people, time without end, this intangible force that is now Knute Rockne, will come like a cool, refreshing wind from that spot in the Kansas skies to strengthen the weak, to encourage the weary, to stimulate the right and to sanction the strong.

"Those who embrace Knute Rockne's religion, those who understand the full significance of that beautiful statue of Our Lady on the Dome at Notre Dame, know that above the peaks, as men meas-

ure peaks, there is a future that humbles these heights. Knute
Rockne's life must have led him there."

An emergency Religious Bulletin edited by Rev. John F. O'Hara:
"Knute Rockne has had a wider influence in developing the ideals
of fair play than any other man of his generation; he did it under
the banner of the Mother of God. We may feel that she took care of
him in his hour of need."

Rev. John W. Cavanaugh, who, as president of the university, admitted Rockne, gave this eloquent valedictory: "Rockne's earliest
fame was won in the air. On the plains of Kansas he died in the air.
His friends and familiars often spoke of him as 'the Bald Eagle.'
Like an eagle poised in incommunicable sunshine, he held a place
apart. Like an eagle stricken in the sky, he came to the end of his
course.

"Some will say his field of achievement was too trivial and limited
to warrant his canonization among the immortals, but this man was
vastly more than a football coach. There was a touch of Napoleon
in Rockne. He had the love of combat, the interest in strategy, as
well as the genius for it, that marked 'the Little Corporal.'

"There was something of Lincoln in the little immigrant from Norway who became the foremost civilian of his day. Lincoln's influence
is all the greater because assassination struck him at the peak of his
power. Rockne's fame and influence may ultimately grow into a myth
of epic proportions because tragedy smote him in the strength and
splendor of his noonday."

(Father Cavanaugh's reference to Lincoln is all the more valid
because Carl Sandburg, then deep in his studies of Lincoln, was reported "keenly aware" of the Rockne story. He was quoted as saying:
"The pure Norse strain made it inevitable for Rockne to push out-
ward as soon as he was conscious of a limit." True enough—but not
quite so simple as that.)

Father Cavanaugh reported that in preparation of the Postscript
to the *Autobiography:* "More than half the printed materials came
from women! Usually they were albums or scrapbooks. Many came
from young women who merely said that Rockne was their ideal
manly man; and that his teams had thrilled them. Mothers of sons
thought of him as a superb exemplar, a despiser of whatever was
cheap and shoddy in character or in living; a knight errant of chivalry

and honor. Consecrated sisters and other teachers in the classrooms of the nation exalted Rockne as a manly model and encouraged students to gather information about him. Priests have often said that any reference to him in a sermon at once stimulated interest."

It was Father Cavanaugh who emphasized the basic thought which infiltrated almost all of Rockne's public utterances: "Rockne often rebelled against the softness and self-indulgence of this day and their enervating effects on life and labor and play! Innumerable parents utter the same lament and recognized in the great coach the David of their deliverance. No wonder grandmothers caught up and safely preserved anything they found that explained or glorified Rockne. No wonder parents dreamed of the day when their sons would sit at Rockne's feet and catch his heroic feelings and learn what lessons of life he could teach. No wonder the pleasure-seeking world, lustful as ever of bread and circuses, of softness and thrills, looked with mixed envy and pride on the clean-limbed, clean-thinking, clean-hearted young giants whom Rockne set up as models of youth . . . Merely as a moral teacher, Rockne deserves to be, like Saul, among the prophets!"

How has he endured at Notre Dame? Almost thirty years after Cavanaugh wrote, Rev. Edmund P. Joyce, executive vice-president of the university, one of the young ones who never knew Rockne, authorized this quote for this book: "Knute Rockne's contribution to the fame of Notre Dame football teams is well known. What is often overlooked, however, is his contribution to the university's educational prestige. This flows not so much from his work in the classroom as a chemistry professor, notable though this was, but from the spirit which emanated from him—a burning commitment to excellence, a scorn of mediocrity—and which had its emulation in many other areas of the university, academic as well as athletic.

"There is one event each year which, for me, offers dramatic proof of the special devotion which Knute Rockne engendered. This is the annual pilgrimage to his grave, preceded by Mass and a Communion breakfast, and attended each year by a hundred or more of his former players and friends. How many of the world's celebrities, I wonder, are thus honored so many years after their death. I suspect you could count them on the fingers of one hand."

Dr. Nigro has kept the name of his friend green with a Rockne

Club, which meets annually in Kansas City. There is a small town in Texas, named Rockne by its school children. There are Rockne Communion breakfasts in other Notre Dame alumni clubs. There are Rockne camps for boys; one of which, in California, was modeled after Boys Town, Nebraska.

The "lone Norse Protestant" who invaded the Irish Catholic stronghold, seems to have taken it, as he took all other schools; to have graduated among its elect as well as its elite.

LVII

Latent in the spontaneous national tribute to Rockne was the haunting question: What now? What happens to the monument so many people thought so important? Can Notre Dame find another man to fill the popular image Rockne created? The privileged obligation of the school to measure up to the task was the theme of many of the poetic tributes.

In his radio address to alumni on Universal Notre Dame Night, within the octave of the death, Father O'Donnell faced the problem and set the mood for the future by quoting from a poem by Major Maurice Baring to a companion lost in the war:

> Because of you we will be glad and gay
> Remembering you, we will be brave and strong.
> And hail the advent of each dangerous day
> And meet the last adventure with a song.
> And as you proudly gave your jeweled gift
> We'll give our lesser offering with a smile,
> Nor falter on that path, where all too swift,
> You led the way and leapt the golden stile.
> Whether new paths, new heights to climb, you find,
> Or gallop through the unfooted asphodel
> We know you know we shall not lag behind
> Nor halt to waste a moment on a fear.
> And you will speed us onward with a cheer
> And wave beyond the stars that all is well.

How has Notre Dame carried on, in its own tradition and the public image created by Rockne, in the years since his death? That is another story which would take another volume. I will give you some highlights.

There are four factors which determine the quality of a football squad:

1. *School policy.* Does the school operate under a climate favorable to good football?

2. *Spirit.* Does it have a football tradition? A shrine of past heroes and glorious deeds—whose ghosts can be invoked when the cheer leaders or the coaches call for extra efforts?

3. *Material.* Does the school normally attract students who are good football players? Is the school background conducive to the development of good football?

4. *Coaching.* What is the quality of the coaching?

These factors are interrelated. Usually the school with a favorable policy has an ancient tradition; and does not entirely depend for its material upon what the stork drops in. When the other three factors are fairly equal, as they are at most major football schools, the deciding factor is the coaching. That's why so many schools tried to hire Rockne.

What are the rules for judging a coach? Usually the students, with their handy hanging trees, and the alumni, with their pens-in-hand, make the first judgments. The financial ledgers speak strongly. But there are simple and almost infallible rules which, if properly applied, can save a lot of grief and money to any college which has a coaching problem.

1. A football squad, over a reasonable period of time, invariably reflects the personality of its coach.

2. A new coach should seldom be judged on the results of his first season, be they good or bad, because he is, during that season, working with a squad that has been coached by his predecessor; and still reflects his predecessor's personality.

3. In his second season a coach has had an opportunity to impose his personality and methods on the squad generally; but especially on the sophomores. Usually he will begin to show results, good or bad, about mid-season in his second year.

4. A coach can safely be judged by the results of his third year. During that season he will have had the juniors under his control for two seasons; and his sophomores will be those he has personally recruited. If he hasn't begun to show marked improvement by then, it's time to start looking again.

Now let's see how these theories have worked out in the long history of the most successful of all football schools.

1. *Policy.* Notre Dame has had a realistic football policy through the years. It keeps within the rules but it recognizes and welcomes the benefits that come from good football teams: in money, student morale, alumni enthusiasm, public interest, and financial help.

2. Notre Dame *spirit,* based on successful tradition, has always been supreme.

3. Notre Dame draws a rugged, virile type of student from every state in the Union. Rockne was the prime example.

4. *Coaching.* With the other three factors always favorable, Notre Dame should always be as good as its coaching. Its phenomenal modern record has been due primarily to the presence, during 24 of the last 41 years, of two of the great Masters, Rockne and Leahy; and the fact that all of its coaches have been home-grown. But the Irish have had their football troubles too, mostly in recent years, as the following chart will reveal.

COACH	YEARS	PERIOD	TOTAL GAMES	WON	LOST	TIED	PER CENT
All	70	1887–1959	594	452	108	34	.807
Rockne	13	1918–30	122	105	12	5	.897
Anderson	3	1931–33	27	16	9	2	.640
Layden	7	1934–40	63	47	13	3	.783
Leahy	11	1940–43 1946–53	107	87	11	9	.888
McKeever	1	1944	10	8	2	0	.800
Devore	1	1945	10	7	2	1	.778
Brennan	5	1954–58	50	32	18	0	.640
Kuharich	1	1959	10	5	5	0	.500

POST-ROCKNE YEARS

25	1931–55	237	182	40	15	.820
4	1956–59	40	20	20	0	.500
29	1931–59	277	202	60	15	.767

(No games were played in 1890 and 1891 . . . Winning percentages do not include tie games . . . Ed McKeever and Hugh Devore each coached one year while Leahy was in service.)

Here are the reasons for the coaching changes:

Heartley Anderson—*The Top Sergeant* . . . Hunk was appointed on a stopgap basis. His appointment was made permanent after he scored six victories and one tie in the first seven games. The authorities forgot this was a Rockne-coached squad. The slide began almost immediately after the permanent appointment. Hunk resigned, became a very successful pro coach. By profession an engineer, he is now in the steel business and is often called upon for help by Irish coaches. He now probably comes close as any other to being The Grand Old Man of Notre Dame football.

Elmer Layden—*The Businessman* . . . Layden was the best combination coach-athletic director of all the Rockne successors. During his period the administration leaned over backward in observing rules. Layden finished the Rockne job of schedule building. His 18–13 victory over Ohio State in 1935 rivals the best of the Rockne spiritual uprisings. He resigned, without pressure, to become Commissioner of National Professional League.

Frank Leahy—*The Robot* . . . Leahy did such a successful job of imitating his idol, Rockne, that his actual coaching record approaches that of the Master. He went undefeated in the four postwar seasons 1946–49. Thereafter his record tailed off; he lost eight games and tied three in '50, '51, '52; but went undefeated for another national title in his final year. The schedule deteriorated as Leahy failed to match Rockne in charm and diplomacy. Ill health forced him to quit.

Terry Brennan—*Youth* . . . Appointed at the age of twenty-six after high-school coaching. First two years, an excellent 17–3; but slipped to 2–8 with his own sophomores in '56. Record for last three years 15–15. Defense the big trouble. The 1956 team gave up 289 points; 1958 team, 173 points. School regretfully made a change.

Joe Kuharich—*The Pro* . . . The first year record the third worst in Irish history. After eight games it was 3–5, and the day of the Pitt defeat was a sad one as team lacked spark and failed in fundamentals. Two "upset" victories over Iowa and Southern Cal improved the atmosphere. Kuharich could not be judged on his first year which saw harmful injuries, especially to passer George Izo. The defense improved as spirit soared in final two upset victories.

An Associated Press survey for the twenty-five years between 1934 (the beginning of the Layden regime) through 1958 (end of the Brennan tenure) revealed that Notre Dame had actually led all other schools in winning percentage over that period. (The remaining schools in the top ten were Oklahoma, Tennessee, Army, Michigan State, Duke, Ohio State, Michigan, Alabama, Georgia Tech.) This record indicates that the Irish have carried on for Rockne, and have kept their position as the school which, in the public mind, is synonymous with magical victory. Every Notre Dame coach, including Anderson and Brennan, has come up with at least one of those sensational copyrighted Irish uprisings.

But the other side of the coin shows a dismal picture. In the last ten years Notre Dame has not had a perfect season, and only once was undefeated (1953–9–0–1). In the "frustrated fifties" the record was 64–31–4, for an average of .676. In the last four years it was 20–20 for a .500 average. This is obviously not championship football; nor by any stretch, Rockne football. That's why, if Notre Dame was to stay anywhere near the spot Rockne had placed it, a coaching change was imperative after '58; and could be again, if Kuharich is not the answer.

Notre Dame, and now I believe I am interpreting administration, alumni, and student thought, does not hope to find another Rockne. There has been no other Rockne in all the history of football, before or after his time, at any school.

Rockne was, without a doubt, not merely a football genius, but a rare human being who rated phenomenally high in every factor found in man. The Common Estimation sought him out; and knighted him *American*. It did not say that this man was merely a football coach who was therefore unimportant. It said, in effect, this was a great man who made us realize just what an important position sport must have in our national life, when it could absorb the talents of such a man.

That's why Notre Dame will continue to try to have fine football teams; for the tradition, for Rockne, for the students, the alumni, the little old ladies, the unattached men, all the people who, having no champion, have adopted Notre Dame as their own.

Who can estimate the influence of a Rockne, of a Notre Dame, of men like him, of schools like Notre Dame, high schools as well as colleges, on the growing boy? The boy makes the man; and Rockne's message to the boy, and to the country, was, *Stay clean; stay strong.*

Who knows what goes on in the hearts and minds of children? Mrs. Catherine Jonas of Joliet, Illinois, found this poem among the papers of her young son after Rockne died:

> K is for keenness—he was always so alert;
> N is for nobleness—felt by anyone who knew him;
> U is for his unionism—he stressed it till it hurt;
> T is for his tenderness—while he watched the game before him;
> E was his effectiveness—it never failed to work.
>
> R stands for Rockne, a name that shines alone.
> O is for the odds at which he placed each struggling team;
> C is for the criticism that cut clear to the bone;
> K this time for kindness, his acts were just and clean;
> N is for the niceness that was his at school or home;
> E is for the wonder eyes now closed from earthly scene.

And Father O'Donnell received this letter:

Dear Father: I feel that I must express the sympathy and the heart feelings of myself and my family on the terrible loss suffered by the University of Notre Dame and the entire world in the death of Knute Rockne.

I am the father of a crippled boy, twelve years of age. He cannot leave the house and lives on the radio. He is a great boy for baseball and football, and Knute heard of him last November at the time he was most hard pressed. He wrote Eddie a letter and sent him an autographed picture of himself.

Father, when at noon Tuesday he heard the announcement over WTAM, Cleveland, that Knute Rockne was killed, he simply shut off the radio and cried; and when I came home that night he said: "Dad, the best man in the world was killed and I can't help him." Well,

Eddie and I knelt down and said the rosary for Knute, and I know he heard the crippled boy pray for him, and I know he appreciated it.

We sat and heard your wonderful sermon today at the funeral, and I am forty-six years old and not ashamed to say I cried, for the whole world lost a friend when we lost Knute Rockne. And a man who would write to a crippled boy and try to make his life happier under the conditions Knute was fighting under last fall, is a *man*.

Knute's picture is draped in black in my home tonight, and the kiddies all knelt before it and said the rosary for Knute Rockne. But little Dick, six years old, said, "Dad, will there be a Notre Dame next year?" I said, "Yes son, next year and every year. Notre Dame will be there fighting with the Rockne spirit."

So, Father, when all this is over, if you see Mrs. Rockne, please tell her of Knute sending his picture to little Eddie Carty, a crippled kid out in Ohio, and that Eddie is going to pray every night for the one he calls his old friend Knute.

That was 29 years ago.

Last November, at the low point of the season, when Notre Dame was trailing 27–7 in the cold rain, a banner was raised in the section of the Pitt Stadium behind the goal posts, high up. It dripped and drooped like the Irish spirits everywhere that afternoon when there seemed no hope for the future. It read like a forlorn little prayer:

KNUTE ROCKNE CLUB OF ELIZABETH, N.J.

Notre Dame scored a touchdown against Pitt: and upset Iowa and Southern Cal, winning going away.

So, who knows?

INDEX